To Thérèse

With love

Samuel

John May   2012

INSIDE THE DEPARTMENT OF ECONOMIC AFFAIRS

Samuel Brittan

the Diary of an 'Irregular', 1964–6

Records of Social and Economic History is a British Academy Research Project.

The British Academy, established by Royal Charter in 1902, is the national academy for the humanities and social sciences, promoting, sustaining and representing advanced research. As an academy composed of senior scholars throughout the UK, it gives recognition to academic excellence and achievement, and plays a leadership role in representing the humanities and social sciences nationally and internationally. As a learned society, the British Academy seeks to sustain the health and promote the development of the various academic disciplines that make up the humanities and social sciences. And as a grant-giving body, the British Academy facilitates the research of individuals and groups of scholars.

More information can be found at *www.britac.ac.uk*

Frontispiece. Samuel Brittan in the 1960s. This photograph appeared on the rear cover of *The Treasury under the Tories, 1951–1964* (1964).

RECORDS OF SOCIAL AND ECONOMIC HISTORY
NEW SERIES 48

INSIDE THE DEPARTMENT OF ECONOMIC AFFAIRS

Samuel Brittan
the Diary of an 'Irregular', 1964–6

EDITED BY
ROGER MIDDLETON

Published for THE BRITISH ACADEMY
by OXFORD UNIVERSITY PRESS

Oxford University Press, Great Clarendon Street, Oxford OX2 6DP

Oxford New York

Auckland Cape Town Dar es Salaam Hong Kong Karachi
Kuala Lumpur Madrid Melbourne Mexico City Nairobi
New Delhi Shanghai Taipei Toronto

With offices in

Argentina Austria Brazil Chile Czech Republic France Greece
Guatemala Hungary Italy Japan Poland Portugal Singapore
South Korea Switzerland Thailand Turkey Ukraine Vietnam

Published in the United States
by Oxford University Press Inc., New York

British Library Cataloguing in Publication Data
Data available

Library of Congress Cataloging in Publication Data
Data available

Typeset by
4word Ltd, Bristol

Printed in Great Britain on acid-free paper by
CPI Group (UK) Ltd, Croydon, CR0 4YY

ISBN 978–0–19–726500–0

Foreword

This edition of the diary, kept by Sir Samuel Brittan while a civil servant in the newly created Department of Economic Affairs (DEA) for the bulk of the period of Harold Wilson's Labour government in office between the elections of October 1964 and March 1966, constitutes a 'first' for the Records of Social and Economic History series in two particular respects. First, it is the only volume in this long-running series so far published that provides an edition of a source concerning the economic history of Britain after 1945. Second, it is unique in being an edition of a document created by an individual who is still living and who has therefore been able to engage with the editor on issues of meaning and context. Samuel Brittan must be thanked for allowing the diary to be published and for the assistance that he has given Professor Middleton in preparing this edition.

The DEA, when established in 1964, was an experimental government department that was promoted in principle to play a key role in the new Labour government's economic policy of the mid-1960s and was headed by George Brown. Samuel Brittan joined that ministry within three weeks of the Labour Government's very narrow election victory and was in post for the following 14 months. He has previously been the Economics Editor of the *Observer* and on leaving his post in the DEA went on to have an exceptionally successful and influential career with the *Financial Times* as one of Britain's leading economic journalists. The diary is of inestimable value in revealing life in the fullest sense in what was a totally new government department and providing insights into policy debates leading up to and following the inauguration of the DEA. We see the expectations and the frustrations of those who viewed this department as truly innovative in the making and implementation of economic policy, as well the tensions and conflicts that led ultimately to the DEA's failure. We are able to see from within the DEA Brittan's own role in, and unrestrained observations on, issues as varied as prices and incomes policy, the drafting of the National Plan and the constant preoccupation with the balance of payments. In particular, we observe Brittan's own frustrations with a policy that initially remained locked into preserving fixed exchange rates. A distinctive feature of the diary is the light it casts on the personalities active in the management of economic affairs in this period, ranging from government ministers, leading civil servants and the host of academic economists who flooded into advisory positions after the election in October 1964.

Professor Middleton provides a truly comprehensive introduction to the edition which sets out the debates about the perceived problems of Britain's economic growth prior to the election of 1964 and the wider issues involved in the tensions that existed between the DEA and the Treasury and the personalities working within them. He also provides a valuable array of appendices that list the 180 persons mentioned in the diary and their posts and roles in a *Dramatis Personae* as well as a calendar of key events and a host of contemporary economic statistics and later revisions to them. Professor Middleton's careful attention to context greatly enhances the value of this edition and we are very grateful to him for the task he has undertaken. We must also thank Professor George Peden, the member of the Records of Social and Economic History Committee, who acted as the link between the editor and the British Academy and gave this project much attention to detail as well as his expert knowledge of the subject.

November 2011   Richard M. Smith
                                          Chairman, Records of Social
                                          and Economic History Comittee

Contents

Boxes, Figures and Tables

Acknowledgements

This project, conceived in 2004, has taken rather a long time to bring to fruition and in the process I have incurred a number of debts.

First, I thank Sir Samuel Brittan for permitting his diaries to be published, for allowing me to interview him closely on their content, for answering many subsequent queries by email and by letter, and then for his forbearance over my inability to transform the diaries into print in anything like the time that I initially promised. Second, I thank my Faculty's Research Committee for funding this project and again for their forbearance on the date of its completion. Third, various archives and university libraries have as ever provided a sterling service. Thus I thank the LSE Archive, home to Coll. Misc. 745/1–5, for easy access and accurate copying of the diary MS; the Bodleian (and in particular Colin Harris) for, in a rushed day, producing files from the George Brown papers speedily; the Thatcher Archive (and in particular Andrew Riley) for answering queries; The National Archive, not least for the wisdom of permitting digital cameras to increase enormously the productivity of a visit to Kew; the Penguin Archive (and in particular its former archivist, Rachel Hassell) located in Bristol due to the hard work of my colleagues Dr John Lyon, Mr George Donaldson, Dr Hugh Pemberton and other members of the AHRC financed Penguin Archive project; the IMF archive; and to my own university library for their customary good service, and particularly their patience with respect to the huge volumes of *Monthly Digest of Statistics* that I so frequently requested.

Fourth, debts of a more personal kind include calls upon, first, Samuel Brittan's network of colleagues and friends from the 1960s and beyond (Wynne Godley, Brian Reading, John Grieve Smith) and, secondly, my own network of historical experts on the 1960s: Forrest Capie, Lewis Johnman, Scott Newton, Glen O'Hara, Michael Oliver, Hugh Pemberton, Neil Rollings, Catherine Schenk and Jim Tomlinson. Fifth, I thank Scot Newton and Glen O'Hara for their most helpful comments on the introduction and Appendix IV, and Michael Oliver for making available the data which forms Figure 8. Sixth, I thank George Peden who read the book in draft and, in his role in the British Academy's Records of Social and Economic History Committee, saw the volume through to publication. It is a much better volume as a consequence of his close attention to detail.

Seventh, the Committee's anonymous reader performed sterling service, saving me from errors and helping to improve greatly the readability and utility of the final manuscript. Finally, and above all, I thank my wife Liz for reading the Brittan diary MS in its entirety and thereby saving me from transcription and other errors.

January 2011

Roger Middleton
Bristol

Abbreviations

BCC	British Chambers of Commerce
BEC	British Employers' Confederation
BIS	Bank for International Settlements
BoE	Bank of England
BoP	Balance of Payments
BoT	Board of Trade
BPP	British Parliamentary Papers
CAP	Common Agricultural Policy
CBI	Confederation of British Industries
CEDC	Cabinet Economic Development Committee
CRU	Composite Reserve Unit
CSO	Central Statistical Office
DEA	Department of Economic Affairs
DVA	Douglas Allen
ECGD	Export Credit Guarantee Department
EDC	Economic Development Committee
EEC	European Economic Community
EF	Economic Forecast
EFTA	European Free Trade Association
ELDO	European Launcher Development Organisation
EPC	Economic Policy Committee
EPU	European Payments Union
ER	Eric Roll
ESRC	Economic and Social Research Council
ET	*Economic Trends*
FBI	Federation of British Industry
FO	Foreign Office
FTA	Free Trade Area
G10	Group of Ten countries
GATT	General Agreement on Tariffs and Trade
GB	George Brown
GDP	Gross Domestic Product
GNP	Gross National Product
GW	[Patrick] Gordon-Walker
HP	Hire Purchase

HW	Harold Wilson
ICFC	Industrial and Commercial Finance Corporation
IDI	Illegal Declaration of Independence
IMF	International Monetary Fund
IR	Inland Revenue
IRC	Industrial Reconstruction Corporation
IRFC	Industrial Reorganisation Finance Corporation
JG	John Groves
LDCs	Less Developed Countries
LJC	James Callaghan
MacD	[Donald] MacDougall
MCA	Monetary Compensatory Amounts
MDS	*Monthly Digest of Statistics*
MoD	Ministry of Defence
MoL	Ministry of Labour
MoT	Ministry of Transport
NABM	National Association of British Manufacturers
NATO	North Atlantic Treaty Organisation
NBPI	National Board for Prices and Incomes
NCB	National Coal Board
NEDC	National Economic Development Council
NEDO	National Economic Development Office
NIER	*National Institute Economic Review*
NIESR	National Institute of Economic and Social Research
NIF	National Income Forecast
NSA	Not Seasonally Adjusted
NZ	New Zealand
O&M	Organisation and Management
OECD	Organisation for Economic Cooperation and Development
OF	Overseas Finance
OGIP	Official Group on Incomes and Prices
ONS	Office for National Statistics
OSA	Overseas Sterling Area
PEP	Political and Economic Planning
PESC	Public Expenditure Survey Committee
PM	Prime Minister
PO	Post Office
PPS	Parliamentary Private Secretary
QRS	Quantity restrictions on trade
RM	Reginald Maudling

RPM	Retail Price Maintenance
SA	Seasonally Adjusted / Sterling Area
SB	Samuel Brittan
SET	Selective Employment Tax
T	Treasury
TFX	General Dynamics F111A jet fighter (superseded TSR2 project)
TIC	Temporary Import Controls
TNA	The National Archive
TUC	Trade Union Congress
TVA	Taxe sur la Valeur Ajoutée
UDI	Unilateral Declaration of Independence
UK	United Kingdom
UKAEA	United Kingdom Atomic Energy Authority
UNCTAD	United Nations Conference on Trade and Development
VAT	Value Added Tax
WA	William Armstrong
WAN	William A Nield
WEP	World Economic Prospects
WP	Working Party
WPTIC	Working Party on Temporary Import Controls
WRM	William Rees-Mogg

Editorial Principles

If G. B. [George Brown] misses any more meetings through 'morning sickness' we will be wondering whether he is going to give birth to a 'little Neddy'. [Diary, 22 January 1965]

The Samuel Brittan diary for his period as an 'irregular' civil servant in the Department of Economic Affairs (DEA) covers the period 2 November 1964 to 29 January 1966, during which he served in the Information Division on 'Special Duties',[1] being assistant to the Chief Information Officer, John Groves* (see Box 1; hereafter, for the first mention, * indicates an entry in Appendix I. Dramatis Personae, pp. 159--78). Now deposited in the LSE Archive (Coll. Misc. 745/1–5),[2] the diary comprises a typed manuscript with handwritten insertions, other marginalia and the occasional additional material. The diary is chronological, though occasionally dates are out of sequence in the MS, and the final file has a series of 'Reflections' which almost wholly repeat material in the regular entries. Where they introduce new material, these 'Reflections' have been embedded in chronological order with the regular diary entries; they are indicated by an R after the date.

In transcribing the Brittan diary to produce this edition I have tried to be a largely parsimonious editor. In part, this has been a consequence of one advantage often enjoyed by contemporary historians; thus, I have had free access to the diary's author, and he has given freely of his time to check the transcription and to answer my queries where meaning and/or names are unclear. Parsimony was also underpinned by principle. Subscribing as I do to the view that diaries are key historical primary sources, and should accordingly only be subject to the lightest of editorial touches, I have done very little to alter Brittan's original text.[3] They thus retain their

---

[1] The term 'irregular' was invented by Brittan, being a new incarnation of the wartime 'temporary' class of civil servants; see S. Brittan, 'The Irregulars', *Crossbow*, 10 (1966), pp. 30–3; revised and expanded as idem., 'The Irregulars', in R. Rose, ed., *Policy-Making in Britain: A Reader in Government* (1969), pp. 329–39.

[2] The diary had been used by Peter Hennessy before the LSE Archive secured its deposit; see *Whitehall* (rev edn, 1990), pp. 184ff. Hennessy first signalled its existence in 'Whitehall Watch: Prime Ministerial Mistrust of the Treasury is Not New', *Independent*, 6 November 1989 (copy in Coll. Misc. 745/5).

[3] See P. Catterall *et al.*, 'Editing Political Diaries', *Contemporary Record*, 7.1 (1993), pp. 103–31.

'News in Brief', *The Times*, 10 November 1964, p. 6 reported Brittan's appointment for 'special information assignments'. TNA EW4/50 C. Raphael, 'Co-operation on Information Work between the Department of Economic Affairs and the Treasury', 28 October 1964 contains two schemas for DEA external relations. Brittan is listed as 'Special Writer (CIO-B)'. In Brittan's first year in the DEA, the *British Imperial Calendar and Civil Service List* records the Information Division as comprising just Groves and Brittan, whereas in the second year the Division had been expanded to include two Principal Information Officers and four Senior Information Officers.

In the *British Imperial Calendar and Civil Service List* for 1965 and 1966 Brittan is listed as on a salary of £3,000 per annum (equivalent to approximately £46,725 and £92,500 in 2011 using the Office for National Statistics' RPI and average earnings indices respectively). His superior, Groves, was in the salary range £3,050–3,900, the Assistant Secretary scale. The scale for Principals was £1,951–2,725 (an inner London allowance was also payable on all of these scales of £65 per annum; £85 from 1 January 1964). These were the 1 August 1963 higher civil service scales; these were raised in December 1964 (backdated to 1 January 1964) and the Assistant Secretary scale increased to £3,300–4,300 with a recommendation that there be a further rise from 1 September 1965 to the range £3,500–4,500: 'Civil Service (Pay)', *Parliamentary Debates* (House of Commons), 5th ser. 721 (25 November 1965), col. 775.

The median salary for the administrative class is not available for this time, but G. Rooth, *Occupation and Pay in Great Britain, 1906–60* (Cambridge, 1965), pp. 70–1 provides some useful contextual and trend data. Substantial nominal rises had occurred as a consequence of the Priestley commission (Royal Commission on the Civil Service, *Report*, BPP 1955–6 (9613), xi, 925), but there were perpetual complaints that administrative class salaries remained significantly below those available for comparable private sector roles in London.

Box 1   Samuel Brittan as an 'irregular'.

immediacy, written on the day or not long after, although Brittan does admit to some subsequent tinkering and there are also the 'Reflections'. I have also excised very little, and such excisions as there are purely on grounds that they relate to material that is marginal to Brittan and/or the DEA. Nothing has been excised to save the sensitivities of the living or of the relatives of the dead. As befits verity to an historical source, the text here reproduced is that as written save that I have corrected typing errors (such is their frequency that it would have marred the text to have continual editorial marks for such changes) and have standardised abbreviations of names, departments and other institutions (all recorded in Abbreviations, pp. xiii–xv).[4] Additionally, some editorial insertions have been made to maximise clarity, but they are minimal in number and are always denoted appropriately by square brackets. The style of dating has been standardised; all omissions from the text are indicated by ellipses; and [sic] has been inserted to confirm that a passage is the original text rather than a transcription error or other failure.

Bridging passages (in italics) have been kept to a minimum, but relatively full biographical notes have been provided for individuals and episodes. As Alex Cairncross* has shown with his diaries,[5] and with those that he edited of his predecessor as Economic Adviser to HM Government, Robert Hall*,[6] for the advisers, whether established civil service or irregulars such as Brittan, Whitehall was truly at this time a 'village':[7] a community, cohesive by virtue of a large commonality of upbringing and outlook and with networking a *sine qua non* for advancement. Brittan, who was just about to publish his career-making first book, *The Treasury under the Tories, 1951–64* (1964), was already a consummate networker when he entered the DEA. That this was so shines through in his diary which records over 180 individuals in his network in the fourteen months of his tenure as an 'irregular' in the DEA. Much later, Brittan recorded that his time at the DEA 'was important mainly for the contacts I made and

---

[4] Where provided full names/surnames are retained, but where abbreviations are used they have been standardised. Thus, for example, Douglas Allen (later Lord Croham), a key figure in the DEA and later the Treasury, is rendered in the diary variously as: Allen, Douglas Allen, D. Allen, D. A. V. Allen, D. A. V, D. A. V. A. and D. V. A. After the first mention, DVA is then used throughout where an abbreviation was used in the diary. This practice has been adopted for other key characters (notably GB, George Brown; ER, Eric Roll; MacD MacDougall).The rendering of years, percentages (%), quantities (m and bn) has also been standardised. In a few places the MS is indecipherable and [...?] has been inserted.

[5] A. K. Cairncross, *The Wilson Years: A Treasury Diary, 1964–1969* (1997) and idem, *Diaries: the Radcliffe Committee and the Treasury, 1961–64* (1999).

[6] A. K. Cairncross, *The Robert Hall Diaries*, I: *1947–53* (1989); II: *1954–61* (1991). Additionally, Hall's predecessor, James Meade (later Nobel laureate), kept a diary: S. K. Howson and D. E. Moggridge, eds, *The Wartime Diaries of Lionel Robbins and James Meade, 1943–45* (1990) and idem., eds, *The Collected Papers of James Meade*, IV: *The Cabinet Office Diary, 1944–46* (1990).

[7] As described H. Heclo and A. Wildavsky, *The Private Government of Public Money: Community and Policy inside British Politics* (1974).

9.11.64. Came in in the morning and found three telephones on my
desk. Then one was put on the floor and started ringing! A
grey-beige one was put in and then disconnected and then put
in again.

Reflection. Machine works through Private Office.
                           complained of
10-11 F. Atkinson:/New establishment versus old.

Crosland: Some sympathy with officials about 9.30 a.m.
G.B. wants masses of people there, including Parliamentary
Private Secretaries! Says point of maximum demoralisation reached
in battle over rank and status. Chief difficulty is insiders
versus outsiders.

Crosland. Devaluation ruled out within couple of hours of new Government. Those of us who are very unhappy about this must accept
the issue has been shelved if we are to retain any influence at
all. Export subsidies would have been a much greater breach
in international trading rules than the levy. Officials and
international bodies would then have displayed rabid hostility
instead of just neutrality.

Atkinson. Old school not trusted. Two people from NE1
have come over with Allen. Brown only trusts MacD.' people.
Labour Party somehow associated with Cairncross with Selwyn
Lloyd's policy and does not trust him. Cairncross was away
with pneumonia during transition. He said the Labour Party
would have to make up its mind whether to sack him and introduce the
spoil spoil system. (Atkinson thought I was old friend of G.B.!)

COLL. MISC. 745/1 (6)

Figure 1. A page from the diary, dated 9 November 1964. Reproduced with permission of the Library
of the London School of Economics and Political Science (LSE Archive, Coll, Misc. 745/1–5).

the subsequent beliefs of people that I was writing about Whitehall from experience.'[8] The importance of these contacts and of the 'village' — of British government and bureaucracy, as revealed by Heclo and Wildavsky,[9] as one of intimates as against strangers — underlies the strenuous efforts made to identify everyone who makes an appearance in the diary; details of which are recorded in the Dramatis Personae.

---

[8] S. Brittan, 'Samuel Brittan (b. 1933)', in R. E. Backhouse and R. Middleton, eds, *Exemplary Economists* (Cheltenham, 2000), II, p. 280.
[9] Heclo and Wildavsky, *Private Government*, p. 9.

The Department of Economic Affairs

The publication by the Government of a plan covering all aspects of the country's economic development for the next five years is a major advance in economic policy-making in the United Kingdom. Prepared in the fullest consultation with industry, the plan for the first time represents a statement of Government policy and a commitment to action by the Government.

...

The plan is a guide to action.[1]

[The National Plan:] conceived October 1964, born September 1965, died (possibly murdered) July 1966.[2]

1. Introduction

The Department of Economic Affairs (DEA) was one of a 'flurry of machinery of government changes'[3] which quickly followed upon Labour's extremely narrow election victory on 15 October 1964 (see Box 2). This ended thirteen years in opposition but yielded a majority so small as to guarantee a further election in the short-term and highly tactical politics meantime, by both the political and bureaucratic elites.

In addition to the DEA, four other departments were established by Harold Wilson*, the new Prime Minister: the Ministry of Overseas Development, the Ministry of Technology (known as MinTech and, with the DEA, the institutional manifestation of Wilson's much cited — and misunderstood — 'white heat of technology' speech),[4] the Welsh Office and the Ministry of Land and Natural Resources. The DEA formally lasted until October 1969, but as we shall see was critically injured within twelve

---

[1] Foreword by the First Secretary of State, *The National Plan*, BPP 1964–5 (2764), xxx, p. iii. The Plan was published on 16 September 1965.

[2] R. G. Opie, 'Economic Planning and Growth', in W. Beckerman, ed., *The Labour Government's Economic Record, 1964–1970* (1972), p. 170.

[3] K. Theakston, *The Civil Service since 1945* (Oxford, 1995), p. 89.

[4] Labour Party conference speech, Scarborough, 1 October 1963, published in H. Wilson, *Purpose in Politics: Selected Speeches* (1964), pp. 18–27. For a balanced assessment, see B. Pimlott, *Harold Wilson* (1992), pp. 302–5 and S. Fielding, '"White Heat" and White Collars: The Evolution of "Wilsonism"', in R. Coopey, S. Fielding and N. Tiratsoo, eds, *The Wilson Governments, 1964–1970* (1993), pp. 29–47.

The 1959, 1964 and 1966 general elections can be summarised thus:

Election	Turn-out	Vote shares (%)				No of seats				Butler 2 party swing
		Cons	Lab	Lib	Other	Cons	Lab	Lib	Other	
08.10.59	78.7	49.4	43.8	5.9	0.9	365	258	6	1	+1.7
16.10.64	77.1	43.4	44.1	11.2	1.3	304	317	9	0	-3.1
31.03.66	75.8	41.9	47.9	8.5	1.7	253	363	12	2	-2.8

The 1959 general election, which re-elected the Conservatives for a third period in office, produced an unequivocal result. However, the October 1964 election was one of the tightest contests of the twentieth century, such that the Labour and Conservative shares of the popular vote (respectively 44.1 and 43.4 per cent) were so close that Labour secured a Parliamentary majority of only four (five with the Speaker). Moreover, this was soon to be diminished by by-elections, such that Labour's majority was only two by the time that Parliament was dissolved on 10 March 1966. At the subsequent general election, Labour increased its share of the vote to 47.9 per cent, achieving a 2.8 point swing, and a much increased majority, now at 97: see D. E. Butler and A. King, *The British General Election of 1964* (1965), pp. 303, 304; idem, *The British General Election of 1966* (1966), pp. 1, 297, 326; and *Contemporary British History*, 21. 3 (2007), pp. 283–387, a special issue 'The 1964 General Election - the "Not Quite, But" and "But Only Just" Election', ed P. Barberis.

It is not insignificant that Labour's election victory in 1964 was, despite an enlarged electorate, secured on the basis of fewer votes than 1959 as 1.75 million former Conservative voters either did not vote or (temporarily) shifted their allegiance to the Liberals, a result that some commentators saw as highly significant: for example, the period October 1964 to May 1966 has been described as 'eighteen months at Dunkirk': P. Foot, *The Politics of Harold Wilson* (Harmondsworth, 1968), p. 155. The end of thirteen years of Conservative rule was thus the end of duopolistic postwar politics and Wilson had very good grounds for caution during the 'Dunkirk era'.

Box 2. The General Elections of 1959, 1964 and 1966.

months. It was largely a spent force less than eighteen months later (the July 1966 measures, as is indicated above by Roger Opie* who served in the DEA at the same time as Brittan), and by August 1967 it had entered its final phase of existence with diminished responsibilities and under closer prime ministerial control than hitherto.[5] Hennessy notes that 'For such a short-lived department ... the DEA acquired a formidable legend' and not just for the 'celebrated story that it was born in the few minutes it took a London taxi to carry Wilson and George Brown[*] from a meeting with the TUC ... back to the House of Commons.'[6] In one recent popular history of postwar Britain, the legends of the DEA are expanded into a titanic struggle: a turf war between the new department, led by the 'knight commander of the British economy', and the Treasury representing the bastion of economic orthodoxy and civil service obstructionism. For Marr, at the Treasury 'some of the brightest minds were planning how to frustrate Brown's intended coup' of British economic policy, whilst the upstart DEA was forced, in 'scenes which might have come from the post-1980 television satire *Yes, Minister*,' to indulge in covert operations in order to secure first the accommodation, equipment and staff for the new department and then the economic intelligence that would allow it to function effectively in the ultra competitive and secrecy-obsessed Whitehall of the 1960s.[7]

In this introduction we detail the truer and fuller story of the DEA's origins, but here signal that the DEA was quite particular to time and place. These conditions set its significance and why the Brittan diary is of such particular historical value for what it reveals about life inside the new department and new government.[8] Additionally, of course, Brittan would in the years following his service in the DEA become one of the most, if not the most, distinguished of Britain's financial journalists; indeed, he was knighted for his services to economic journalism in 1993,[9] and he

---

[5] The most recent and fullest history of the DEA is C. Clifford, 'The Rise and Fall of the Department of Economic Affairs, 1964–69: British Government and Indicative Planning', *Contemporary British History*, 11.2 (1997), pp. 94–116; also idem. and A. McMillan, eds, 'Witness Seminar: The Department of Economic Affairs', *Contemporary British History*, 11.2 (1997), pp. 117–42. Additionally, see J. Leruez, *Economic Planning & Politics in Britain* (Oxford, 1975), ch. 6; P. Hennessy, *Whitehall* (rev. edn, 1990), pp. 182–8; C. Pollitt, *Manipulating the Machine: Changing the Pattern of Ministerial Departments, 1960–83* (1984), esp. pp. 51–6, 66; K. Theakston, 'Whitehall Reform', in P. Dorey, ed., *The Labour Governments, 1964–1970* (2006), pp. 147–67; and J. D. Tomlinson, *The Labour Governments, 1964–70* (Manchester, 2004), III, ch. 4.

[6] Hennessy, *Whitehall*, p. 182.

[7] A. Marr, *A History of Modern Britain* (2007), pp. 242–3.

[8] For a memoir which includes an account of his fourteen months in the DEA, see S. Brittan, 'Samuel Brittan (b. 1933)', in R. E. Backhouse and R. Middleton, eds, *Exemplary Economists* (Cheltenham, 2000), II, pp. 270–95.

[9] 'Top Award for Mr Samuel Brittan', *The Times*, 26 April 1971, p. 17 reported that Brittan had been selected as Financial Journalist of the Year, noting that since leaving the DEA for the *Financial Times* he had 'pioneered a distinctive category of "economic" journalism which had since been adopted in other papers.'

features very heavily indeed in the academic literature on British economic policy and performance from the early 1960s to the present day (Table 1 provides brief biographical detail and an event history, the latter focused on Brittan's period of major public prominence, the 1960s to the 1990s).[10]

2. The Significance of the DEA

The DEA's significance is manifold: its inception and subsequent life cycle mirror Britain at a very particular point, one of convergence of a number of longer-term forces which were then exacerbated by the short-term difficulties experienced by the new government, long in opposition, and operating with a bare working majority.

First, this was the era of a 'great reappraisal' in British economic policy. The phrase is Brittan's; it appears in his first book, *The Treasury under the Tories* (1964) (hereafter, his Treasury book),[11] published just after Brittan entered the DEA (the date is of considerable significance, upon which see pp. 27–30). It is this book, one based in part upon official and somewhat unofficial interviews with Treasury and other civil servants,[12] which consolidated his reputation as a premier economic journalist. Moreover, he had already been identified as having skills that would be valuable for the new department by Brown and his proto-members of the DEA, all of whom, as we shall see (pp 18–22), had been planning actively since summer 1963 in the event that Labour won the election. This 'great reappraisal' was not a discreet event but a process; indeed quite a prolonged process, as the new 'growth consciousness'

---

[10] See my essay 'Brittan on Britain: "The economic contradictions of democracy" redux', *Historical Journal*, 54.4 (2011), pp. 1141–68; for his place in the 'declinism' literature, see J. D. Tomlinson, *The Politics of Decline: Understanding Post-War Britain* (2000), esp. p. 89 and R. English and M. Kenny, eds, *Rethinking British Decline* (2000), ch. 7.

[11] Chapter 7, 'The Great Reappraisal'. Published by Penguin Books as a Pelican, the series for non-fiction contemporary issues. A simultaneous hardback was planned with Secker & Warburg, but in the event there was no hardback edition until the second revised edition, published as *Steering the Economy: The Role of the Treasury* (1969). The Penguin Archive (PA) has two files (DM1107/A722 and DM1107/A1252) of correspondence between Brittan and his Penguin editors covering the period 1962–9.

[12] PA DM1107/A722, Samuel Brittan to Anthony Godwin, 17 November 1964. The accompanying document ('List of complimentary copies') records the names of 46 persons who comprised the private interviews. Starting with William Armstrong*, then Joint Permanent Secretary, Treasury, and including the Prime Minister and Chancellor of the Exchequer, and his predecessor, this list comprises a veritable 'who's who' of British economic policy-making at this time.

took root.[13] It began under Selwyn Lloyd's* Chancellorship, whereby the Conservative government responded to perceptions of relative economic decline with an explicit growth target and a new demand- and supply-side policy mix of fiscal activism and indicative planning. This was then developed by Labour in opposition in the form of an even higher growth target and a more developed 'National Plan' to be designed and implemented by a new planning ministry (not yet called the DEA). Latterly, these policies pursued first under the Conservatives and then Labour have become known as 'Keynesian plus', thereby implying a certain degree of cross-partisan agreement, at least in principle, that the 'classic' short-term Keynesian demand management techniques needed to be augmented with a range of supply-side measures if higher growth was to be achieved.[14] Subsequently, as Pemberton observes, 'What had seemed at the time to be a major shift in the framework of economic policy had come to naught, or at least to very little.'[15] The Brittan diary provides a unique insight into the failure of Keynesian plus policies.

Secondly, institutions played a key role in the Keynesian plus era. The DEA was part of a period of 'intense interest in machinery of government reform by Labour politicians'.[16] Arguably, this was also the case for their predecessors, though the motives were different and pragmatism was more to the fore as the Macmillan-Home government remained consonant with the long-run 'reluctant collectivism' of postwar conservatism.[17] Thus the period 1961–4 was one of considerable innovation, being of interest to historians and political scientists

[13] R. Middleton, 'Economists and Economic Growth in Britain, c.1955–65', in L. A. Black and H. Pemberton, eds, *Affluent Britain: Britain's Postwar 'Golden Age' Revisited* (Aldershot, 2004), pp. 129–47; see also T. W. Hutchison, *Economics and Economic Policy in Britain, 1946–1966: Some Aspects of their Interrelations* (1968), pp. 207–33, to many in the British economics establishment a notorious work — 'the publishing outrage of the year', according to an anonymous Oxford economist (*New Statesman*, 1 November 1968) — dedicated to deflating expectations about what economics as a discipline might achieve and examining forensically every forecasting and policy error committed by leading economists during this review period. It is noteworthy that Brittan (pp. 122–3 n.1) did not escape Hutchison's critical eye, though by comparison with his elders Brittan escaped lightly indeed.
[14] A. M. Gamble and S. A. Walkland, *The British Party System and Economic Policy, 1945–1983: Studies in Adversary Politics* (Oxford, 1984), pp. 80–5.
[15] H. Pemberton, *Policy Learning and British Governance in the 1960s* (2004), p. 5; see also G. O'Hara, *From Dreams to Disillusionment: Economic and Social Planning in 1960s Britain* (2007), pp. 22–3.
[16] Clifford 'Rise and Fall', p. 94.
[17] The phrase comes from V. George and P. Wilding, *Ideology and Social Welfare* (1985), p. 4; on Conservative ideology, see E. H. H. Green, *Ideologies of Conservatism: Conservative Political Ideas in the Twentieth Century* (Oxford, 2002), esp. ch. 9.

Table 1. Samuel Brittan: biographical and event history

Date [1]	Event		Date [1]
29.12.1933	Born		
1944–52	Kilburn Grammar School		
1952–5	Jesus College, Cambridge, economics tripos, 1st class		
1955–61	Financial Times (Economics Correspondent, 1960–3)		
1961–4	Economics Editor, the Observer		
		Labour government takes office	16.10.1964
01.11.1964	Joined DEA		
10.12.1964	The Treasury under the Tories published (Penguin)		
31.01.1966	Left DEA		
01.02.1966	Financial Times (Economics Editor, 1966–78; Assistant Editor, 1978–96)		
		Labour government re-elected	01.04.1966
1967	'Inquest on planning in Britain' published (PEP)		
1968	Left or Right: The Bogus Dilemma published (Secker & Warburg)		
1969	Steering the Economy published (Penguin/Secker & Warburg)		
1970	George Orwell prize for political journalism		
		Conservative government takes office	19.06.1970
?09.1970	The Price of Economic Freedom: A guide to Flexible Exchange Rates published (Macmillan)		
?01.1971	Steering the Economy, 2nd edn. Published (Penguin)		
26.04.1971	Wincott Foundation Financial journalist of the year		
1972	Government and the Market Economy published (Institute for Economic Affairs)		
?04.1973	Capitalism and the Permissive Society (Macmillan) and Is there an Economic Consensus (Macmillan) published		
		Labour government takes office	04.03.1974
		Labour government re-elected	10.10.1974
1973–4	Fellow, Nuffield College, Oxford		
1974–82	Visiting Fellow, Nuffield College, Oxford		
1975	'The Economic Contradictions of Democracy' published (British Journal of Political Science)		
1975	Second Thoughts on Full Employment published (Centre for Policy Studies)		

Year	Event	Conservative government
1977	*The Economic Consequences of Democracy* published (Temple Smith)	
1978	Visiting Professor of Economics, Chicago Law School	
1978	'How British is the British Sickness?' published (*Journal of Law & Economics*)	
		Conservative government takes office 04.05.1979
1981	*How to End the Monetarist Controversy* published (Institute for Economic Affairs)	
1983	*The Role and Limits of Government* published (Temple Smith)	
		Conservative government re-elected 09.06.1983
1985	Hon. DLitt, Heriot-Watt University	
1985–6	Member, Peacock Committee on the Financing of the BBC	
1987–92	Honorary Professor of Politics, University of Warwick	
		Conservative government re-elected 11.06.1987
1988	Ludwig Erhard prize for economic writing	
1988	*A Restatement of Economic Liberalism* published (Social Market Foundation)	
		Conservative government re-elected 09.04.1992
1993	Knighted for 'services to economic journalism'; Chevalier de la Legion d'Honneur	
1995	*Capitalism with a Human Face* published (Edward Elgar)	
1996–	Fortnightly column for *Financial Times* in retirement	
1998	*Essays, Moral, Political and Economic* published (Edinburgh University Press)	
2005	*Against the Flow: Reflections of an Individualist* published (Atlantic Books)	

Sources: Personal correspondence, *Who's Who*.
Note: [1] As with Appendix II, as much of the date of an event, or beginning events, is given, with '?' signalling missing information.

(institutions and the problems of securing radical policy reform featured much in the ESRC Whitehall research programme).[18] The Treasury was significantly reorganised in 1961–2, and particularly with the establishment of the Public Sector Group, while 1962 saw the creation of the National Economic Development Council (NEDC, known affectionately as Neddy) and associated Economic Development Committees (EDCs, the little Neddies).[19] The NEDC quickly generated a 4% growth target for 1961–6 (cumulatively 22 per cent), publishing this in February 1963 as *Growth of the United Kingdom Economy to 1966* (known as the green book) and two months later a key background paper, *Conditions Favourable to Faster Growth* (the orange book).[20] The Brittan diaries shed considerable light on institutional innovation and the conditions for success but above all failure during the all-important first year of the new Labour government.

Institutional innovation has a particular resonance for the DEA, forged as it was in the special circumstances following the unexpected death in January 1963 of the Labour Party's leader (Hugh Gaitskell) and the difficulty faced by his successor. Wilson was by no means the heir apparent, and once elected he had to balance the rival demands of his competitors in

---

[18] This project into the changing nature of central government, funded by the ESRC between 1994–9, and blending theory and history in an unparalleled fashion for its subject, involved academics and civil servants, current and retired, in the biggest investigation into the core executive ever undertaken. For the project's overall results, see R. A. W. Rhodes, 'The Changing Nature of Central Government in Britain: The ESRC's Whitehall programme', *Public Policy and Administration*, 13.4 (1998), pp. 1–11 and idem. 'A Guide to the ESRC's Whitehall Programme, 1994–1999', *Public Administration*, 78.2 (2000), pp. 251–82; and, more specifically for the 1960s, R. Lowe, 'The Core Executive, Modernization and the Creation of PESC, 1960–64', *Public Administration*, 75.4 (1997), pp. 601–15; and idem. and N. Rollings, 'Modernising Britain, 1957–64: A Classic Case of Centralisation and Fragmentation?' in R. A. W. Rhodes, ed., *Transforming British Government* (2000), I, pp. 99–118.

[19] For a Treasury insider view of these changes, see R. W. B. Clarke, 'The Plowden Report, I: The Formulation of Economic Policy', *Public Administration*, 41.1 (1963), pp. 17–24; Treasury reorganisation features prominently in G. K. Fry, 'Whitehall in the 1950s and 1960s', *Public Policy and Administration*, 13.1 (1998), pp. 2–25; A. Ringe, N. Rollings and R. Middleton, *Economic Policy under the Conservatives, 1951–64: A Guide to Documents in the National Archives of the UK* (2004); see also A. Ringe, 'Background to Neddy: Economic Planning in the 1960s', *Contemporary British History*, 12.1 (1998), pp. 82–98; idem. *et al.*, 'The National Economic Development Council, 1962–67', *Contemporary British History*, 12.1 (1998), pp. 99–130; and A. Ringe and N. Rollings, 'Responding to Relative Decline: The Creation of the National Economic Development Council', *Economic History Review*, 53.2 (2004), pp. 331–53. For an history of the NEDC, see K. Middlemas, *Industry, Unions and Government: Twenty-One years of NEDC* (1983).

[20] In March 1964 NEDC issued an update on their plan, *The Growth of the Economy*.

the leadership contest of February 1963,[21] respectively Brown and James Callaghan* (comprising in aggregate, the 'triumvirate'). As Heppell notes, 'the manner in which Wilson acquired the Labour Party leadership is central to understanding the complexities of his party leadership tenure and his insecurities which were to be a great impediment to Labour in office.'[22]

Whilst we now know that the taxi journey featured not in the birth of the DEA, a more considered affair, but in Wilson offering Brown the post of Secretary of State for the as yet unnamed department (variously, Ministry of Economic Expansion, Ministry of Production, Ministry of Planning and Production and Ministry of Economic Affairs), we also know that by the time the DEA featured in the Labour Party manifesto[23] it had the underpinning of a concordat by the triumvirate about the division of responsibilities between the Treasury and the new department, but that this was more in the nature of 'verbal truce' and not a formal contract.[24] Indeed, for Douglas Jay*, who would become President of the Board of Trade in the new government, and who had spent many months trying to persuade Wilson against the 'rash experiment' that became the DEA, the new department 'was a prime example of creating bad organization in order to appease personalities — a classical recipe for trouble. Wilson, I am sure, knew the scheme was ill-judged, but for some reason put personal appeasement first.'[25]

---

[21] Candidate support in first (7 February) and second (14 February) ballots:

Wilson	115	144
Brown	88	103
Callaghan	41	n.a.

Source: T. Heppell, 'The Labour Party Leadership Election of 1963: Explaining the Unexpected Election of Harold Wilson', *Contemporary British History*, 24.2 (2010), table 2.

[22] Heppell, 'Labour Party Leadership', p. 163.

[23] Labour Party, *The New Britain* (1964) detailed how the Ministry of Economic Affairs would design and implement the National Plan. Responsibility for the drafting of the manifesto (and 1966) lay with Peter Shore* who would later head the DEA.

[24] Clifford 'Rise and Fall', pp. 96–7. In making this judgement, Clifford drew upon A. Morgan, *Harold Wilson* (1992), p. 258 as well as the memoirs of the triumvirate: G. Brown, *In my Way* (1971), ch. 5; H. Wilson, *The Labour Government, 1964–1970: A Personal Record* (1971), ch. 1; and J. Callaghan, *Time and Chance* (1987), these supplemented by D. P. T. Jay, *Change and Fortune: A Political Record* (1980), ch. 12.

[25] Jay, *Change and Fortune*, p. 295. The rivalry between Brown, Callaghan and Wilson for the post-Gaitskell future of the Labour Party had its proximate origins in the leadership struggle between Gaitskell and Wilson of 1960, was continued by Wilson and Brown in 1962 for the deputy leadership (with Brown the victor) and, whilst ostensibly settled in February 1963, when Wilson became leader, resulted in what was at best an unstable equilibrium; see Heppell, 'Labour Party Leadership', esp. pp. 163–5; A. Howard and R. West, *The Making of the Prime Minister* (1965), esp. ch. 1; and

This leads inevitably to the third dimension: that of the role of personalities and of leadership—for good or for ill, critical in producing good
government or its obverse (unsurprisingly, issues of leadership also
featured prominently in the ESRC Whitehall programme, with the recent
biographical 'turn' in the social sciences now including political science).[26]
For postwar liberal democracies, the growing personalisation of politics
has been ubiquitous; and whilst we must be careful not to conflate the
different strands of the literature (presidentialism, leadership, new political communications, political socialisation),[27] nor artificially telescope
these processes, for Britain there were aspects of presidentialism that well
predate Thatcher.[28] Whilst Wilson might not, *contra* Thatcher, have had
an eponymous existence,[29] and certainly there was no 'cult' of Wilson as
such,[30] amongst the political classes and much of the electorate there was
an expectation of promise which was not routine for British politics at that
time. Hennessy rightly observes that '1963–4 did have something of a
radical dawn about it';[31] but even for those on the left such as Paul Foot*,
already a highly cynical journalist,[32] Wilson's performance between

---

T. Bale, 'Harold Wilson, 1963–76', in K. Jefferys, ed., *Leading Labour: from Keir Hardie to Tony Blair* (1999), pp. 121–4. The multi-dimensional factionalism of the Labour Party in the 1950s and 1960s is explored in both longer-run and broader context in P. Clarke, *A Question of Leadership: Gladstone to Blair* (rev. edn. 1999), chs.11–12.

[26] For example, K. Theakston, *Leadership in Whitehall* (1999); see also idem. 'Comparative Biography and Leadership in Whitehall', *Public Administration*, 75.4 (1997), pp. 651–67.

[27] I. McAllister, 'The Personalization of Politics', in R. J. Dalton and H.-D. Klingemann, eds, *The Oxford Handbook of Political Behavior* (Oxford, 2007), pp. 571–88; D. Kavanagh, *Political Science and Political Behaviour* (1983), ch. 7; and A. King, 'Do Leaders' Personalities Really Matter?', in A. King, ed., *Leaders' Personalities and the Outcomes of Democratic Elections* (Cambridge, 2002), pp. 1–43.

[28] M. Foley, *The Rise of the British Presidency* (Manchester, 1993), pp. 11, 13, 103–6, 116.

[29] See, however, I. Favretto, '"Wilsonism" Reconsidered: Labour Party Revisionism, 1952–64', *Contemporary British History*, 14.4 (2000), pp. 54–80 and N. Thompson, 'The Fabian Political Economy of Harold Wilson', in Dorey, ed., *Labour Governments,* pp. 53–72 for the contrary view: that Wilson was an ideologically-driven strategist as well as a consummate tactician.

[30] D. Walker, 'The First Wilson Governments, 1964–1970', in P. Hennessy and A. Seldon, eds, *Ruling Performance: British Governments from Attlee to Thatcher* (Oxford, 1987), pp. 187, 200–1. For all of its 'instant history', Howard and West, *Making of the Prime Minister* well captures the excitement of the 1964 election without recourse to extravagant claims for Wilson's proto-presidential performance. The other much cited instant history by Anthony Shrimsley*, *The First Hundred Days of Harold Wilson* (1965), is less restrained and takes as its guiding text (cited p. xi) Wilson's speech of 15 July 1964: 'You know we're going to have to tackle all of these problems pretty well at once. What I think we're going to need is something like President Kennedy had when he came in after years of stagna-
tion in the United States. He had a programme of a hundred days—a hundred days of dynamic action.'

[31] Hennessy, *Whitehall*, p. 181.

[32] He would later publish *The Politics of Harold Wilson* (Harmondsworth, 1968).

becoming party leader and the 1964 election elicited expectations of change which will be familiar to those who experienced the new political dawn that was the election of New Labour in 1997. Thus:[33]

> Harold Wilson, with his cheeky, cocky demeanour, his cheerful smile and his Yorkshire burr, summed up the confidence and hope. Here was living proof that Labour could deliver a prime minister who was plainly not a MacDonald or an Attlee — a man who genuinely believed in public enterprise and public endeavour, and would not sell the pass.

The optimism and the spirit of engagement with Labour's programme of modernisation transcended political boundaries. For example, the industrialist Fred Catherwood*, who served as Chief Industrial Adviser in the DEA and then became Director General of the NEDC, expressed the view that:[34]

> If powerful national figures are made responsible for doing something that the country wants and some of the ablest men in government service are redeployed to help them, then a new centre of power has been brought into being in the national decision-making process and major national decisions will, from then on, have a different bias.

The high expectations of Labour in opposition and early government, of course, did eventually turn to disappointment and thence to the widely-shared notion, apparent long before the 1970 election defeat, of a 'breach of promise', this well-captured in a book of that title by Ponting.[35] But for a moment, Hennessy's 'radical dawn', in which Wilson's 'white heat' modernisation agenda attracted technocrats and the newly educated electorate alike, produced a moment of opportunity, and with economic policy an important means for its fulfilment.

Richard Crossman* would later, via his diaries,[36] develop the critique that between 1964–70 Wilson sought to create the impression of Cabinet government when the reality was one of prime-ministerial-cum-presidential

---

[33] P. Foot, 'Obituary: Pipe Dreams', *Socialist Review*, June 1995 <http://pubs.socialistreviewindex. org.uk/sr187/foot.htm> 07.06.10.

[34] *The Times*, 3 May 1966, cited in J. W. Hackett, 'Britain and France: Two Experiments in Planning', *Political Quarterly*, 37.4 (1966), p. 433 n.6. Catherwood was the author of *Britain with the Brakes Off* (1966) which attracted much attention for extolling the virtues of American managerial know how and enterprise; his memoirs, *At the Cutting Edge* (1995), chs 6–7 cover his years at the DEA and NEDC.

[35] C. Ponting, *Breach of Promise: Labour in Power, 1964–1970* (1989), esp. ch. 25.

[36] R. H. S. Crossman, *The Diaries of a Cabinet Minister*, I: *Minister of Housing, 1964–66* (1975); II: *Lord President of the Council and Leader of the House of Commons, 1966–68* (1976); III: *Secretary of State for Social Services, 1968–70* (1977); J. Morgan, ed., *The Backbench Diaries of Richard Crossman* (1981).

government;[37] a view also propounded by Barbara Castle* (who would become the Secretary of State for the new Ministry of Overseas Development) in her diaries.[38] Now that the Crossman diaries have been subject to detailed, very sceptical scrutiny,[39] Wilson's leadership style investigated using some systematic (political science-inspired) evaluation criteria,[40] and the proper discount rate applied to Wilson being the first to use effectively (as against, *pace* Macmillan, understand the potential of) new political communications, we can see the dissonance between rhetoric and reality on the 'white heat' modernisation agenda and why personalities mattered so much for this government and for the DEA in particular.

We know from a variety of studies about the Whitehall village the key role played by the 'trial of personalities' in policy-making (the diary provides much new source material), by which Heclo and Wildavsky meant that there was a constant ruthless appraisal of everyone by everyone, ministerial and official alike.[41] We know also from the more recent literature on the failure of policy reform in the 1960s, and in particular that on the advocacy network for securing faster economic growth through Keynesian plus policies, that the failure was one of institutions, with the heart of the problem being issues of governance: 'the fragmentation of the policy terrain, the interdependence of many of the actors and institutions within it, and the ability of competing networks to resist the reforms promoted by the growth advocacy network'. In short, as Pemberton identified it, a key problem was 'the scale of division within the core executive over the direction of policy.'[42]

Where there is division, strong and effective leadership has the potential to lessen the adverse affect of defective institutions. However, for the new government there was a very mixed endowment of talents. Foremost here was the problem of a new government out of office for thirteen years. Admittedly, Wilson had much experience when last in government, and this of a particular character: first as a wartime civil servant and then as a minister, latterly at a second rank Cabinet level. Additionally, by the

[37] Foley, *Rise of the British Presidency*, pp. 11, 13. The received opinion on how British governments operated in practice is represented at this time in J. P. Mackintosh, *The British Cabinet* (1962).

[38] B. Castle, *The Castle Diaries, 1964–1970* (1986).

[39] K. Theakston, 'Richard Crossman: The Diaries of a Cabinet Minister', *Public Policy and Administration*, 18.4 (2003), pp. 20–40.

[40] V. Honeyman, 'The Leadership of Harold Wilson Assessed Using the Greenstein Model', POLIS Working Paper no. 25, University of Leeds (2007).

[41] Heclo and Wildavsky, *Private Government*, p. 123.

[42] Pemberton, *Policy Learning*, p. 185.

standards of the 1940s Wilson was a professional economist. This gave him a particular authority beyond that of just being prime minister; in particular, for those who had no experience of government, it invested in him especial expertise on machinery of government and economic matters. Subsequently, assessments of Wilson have not rated highly his organisational capacity; indeed, to Hennessy,[43] Wilson's was 'a hugely disappointing premiership in terms of modernizing the instruments of government' with 'The fate of the DEA ... symbolic of Wilson the supreme Whitehall technician — failure at every level, from the Cabinet command post to the interdepartmental bush, where drive, energy and strategy can disappear without a trace.' Wilson's strengths as a leader, his consummate political skills and proficiency as a public communicator, did not translate into being an effective organisational capacity which limited the feasibility of his public policy vision.[44] Hennessy makes much of Wilson's career-long animus towards the Treasury,[45] but also records Callaghan's dissent that there ever could be a 'creative tension' between the DEA and Treasury. Theakston, a political scientist who has studied the postwar British bureaucracy in depth, judged Wilson's position vis-à-vis the civil service as more complicated: in opposition 'he had identified himself with fashionable modernizing thinking' but as premier he 'was clearly something like a permanent secretary *manqué*'.[46] Whatever the verdict on this aspect of his leadership, Walker is right in his verdict that Wilson's success in 1963–4 'was [as] a work of personnel management ... of bonding together into a single electoral entity a Shadow Cabinet comprising Wilson's political enemies and rivals, a sluggish and unilateralist party outside of Parliament and an ageing and cantankerous band of MPs within.'[47]

Such complications are as nothing as we now turn to consider Brown. Our starting point is that such were the structural constraints on the DEA's operation — as we shall see, it had no oversight of budgetary policy, nor much else to do with Treasury macroeconomic policy — that it could only operate at all because it had a distinctive and powerful champion in the form of Brown (and in the background some very effective civil servants with long experience of circumventing the Treasury). The triumvirate

[43] P. Hennessy, *Cabinet* (1986), p. 70.
[44] Honeyman, 'Leadership of Harold Wilson', pp. 13–21.
[45] Hennessy, *Whitehall*, pp. 180, 182.
[46] K. Theakston, *The Labour Party and Whitehall* (1992), pp. 33–4.
[47] Walker, 'First Wilson Governments', pp. 186–7.

was always a delicate compromise and this without factoring in Brown's 'morning sickness' (Diary, 22 January 1965), the DEA euphemism for his alcoholism. The best biography of Brown, which invokes the now standard euphemism for drunkenness ('tired and emotional'), one which had been invented by the satirical magazine *Private Eye* to describe Brown, details him as 'a victim of two afflictions, both of which harmed his career and blighted many of his social relationships, even if they also helped him to attain the status of a beloved national character: one was an addiction to drink, and the other was an inferiority complex induced by his fretful resentment of the class system.'[48] Brown's personality shines through the memoirs of the political elite and, in particular, of those officials who had greatest day-to-day contact with him. For example, Donald MacDougall*, in from the start of the DEA as Director General, recounts a number of episodes of tiredness and emotion, including one in which very late at night after 'we had both had a few drams' Brown temporarily lost the draft National Plan after 'He had thumbed a lift in a Mini driven by a man with a red beard, accompanied by a girl in pink trousers, who took him home.'[49]

On Brown the balance sheet is indeed complicated; he was a man of rare gifts and of enduring disability in the world of Whitehall, if not Westminster. For Tony Crosland*, the DEA's first Minister of State (who had favoured Callaghan for the leadership), 'Brown's temperament could be disastrous in a prime minister, [but] he greatly respected many of George's qualities. "The man has genius," .... George would get hold of an idea and charge off with passion, eloquence, animal vitality of a quite remarkable kind. If he sometimes charged in the wrong direction, he did it with distinction.'[50] A leading member of a later generation of Labour ministers, in writing a guide on *How to be a Minister*,[51] had Brown as 'an exceptionally effective minister ... full of energy and drive, and immensely popular on public platforms', but then noted that quite characteristically he then resigned on the wrong issue in 1968 when he should have gone in 1966 when his going would have been both more understandable and thus career-enhancing. As we have seen Jay was no friend of the DEA, nor indeed of its First Secretary: 'Brown's method of argument was once aptly described to me by someone who had experienced it

[48] P. Paterson, *Tired and Emotional: The Life of Lord George-Brown* (1993), p. 7.
[49] G. D. A. MacDougall, *Don and Mandarin: Memoirs of an Economist* (1987), p. 159, also pp. 144–5; cf. Brown, *In my Way*, pp. 105–6 for a rather different version. Both date this event as 4 August 1964. Brittan reports the episode: Diary, 5 August 1965.
[50] S. Crosland, *Tony Crosland* (1982), p. 131.
[51] G. Kaufman, *How to be a Minister* (rev. edn, 1997), p. 169.

as a "bulldozing rather than reasoning".[52] However, given the poor hand dealt Brown by Wilson, and Callaghan's deep scepticism about the DEA over at the Treasury, bulldozing appeared the minimum strategy to make things happen not least when, first, you have to construct a Ministry from scratch and, second, within the first days of government a decision has been taken (not to devalue sterling) which already has undermined your raison d'etre.

Finally, the diary is of importance because of the dramatis personae (Appendix I): the DEA touched an extraordinary number of civil servants, economists, politicians and other policy makers who, at the time and (for many) subsequently, formed Britain's economic establishment and governing class. The Dramatis Personae (pp. 159–78) lists 180 names, encompassing prime ministers through to junior economists via journalists and industrialists. The economists, in particular, need to be highlighted: the advent of the Wilson government saw an unprecedented (in peacetime) influx of academic economists, and so much so that Opie could not resist the quip, made after he had left the DEA, that 'It might have seemed to an outside observer that on the morning of 16 October 1964 a new era of economic policy had dawned ... [bringing with it] an army of economic advisers unmatched in numbers and talent in peace-time — it was even suggested that any innocent traveller standing on the Oxford platform on that distant morning would have been trampled to death in the stampede of economists boarding the 8.52.'[53] Brittan, a Cambridge-trained economist, travelled in from north-west London but the point was well made that the day of the economist had well and truly arrived in Whitehall. Yet, only four years later, many were lamenting this development as a 'plague of economists', [54] though this sits uneasily with Opie's conclusion about the fate of the influx: 'Welcomed with open arms, as new visitors to the Rockies are welcomed by the grizzlies'[55]

---

[52] Jay, *Change and Fortune*, p. 338; see Diary, 4 January 1965: 'Perhaps, one has to be a bit of a bastard to get anything done.'

[53] R. Opie, 'The Making of Economic Policy', in H. Thomas, ed., *Crisis in the Civil Service* (1968), p. 54.

[54] R. Middleton, *Charlatans or Saviours?: Economists and the British Economy from Marshall to Meade* (Cheltenham, 1998), pp. 21–3, 202; for the role and influence of economists in government in the 1960s, see L. M. Allan, 'Thatcher's economists: ideas and opposition in 1980s Britain', University of Oxford DPhil thesis (2008), ch. 3.

[55] Opie, 'Making of Economic Policy', p. 55.

3. The Origins of the DEA

The origins of the National Plan and thus the DEA lay with the Labour Party's growing preoccupation with apparent economic decline by the late 1950s.[56] There were many aspects to this, but common themes included harnessing new technology, securing higher investment and greater planning to break free of the constraint of what were then called 'Stop-Go' policies, the last of these a bête noire of Brittan in his Treasury book.

The proximate origins lie with the proposal to prepare and implement a 'national plan' contained in *Signposts for the Sixties*, the Labour Party policy document produced by the NEC's Home Policy Subcommittee for the 1961 party conference; this based on an earlier policy document, *Labour in the Sixties* presented to the previous year's conference.[57] As chairman of the sub-committee, Wilson together with Peter Shore and Thomas Balogh* had been closely involved in both documents which, in effect if not in design, contributed towards closing the gap between the right and the centre-left of the party after the Clause IV revision dispute. Pimlott sees both as revisionist documents, clearly influenced by Crosland's *The Future of Socialism* (1956) but with added emphasis on planning.[58] Planning had 'captured the high ground of Labour Party policy-making' by 1961, with Wilson having earlier published a plan which sought a targeted 50 per cent rise in investment in the quinquennium 1961–6.[59] *Signposts for the Sixties* was adopted by the party as the appropriate guide to economic and a whole range of other policies issues, and in the next two years Wilson and Balogh worked intermittently on developing the inchoate proposals in the 'Planning for expansion' chapter.

Wilson's mature thinking on this and associated economic topics were expressed in a series of speeches published as a Penguin special just before the election.[60] Here he drew a sharp distinction between the problem of maintaining short-term expansion, pace 'Stop-Go' destabilisation, and the longer-term problem of securing 'those structural changes

[56] Tomlinson, *Politics of Decline*, pp. 35–7.

[57] Labour Party, *Signposts for the Sixties* (1961), p. 13; idem, *Labour in the Sixties* (1960).

[58] Pimlott, *Harold Wilson*, p. 272; for these documents and the broader environment, see T. Jones, *Remaking the Labour Party: From Gaitskell to Blair* (1996), ch. 4; J. Cronin, 'Labour's "National Plan": Inheritances, Practice, Legacies', *The European Legacy*, 6.2 (2001), pp. 215–32 and idem, *New Labour's Pasts: The Labour Party and its Discontents* (2004), ch. 2.

[59] Tomlinson, *Labour Governments*, pp. 72–3; H. Wilson, 'A Four-Year Plan for Britain', *New Statesman*, 24 March 1961, pp. 462–8.

[60] H. Wilson, *The New Britain: Labour's Plan* (Harmondsworth, 1964), esp. chs. 2, 5.

which are necessary to strengthen the economy.' The two were inextricably connected, for avoiding Stop-Go through strengthening the balance of payments required higher medium- to longer-term investment to build productive capacity. For Wilson, 'the urgent need is to make these structural changes in British industry that will help our export-import relationship and, at the same time, to repair those gaps in the economy — whether of capital equipment or of skilled manpower — which are such a serious limiting factor to continued expansion.' He concluded that 'The problems we are facing underline the need for effective economic planning covering industrial policy, financial policy, and the application of science to industry', with a Minister of Economic Planning envisaged to ensure that an 'effective national plan is worked out' to attain these objectives. Thus 'What Neddy [the NEDC] has begun, this Ministry must carry through, with effective powers for the job.'[61]

As Cronin notes, Labour was here exploiting the 'new respectability of planning' which offered it 'an unprecedented opportunity, for it shifted the terms of the debate about national economic policy onto a new terrain — a terrain on which Labour was not only comfortable ideologically, but where they could claim superior expertise.'[62] However, there was a difficulty, and this is where short- and longer-term policy problems and the underlying diagnoses of declinism merged together in the form of Balogh's long-standing and highly influential critique of what was wrong with the British civil service and thus economic policy.[63] For Balogh, 'The post-war record of British economic policy inevitably leads to the conclusion that a Civil Service reform as fundamental as that undertaken by Northcote and Trevelyan is long overdue'; the problem was the 'substitution of "Snowesque" scientific dilettantes for "Bridgesian" humanistic amateurs.'[64] Balogh, one of two Hungarian-born economists who would rise to influence (the other was Nicholas Kaldor*), had been a policy adviser to Wilson since the late 1940s; he had since 1943 been a member of the Party's Economic and Financial Committee; and as the

---

[61] Wilson, *New Britain*, pp. 27, 28, 30, 36–7.

[62] Cronin, *New Labour's Pasts*, p. 64.

[63] T. Balogh, 'The Apotheosis of the Dilettante: The Establishment of Mandarins', in H. Thomas, ed., *The Establishment* (1959), pp. 83–126; idem. *Planning for Progress: A Strategy for Labour* (1963); and Fabian Society, *The Administrators: The Reform of the Civil Service* (1964). On the last of these, Balogh was a member of the working group which produced this report, along with Crossland, Shirley Williams*, Robert Neild*, David Henderson, Michael Shanks* and John Grieve Smith*. On Wilson and Balogh, see Pimlott, *Harold Wilson*, pp. 275–6.

[64] Balogh, *Planning for Progress*, pp. 30, 31.

1964 election drew near he articulated a vision of administrative modernisation to achieve the purposeful planning that must underpin faster
economic growth that had much to commend it in terms of the right blend
of statecraft and economic potential at that time.[65]

After the general election, Balogh would be appointed economic
adviser to the Cabinet; in preparation, according to Clifford, in May 1963,[66]
Wilson gave him 'the job of designing planning policy'.[67] Here Balogh's
influence was twofold: first, as a member of the Fabian working party
which, on Wilson's instigation, was investigating the case for, and feasibility of, a new central economic department; and, secondly, more directly
with Wilson and (from the July 1963 announcement of his appointment)
Brown as minister in waiting. Michael Shanks, like Brittan an economist-
journalist, and soon to be a DEA 'irregular', was a member of the Fabian
working group and has argued that the DEA's creation was a direct result
of its report.[68] The Fabian group's central conclusion was that 'administration was too important to leave to administrators' and this made the case
for the careful deployment of irregulars, and especially economists, within
government: this in general to dilute the cult of the amateur supposedly
pervading the civil service and, in particular, to ensure that there were
adequate intellectual guns ranged against the Treasury.

The Fabian report (which was completed in February 1964)[69] has been
investigated by historians and political scientists as part of research into
the background to the 1968 Fulton report on the civil service;[70] it only

[65] A. W. M. Graham, 'Thomas Balogh (1905–1985)', *Contemporary Record*, 6.1 (1992), pp. 194–207;
see also M. Shanks, 'The "Irregular" in Whitehall', in P. Streeten, ed., *Unfashionable Economics:
Essays in Honour of Lord Balogh* (1970), pp. 244–62.

[66] According to Clifford and McMillan, 'Witness Seminar', p. 122. Participants in this
seminar chaired by Peter Jay* included: Alec Cairncross*, Callaghan, Tom Caulcott*, Douglas Allen
(later Lord Croham)*, Edmund Dell*, Ronald McIntosh*, Anne Muller* and Eric Roll*.

[67] Wilson's scientific adviser Patrick Blackett* also played a significant but as yet undocumented role
in the origins of the DEA (Clifford, 'Rise and Fall', p. 95), whereas his role in MinTech has been
investigated, see M. W. Kirby, 'Blackett in the "White Heat" of the Scientific Revolution: Industrial
Mobilisation under the Labour Governments, 1964–1970', *Journal of the Operational Research
Society*, 50.10 (1999), pp. 985–93.

[68] Shanks, '"Irregular" in Whitehall', p. 244.

[69] Lord George Brown Papers (LGBP) MS Eng c4986, Shirley Williams to George Brown, 11 February
1964. Williams listed those that had been interviewed. This included a number of economists: Robert
Hall*, Bryan Hopkin*, MacDougall.

[70] Committee on the Civil Service (Fulton Committee), I: *Report of the Committee, 1966–8*, BPP
1967–8 (3638), xviii, 129; see G. K. Fry, *Reforming the Civil Service: The Fulton Committee on
the British Home Civil Service of 1966–1968* (1993); Theakston, *Labour Party and Whitehall*; and
R. Lowe, *The Official History of the British Civil Service*, I: *Reforming the Civil Service, the Fulton
years, 1966–81* (2010).

features incidentally in such histories of the DEA as have to date been prepared.[71] Tomlinson writes:[72]

> For Wilson, [a] planning organization needs to acquire its authority from the Cabinet and the economic departments if it is to be able to call, in the national interest, for the co-operation that will be required. For Labour, the NEDC could not be the apex of the planning machinery; for that, a new ministry with a senior minister in charge would be necessary.

Balogh had deeper criticisms of the NEDC; above all, as Pimlott argues (citing Balogh in part), he was adamant that the new department 'be led by a non-Treasury, non-Whitehall "economic visionary with energy and technical knowledge backed by the best available brains working in applied economics".'[73] With Brown the 'economic visionary', the search then turned to building a department and securing the 'best available brains'. In tracing the sequence of what then happened we need first to make an important point about evidence: hitherto, we have made some use of memoirs with the politicians, but in exploring the recruitment of like-minded economists who were already serving civil servants we become very dependent on this type of source, and such is the dissonance between the aspirations for, and the agreed achievements of, the DEA the memoirs must be treated with some caution until they can be augmented by supporting correspondence between the key parties.

So far as we can reconstruct events,[74] during the early summer of 1963 Brown was in conversation with Eric Roll (who would become DEA Permanent Secretary), at that time about to be based in Washington in an international economic diplomacy role, and MacDougall, NEDO Economic

---

[71] Clifford, 'Rise and Fall', albeit brief on the origins, is both the most detailed and based on primary sources in TNA and Labour Party archives.

[72] Tomlinson, *Labour Governments*, p. 75 and note 25.

[73] Pimlott, *Harold Wilson*, pp. 278–9, citing in part T. Balogh, *Unequal Partners* (Oxford, 1963), II, p. 269; see also TNA CAB 147/9, Thomas Balogh to Prime Minister, 25 February 1965 for his early reflections on the establishment of the DEA and in particular in relation to the Treasury, the 'monolithic supremacy' of which had now been challenged successfully.

[74] See Pollitt, *Manipulating the Machine*, pp. 51–3, this based in part upon interviews with key politicians and officials, of whom Laurence Helsby* played a key role in liaising with Labour in opposition under the Douglas-Home rules; and Clifford, 'Rise and Fall', pp. 122–3 which unfortunately cites no sources. See also 'Tory Question on Brown Article', *The Times*, 10 April 1968, p. 1 which reports on the stir created retrospectively by a Conservative backbencher after Brown wrote about the events of 1963–4 in the *Sunday Times*, 31 March 1968. Here he named MacDougall, John Jukes*, Catherwood and Roll as participating in discussions before the election as part of a series of 'conferences and seminars with academics, industrialists, trade unionists and civil servants.'

Director.[75] Taking each in turn, Roll provides quite a full account in his aptly entitled memoirs of the 1963–4 discussions which led to him becoming the new department's permanent secretary.[76] He records that at the initial discussion he was cautious about what a new planning department might achieve and the stance that the Treasury might adopt towards such a newcomer. Nonetheless, sufficient enthusiasm must have been perceived by Brown who, upon meeting Roll in autumn 1963, made clear that given the imminent election he ought not to put down deep roots in the US;[77] and by April 1964 Roll must have been deeply involved in DEA planning for he commented critically but not destructively upon a report, which derived from NEC discussions,[78] which, via MacDougall, established what would remain the preserve of the NEDC and the Treasury and what would be within the purview of what at this stage was called the Ministry of Planning.[79] Roll recorded in his memoirs that in 1964 he was 'very sceptical about the exaggerated hopes for the DEA entertained by many',[80] but this impression becomes slightly stronger and probably more accurate in Francis Cairncross' *Dictionary of National Biography* entry that Roll 'reluctantly became permanent secretary'.[81] In part, this was unsurprising for Roll had to spend the first three months of his appointment shuttling between Washington and London because no successor could be found for his Treasury post,[82] including the job being turned down by Francis'

---

[75] The Roll papers, if they exist, are not yet available; the MacDougall papers, deposited in the Churchill Archive, have nothing of relevance for the DEA part of his career, though there is material on the NEDC period (MACD 32 iii) and a longer version of his memoirs (MACD 40 ix); but the Brown papers (LGBP) do contain some correspondence involving all three parties and latterly Brittan; see p. 27.

[76] E. Roll, *Crowded Hours: An Autobiography* (1985), pp. 149ff; see also his 'The Machinery for Economic Planning: I, The Department of Economic Affairs', *Public Administration*, 44.1 (1966), pp. 1–11.

[77] Brown, *In my Way*, p. 97 also reports this.

[78] Clifford, 'Rise and Fall', p. 96 and n. 18 refers to discussions between autumn 1963 and spring 1964 in the Home Policy Committee and the Finance and Economic Policy Sub-Committee; see also Brown, *In my Way*, p. 95 and Cronin, *New Labour's Pasts*, p. 69 n. 33. LGBP c5000 has a copy of 'The requirements of Economic Planning: An Outline', March 1963 prepared by the Finance and Economic Policy Sub-Committee.

[79] LGBP MS Eng c5000, 'The machinery of economic policy', February 1964. Committee members included Jeremy Bray* (who would later become a PPS in the DEA), Neild, Richard Pryke*, Douglas Jay and Kaldor.

[80] Roll, *Crowded Hours*, p. 164.

[81] F. Cairncross, 'Roll, Eric, Baron Roll of Ipsden (1907–2005)', *Oxford Dictionary of National Biography*, <www.oxforddnb.com/view/article/96608>, 29.06.10.

[82] Roll, *Crowded Hours*, p. 155. Roll was succeeded by John Stevens, a banker, on 15 January 1965.

father,[83] Alec Cairncross, who was fighting a turf war over at the Treasury, which was also occasioned by the advent of the new government with its influx of Labour-sympathising economists as Special Advisers.[84] Brown in his memoirs admitted to having made a 'grave misjudgement' about this appointment and muses that William Armstrong would have been a better choice, not least that in moving from the Treasury he would have solved the tensions between the two departments.[85]

MacDougall played a key role in recruitment to the DEA, including in the event transferring half of the NEDO economists to the new department once it was established. The extant evidence for his involvement with Brown and DEA planning is from early 1964, but it was undoubtedly earlier as, unlike Roll, he was already right at the heart of the economic machinery of government; indeed, one journalist, very much a cheerleader for Labour at this time, has MacDougall and Fred Catherwood as proposing Roll.[86] MacDougall's stance towards the DEA was framed within a complex of short-term and long-term factors: first, and most immediately, he was much influenced by his then current NEDO perspective on Keynesian plus policies and their necessary institutional foundations; secondly, he was already resolved that devaluation was a *sine qua non* 'if we were to get sustained growth and avoid endless balance of payments troubles';[87] and thirdly, his long experience of government service had included proximity to the fraught 'Operation Robot' episode, this a failed attempt of 1952 to secure a floating exchange rate and thus to break free of the balance of payments constraint.[88] From this episode he was highly 'doubtful about the wisdom of giving such a virtual monopoly of general economic knowledge and power to the Chancellor and the Treasury'.[89]

MacDougall recorded in his memoirs that in the months before the general election he was allowed—this under the new Douglas-Home

---

[83] Cairncross, 'Roll, Eric,'.

[84] A. K. Cairncross, *The Wilson Years: A Treasury diary, 1964–1969* (1997), pp. 1–2.

[85] Brown, *In my Way*, p. 97; cf. Theakston, *Leadership in Whitehall*, p. 182 on why this was neither a likely event nor necessarily a better one for the DEA.

[86] Shrimsley, *First Hundred Days*, p. 42–3.

[87] MacDougall, *Don and Mandarin*, p. 148.

[88] P. Burnham, *Remaking the Postwar World Economy: ROBOT and British Policy in the 1950s* (2003), esp. pp. 71, 74–8. The plan was defeated, with MacDougall and Maurice Allen, the Bank of England chief economist, particularly effective amongst the economists—and non-economist advisers—who opposed the abandonment of the fixed exchange rate regime.

[89] G. D. A. MacDougall, 'The Machinery of Economic Government: Some Personal Reflections', in D. Butler and A. H. Halsey, eds, *Policy and Politics: Essays in Honour of Norman Chester* (1978), p. 175.

rules[90] — to 'discuss with Opposition leaders possible changes in the organisation of departments'; and that, asked whether he would join the planned new department if Labour won the election, he indicated that he would do so, though he had clear reservations about leaving NEDC work unfinished and about the exact distribution of responsibilities between the planned new department, the NEDC and the Treasury.[91] His assessment of the effectiveness of the DEA, which he left in 1968 to replace Cairncross as chief economic adviser to the Treasury, revolved around the issue of the 'creative tension' between the two departments: 'The long run is a succession of short runs, and, in the event of a clash of interests, the Treasury was bound to win, at least so long as we had severe balance of payments difficulties.'[92] That said, he was more positive than Roll about the case for the DEA: 'there was a need, in the early years of the Wilson Government, for a senior Minister, with a Department like the DEA, to coordinate the many other economic policies, outside the traditional Treasury responsibilities, which a Chancellor could not possibly have had time to cope with adequately, especially as he has recurring external crises on his hands.'[93]

4. The DEA and the Institutions of Economic Policy

Before coming to the diaries and to Brittan's fourteen months in the DEA we take a brief detour to situate the DEA within the machinery of government and then to detail the structure of the DEA, of which the Information Division, in which Brittan was located initially, was one of five divisions in a department which by 1 October 1965 already had an establishment of 544 staff (as against 1,580 in the Treasury and 9,500 in the Board of Trade).[94] Appendix II provides a list of DEA ministers and senior officials.

In Figure 2 we reproduce Leruez's most helpful organisational chart for the incoming government:[95] this comprising a core executive led by

---

[90] Initiated in advance of the 1964 election, a new provision whereby informal contact was permitted between the civil service and the Opposition even before Parliament was dissolved; see P. Catterall, 'Handling the Transfer of Power: A Note on the 1964 Origins of the Douglas-Home Rules', *Contemporary British History*, 11.1 (1997), pp. 76–82.

[91] MacDougall, *Don and Mandarin*, pp. 148.

[92] MacDougall, *Don and Mandarin*, p. 174.

[93] MacDougall, *Don and Mandarin*, pp. 174–5.

[94] E. Roll, 'Machinery for Economic Planning', p. 6.

[95] 'Corridors of Economic Power', *The Times*, 12 November 1964, p. 20 provides a more detailed organisational chart (including senior officials by name as well as those of ministers) but it is too large and too complex to reproduce here.

the Prime Minister and a coordinating role for the DEA in terms of, first, other key departments, having in part or wholly economic functions; and, second, a series of administrative bodies (pre-eminently the NEDC and the NBPI) and, via the Treasury, the Bank of England. Additionally, Leruez also included and spatially located Cairncross as chief economic adviser, Kaldor as special adviser to the Chancellor and Neild as economic adviser to the Treasury, but not Balogh who was in the Cabinet Office. MacDougall, the last of the five key economic advisers, is also not identi-fied. Figure 2 is far from being a full policy network in the sense used by public policy analysts. This would need to incorporate dimensions for organised capital (for Britain, a specifically financial element as well as industrial-commercial interests) and labour,[96] but we are excused such a requirement here for it was the very novelty, pivotal position and person-ality attributes of key agents (not least Brown) which made the DEA an institution at least with the potential to create a unique policy network in this wider sense. Indeed, it had to do so, for lacking executive functions its raison d'être 'was one of co-ordination and therefore its links with other departments were of prime importance.'[97]

In Figure 3, we reproduce a chart prepared by Robert Shone*, NEDC Director General,[98] which foregrounds the NEDC but makes clear the interconnection with the DEA and thence, via Figure 2, to the broader economic machinery of government. In delineating the DEA's role, Roll, who drew heavily upon Otto Clarke's* assessment of the Treasury's post-1962 reorganisation responsibilities,[99] made clear that 'the purpose of the Department may be thought to be virtually co-terminous with govern-ment economic policy as a whole': 'to co-ordinate the activities of the economic departments ... so that their decisions are consistent with the achievement of a faster rate of growth while avoiding inflationary pres-sures; and through our relations with both sides of industry to secure a wide acceptance of the need to change our approach towards those factors in our economic life which impede economic growth.'[100]

---

[96] Pemberton, *Policy Learning and British Governance*, ch. 2 addresses this lacuna.
[97] Clifford, 'Rise and Fall', p. 103.
[98] TNA CAB 124/1440, Speech by Sir Robert Shone ... at the Opening Plenary Session of the Conference on "Productivity: The Next Five Years" at Eastbourne, on Tuesday, 26th November, 1963' provides a useful position statement, both personally and in relation to the NEDC in the pre-DEA period.
[99] Clarke, Plowden report', pp. 20–1; for his later views on the DEA, see 'The Machinery of Government', in W. Thornhill, ed., *The Modernization of British Government* (1975), p. 70.
[100] Roll, 'Machinery for Economic Planning', p. 3.

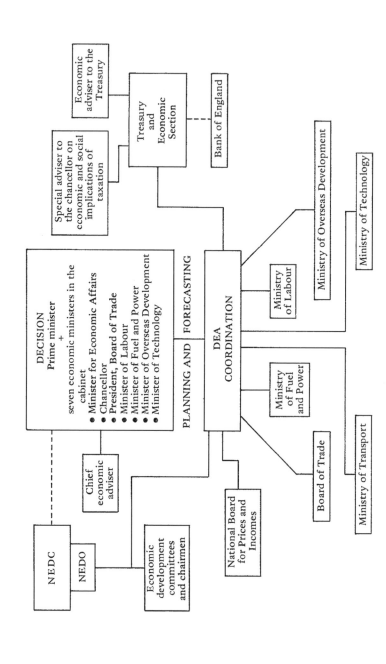

Figure 2. Government economic machinery, late 1964.
Source: Leruez, Economic Planning and Politics in Britain, figure 6.1.

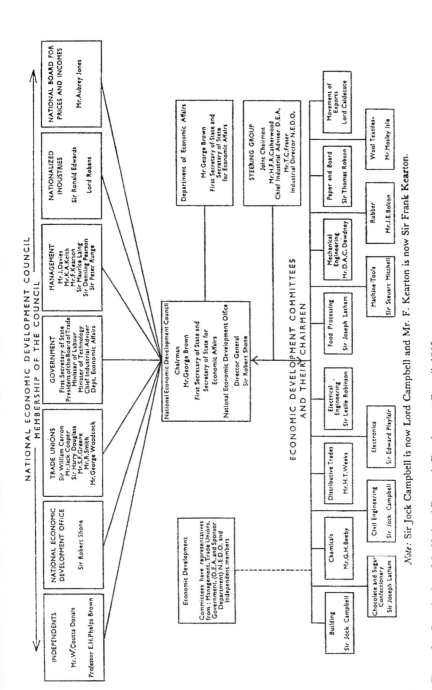

Figure 3. Organisation of the National Economic Development Council, 1965.

Source: Shone, 'Machinery for Economic Planning', p.17. Reproduced with permission of John Wiley and Sons Ltd.

Note: Sir Jock Campbell is now Lord Campbell and Mr. F. Kearton is now Sir Frank Kearton.

All of this was reflected in the divisional structure (divisional head, at Deputy Secretary level, in parentheses) which — in contrast to Whitehall norms — was organised on functional lines:[101]

I   Economic Planning (Jukes): the largest division; de facto comprising the previous NEDO Economic Division (assembled by MacDougall); and given the responsibility for preparing the National Plan;[102]

II   Industrial Policy (Ronald McIntosh*): much smaller; working closely with the Economic Planning Division; staffed mainly by 'irregulars'; and acquiring from the NEDC responsibility for the (initially nine but eventually 25 by 1968) EDCs;

III   Economic Co-ordination (Evan Maude* for home coordination; Mitchell[103] for overseas coordination): comprising members drawn from the Treasury's National Economy Group; responsibilities included the all-important income and price policy; and

IV   Regional Policy (Arthur Peterson*): partly staffed by secondments from the Board of Trade, this division operationalised the explicit regional dimension of the National Plan by establishing economic planning machinery (including Economic Planning Councils) in the English regions together with comparable bodies for Northern Ireland, Scotland and Wales.

These four Divisions, together with the Information Division in which Brittan resided temporarily, comprised the DEA which was headed by Roll as Permanent Secretary, Allen as Second Permanent Secretary, MacDougall as Director-General and Catherwood as Chief Industrial Advisor (see Appendix II). At this point, the functions of the DEA, the Plan and the NEDC and EDCs was described by a high-profile visiting group of US economists as follows:[104]

---

[101] In addition to Roll, Shanks, another *FT* journalist who like Brittan served in the DEA, provides a brief outline in *Planning and Politics: The British Experience, 1960–76* (1977), pp. 32–3; see also, Leruez, *Economic Planning*, ch. 6; Pollitt, *Manipulating the Machine*, pp. 51–3; Clifford, 'Rise and Fall', pp. 102–3; Fry, 'Whitehall', p. 15. A useful comparative perspective is provided by G. Denton, M. Forsyth and M. MacLellan, *Economic Planning and Policies in Britain, France and Germany* (1968), esp. ch. 4, this the culmination of a long-running PEP project, of which Denton was the research officer in charge, on economic planning and on the growth of the British economy; see also Political and Economic Planning, *Growth in the British Economy: A study of Economic Problems and Policies in Contemporary Britain* (1960).

[102] Opie, 'Economic Growth', pp. 165–70 provided a detailed insiders guide to the making of the Plan.

[103] Although not in the DEA section of the *British Imperial Calendar and Civil Service List* for either 1965 or 1966, it is highly probable that this is Sir Derek Mitchell (1922–2009) who, falling foul of Marcia Williams*, was from the No. 10 office 'promoted' to the DEA at the end 1965.

[104] D. C. Smith, 'Incomes Policy', in R. E. Caves and Associates, eds, *Britain's Economic Prospects* (1968), p. 118.

The purpose of the plan was to develop a coordinated, internally consistent set of projections of how the economy might develop to 1970 and thereby create expectations that would induce private economic decisions to conform to the projections. The work of the National Economic Development Council was directed more to the establishment and operation of consultative bodies for particular industries: economic development committees, of which there are now over twenty. The function of these committees is to explore problems at the industry level and to suggest ways to reduce them.

5. Brittan and the DEA

It was MacDougall who approached Brittan about the DEA and also made the introduction to Brown.[105] Certainly, Brittan met Brown on 21 July 1964 to discuss the role that the former might play, and between this meeting and his joining the DEA on 1 November 1964 he provided Brown with at least one briefing, portentously on import restrictions.[106] At the time of their meeting Brittan was Economics Editor at the *Observer,* a post in which he was not content as 'The paper needed someone who could take charge of all of its financial coverage, which was not my *forte*';[107] he was also putting the finishing touches to his Treasury book which was due to be published in the late summer but did not appear until a month after he had entered the DEA.[108]

Brittan is brief in his published memoir about the fourteen months he spent at the DEA, describing it as 'important mainly for the contacts I made

---

[105] This section draws upon an interview with Brittan at his home on 11 August 2005. MacDougall, *Don and Mandarin*, p. 150 has him as making the introduction with Brown.

[106] LGBP c4998 George Brown to Samuel Brittan, 22 July 1964; c4997 Samuel Brittan to George Brown, 14 August 1964; c4998 George Brown to Samuel Brittan, 1 September 1964. LGBP c4867 'Desk Diary 1964' has Brown seeing Brittan at 1615 hours on 21 July and then, at 2100 hours, meeting in the French Club with MacDougall, Neild, Shore and Balogh. Brown had dinner with MacDougall on 17 September and it is probable that final arrangements for the DEA were there then made. See also Paterson, *Tired and Emotional*, p. 173.

[107] Brittan, 'Samuel Brittan', p. 278.

[108] PA DM1107/A722 contains correspondence between Brittan and his Penguin editor (Dieter Pevsner) which makes clear that the manuscript (which, as a publishing project, had something of a complex history) was delayed during the summer and autumn, eventually being published on 10 December 1964 (and noted in leading article that day, 'Stop-Go Again?', *The Times*, p. 13). Review copies were made available a week or so earlier, as were personal copies: for example, Cairncross, *The Wilson Years*, p. 21 records in his diary for 1 December that the book had arrived and that '[Edward] Bridges[*] told me he thought passages about himself not too bad.' Given the delay and his impending appointment to the DEA, Brittan was concerned that 'advanced publicity ... [sh]ould emphasise that it was completed in its entirety quite a few months before I took up my present position' (Brittan to Dieter Pevsner, 2 November 1964; for fuller details on the urgency of its publication, see also Brittan to Hans Schmoller, 5 November 1964).

and the subsequent belief of people that I was writing about Whitehall from experience'. In interview he admits that the diary was opportunistic with a secondary purpose of keeping notes and assembling thoughts for a second edition of his Treasury book (the amount of data transcribed into the diary from official sources strongly suggests this as a motive).[109] Additionally, for an Institute of Contemporary British History conference, he provided the following context to summer 1964:[110]

> I had voted Labour in 1964 because I hoped, without much confidence, that Wilson would honour his own pledge and strike a blow against nuclear proliferation by abandoning the British deterrent. But on the economic side I had backed the growth policy of Reginald Maudling (Chancellor from 1962 to 1964) as the most radical show in town and was horrified that the incoming Labour government shattered confidence by shouting from the rooftops about the overall payments deficit it had inherited — very minor by later standards.

This is characteristically Brittan; displaying a combination and complexity of motives for voting, and indeed for joining the DEA, that belies any attempt to define an orthodox partisanship, let alone ideological position. Later, many would highlight Brittan's 'second thoughts' on the Keynesian conventional wisdom,[111] and much has been claimed (and much wrongly so) for his role in the reaction against that wisdom that found expression in Thatcherism,[112] but what is important here is that in 1964 Brittan did not occupy an intellectual position that might be viewed as routinely part of the postwar consensus. His Treasury book was deeply critical of 'Stop-Go' policies and the fetishism that underlay concern for the balance of payments and sterling, but more immediately — and hence the urgency for its publication — Brittan had in the book come out strongly against the sort of planning ministry that transpired with the DEA. One paragraph in particular deserves highlighting, for here Brittan in effect provided an analysis of the failure of the DEA *before* the department even existed let alone his becoming an irregular:[113]

---

[109] Brittan, 'Samuel Brittan', p. 280; Brittan interview.

[110] Brittan, 'A Backwards Glance: the Reappraisal of the 1960s', <www.samuelbrittan.co.uk/spee4_p.html>, accessed 14.03.03.

[111] Especial attention was paid to *Second Thoughts on Full Employment Policy* (1975), though in part this was because it was an early publication from the recently formed Centre for Policy Studies.

[112] Middleton, 'Brittan on Britain'; see also P. Jay, 'Left, Right, Left', *Financial Times Magazine*, 92 (12 February 2005), pp. 25–7, a review of Brittan's most recent book, *Against the Flow: Reflections of an Individualist* (2005).

[113] Brittan, *Treasury under the Tories*, p. 334. This is repeated in subsequent editions which were published as *Steering the Economy: The Role of the Treasury* (1969), pp. 201–2; (rev. edn, Harmondsworth, 1971), pp. 312–13. In noting the durability of this paragraph in subsequent editions,

Much in the preceding pages would point in the same direction as the Production or Economics Ministry favoured by the Labour and Liberal Parties. But the snag in most of these plans is that they assume there is something called 'finance' quite apart from economics and production. In fact, of course, the instruments by which production is influenced in this country are the Budget, monetary policy, exchange rate policy, and one or two very general controls. Despite all the talk of 'physical intervention', this is likely to remain the case. If the Treasury remains responsible for the balance of payments, for taxation, for the Bank Rate, and for the use of devices like the Regulator, it is likely to remain the effective Economics Ministry, whatever nominal changes are made.

The need for unified control of economic policy, and what transpired when it was not achieved, is rightly a staple of the literature on the DEA, at the time and since.[114] It certainly pervades Brittan's diary.

Brittan's Treasury book drew extensively — albeit in an unattributed fashion — on interviews with key officials (from Armstrong downwards through the Treasury and other departments) and politicians, Conservative and Labour.[115] Its publication undoubtedly caused Brown some embarrassment, though he did not acknowledge it or indeed Brittan in his memoirs. In marketing the book, in early 1965 Penguin collected together extracts from reviews, including:[116]

The Observer — Nora Beloff

Miss Beloff picked out for special attention the following paragraph from this book 'No Economic Minister ... who does not have direct and personal control over the Treasury's financial group can really live up to his title.' George Brown was asked if he agreed with this on BBC Television last night. We hear that his answer was rather evasive.

Later, in an interim evaluation of his period as an irregular, Brittan expanded on his 1964 position and on subsequent developments:[117]

Walker, 'First Wilson Governments', p. 204 argues that it 'encapsulated the failure not just of the DEA but of Wilson's macro-economic policy-making: by giving primacy to the maintenance of a singular external value of the pound, domestic production became a dependent variable.'

[114] For example, D. P. T. Jay, 'Government Control of the Economy: Defects in the Machinery', *Political Quarterly*, 39.2 (1968), pp. 134–44 and, from a former Minister of State at the DEA, A. Albu, 'Lessons of the Labour Government: I, Economic Policies and Methods', *Political Quarterly*, 41.2 (1970), pp. 141–6; see also Leruez, *Economic Planning*, chs 6, 9 and Pemberton, *Policy Learning and British Governance*, pp. 185, 189.

[115] PA DM1107/A722 Brittan to Anthony Goodwin, 17 November 1964, enclosing 'List of Complementary Copies' which records 46 names.

[116] PA DM1107/A722 'News from Penguin, The Treasury under the Tories', undated but position in file indicates early January 1965. The *Observer* review, 'Learning to Live with Busy Mr Brown', was published 13 December 1964, p. 4.

[117] Brittan, 'The Irregulars', p. 337.

In *The Treasury under the Tories* I advocated a real Economics Ministry based on, and including, the economic and financial divisions of the Treasury. Contrary to what is sometimes supposed, I came out strongly against any split of responsibility for managing the economy between the Treasury and the D.E.A. The split had a predictable unfortunate effect on the Treasury itself. It has given it encouragement to concentrate on the short-term and to revert at times to some of the attitudes characteristic of an old-fashioned Finance Ministry.

As will be seen from the diary the early months of the DEA involved a process of mutual education and expectation-setting by *all* parties, Brittan included, on what was possible for the new ministry given, first, the deficiencies of the concordat and, second, that the incoming government had within its first three days made the momentous decision that sterling would not be devalued.[118] From the first woeful entry ('Gloomy toilet with no soap or towel', Diary 2 November 1964) Brittan's disappointment with the DEA is palpable. It would be too easy to understand this in terms of how MacDougall characterises Brittan's DEA period:[119]

His year or so in the DEA, while no doubt highly educational, may have been something of a disappointment to him in that George Brown used him more for his journalistic talents and less for his powers of economic analysis than he had been led to believe when I introduced them and George more or less gave the impression that the three of us would run the Department.

The diary conveys well the chaos, but also the excitement, which surrounded the creation of the new department. This is a staple of the literature on the DEA and the diary amplifies in particular the critique that, whatever the rhetoric on Labour's extensive planning in opposition, in practice it had not done sufficient planning for achieving effective government,[120] making laughable the judgement by Shrimsley of 'the incredibly careful preparations made by Wilson and his colleagues whilst in opposition ...[with this] particularly so ... [for] the DEA'.[121] The diaries also shed considerable light on the day-to-day operation of a department whose minister and functions inevitably placed it in the limelight. What results is both different from and a complement to Cairncross' much

---

[118] Middleton, *Charlatans or Saviours?*, pp. 253–7 discusses this decision and, in particular, the role of the economists; see also C. C. S. Newton, 'The Two Sterling Crises of 1964 and the Decision not to Devalue', *Economic History Review*, 62.1 (2009), pp. 73–98 and idem, 'The Sterling Devaluation of 1967, the International Economy and Post-War Social Democracy', *English Historical Review*, 125.3 (2010), pp. 912–45.
[119] MacDougall, *Don and Mandarin*, p. 150.
[120] Theakston, *Labour Party and Whitehall*, p. 65.
[121] Shrimsley, *First Hundred Days*, p. 43.

longer Treasury diaries.[122] In part, Brittan's position as an irregular and junior to Cairncross makes this inevitable, but it is also reflects very different personalities: as one reviewer said of Cairncross' diary for the Wilson years, they were marked by a 'quality of restraint'.[123] Brittan's diary is much less restrained, much more that of a journalist suddenly given privileged access to key source material. Of course, they both share the characteristic of being written contrary to civil service rules. Both present an image of government in perpetual crisis; both add facts and atmosphere to our knowledge of the period, but of the two Brittan has the edge for his reflections on the workings of government and on the process of policy formulation.

Early on, we observe Brittan deepening the understanding of the policy process that he conveyed in his Treasury book. Thus for 24 November 1964 he reflects:

> Spent from noon to 8 p.m. drafting case for Incomes Policy. Mostly re-written by Donald [MacDougall]. Seemed endless process, with bits of paper all over the room; premature drafts retyping and then retyping again. Most of problems seemed to be typing one[s]. I see what Allen means by Donald's method of drafting. Groves thinks Reserves lost £80m on Friday.
>
> Told [Ian] Hudson[*] about book.
>
> *Reflection.* Can waste vast amount of time on speeches which regurgitate all policies. Then on consulting Departments and people within own Ministry, clearing the whole time and constant retyping, and this is quite apart from all the committees.
>
> Officials attend so many meetings with other officials at top and medium level that most of time taken up. Very little time to think. The sheer job of getting something out and agreed and (or clearly disagreed) exerts a great pressure for orthodoxy and following precedent. Any solution must involve more rugged edges, less co-ordination and more breaking up tasks into individual jobs. Different departmental policies should be allowed to emerge. Only high level questions at point of crucial decision should have to involve agreed unified Government action. Too high a price is paid for the myth of Government unity.

Brittan provides a compelling sense of how at the outset the new department was focused less on the National Plan, the fate of which had become inextricably connected with the DEA, and more immediately upon managing the implications of the decision not to devalue and of devaluation thence becoming the 'great unmentionable'.[124]

---

[122] Cairncross, *Diaries: the Radcliffe Committee and the Treasury, 1961–64* (1999) and idem, *Wilson Years*.

[123] A. Howard, 'Fallen on Stony Ground', *Times Literary Supplement*, 23 May 1997, p. 27.

[124] For the first analysis of the external constraint to use the official records in depth, see Newton, 'Two Sterling Crises'.

Such is the wealth of detail in the diary and of the breadth of the DEA's involvements thereafter that we provide in Appendix III a Calendar of Key Events to assist the reader; we have also assembled in Appendix IV Contemporary Economic Statistics and Later Revisions. From the latter we report here in Figure 4 the principal four macroeconomic series (mirroring the postwar policy goals of simultaneous high economic growth, a current account balance of payments surplus, full employment and low inflation) that were closely, if not obsessively, monitored by the authorities together with the industrial production index and an additional balance of payments measure, these both also closely watched by the markets and journalists reporting the markets. (The DEA had an especial interest as economic statistics were part of its brief.) The full data are reported in Appendix IV, but here we chart the first estimates and subsequent revisions (where appropriate) to convey the extreme fluidity of contemporary key performance indicators and consequent uncertainty for policy-makers at a time when, as Macmillan had put it in his famous metaphor, 'We are always, as it were, looking up a train last year's Bradshaw.'[125] In sequence we present in Figure 4 the balance of payment on current account (panel A1), the combined balance of payments on current account and long-term capital transactions (A2),[126] the real GDP growth rate on the previous year (B1), the industrial production index (B2), the unemployment rate (C) and the percentage change in the Retail Price Index (All Items) on previous year (D). As can be seen, and as is discussed in Appendix IV, the data in panels A1–2 and B1–2 were subject to very considerable revisions with consequent difficulties for the economic authorities in gauging the recent past, the current situation and the near future (what we would now call the problem of 'nowcasting') let alone the planning horizon for the Plan.

---

[125] 'Budget Proposals', *Parliamentary* Debates (House of Commons), 5th ser. 551 (17 April 1956), col. 867; on this theme, see G. O'Hara, 'Towards a New Bradshaw?: Economic Statistics and the British State in the 1950s and 1960s', *Economic History Review*, 60.1 (2007), pp. 1–34.

[126] See 'The Balance of Payments: Methods of Presentation', *Bank of England Quarterly Bulletin*, 4.4 (December 1964), pp. 276–86 for the standard presentation at this time. In simplified form (table 1) and with an example of early estimates for 1963 (£ millions), this was constructed as follows:

A. Current account balance	+113
B. Capital account balance	−155
C. Balance of current and long-term capital transactions (A+B)	−42
D. Balancing item	−111
E. Balance of monetary movements (equals sum rows 3+4, inverted sign)	153

In this example, the balancing item (-£111 m) is over twice as large as the visible trade deficit (£49m). A fuller version of this balance of payments account is provided in Table 3.

The problem of 'nowcasting' was understood only too well in the 1960s. 'It is always an obvious problem in this job, to know where one is at a given time.'[127]

Publicly, the first six weeks of the new department were dominated by three issues, here in sequence.[128] First, the urgency of the balance of payments situation which became a crisis because ministers did not effectively question official estimates immediately upon taking office that the 'deficit' (which was being measured not as the current account balance but as including long-term capital items) was unsustainably large. A figure of £800m (approximately 3 per cent of GDP) was allowed to enter into the public domain, whereas even the first published estimate for the current account balance (published March 1965) had it at £374m and current ONS statistics record £327m (Table 2 panel A1).[129] Constructed or otherwise as a crisis,[130] it was to the creation of emergency measures to lessen the balance of trade deficit that the new government had to respond and the DEA was heavily involved in what became the white paper published on 26 October which introduced an immediate imports surcharge, new export rebates and signalled discussions with the IMF about the use of drawing rights and a re-examination of an expensive but highly political Anglo-French project (Concord/Concorde, the supersonic civil airliner produced jointly by Aérospatiale and the British Aircraft Corporation).[131]

---

[127] Robert Hall diary, 2 April 1961, in A. K. Cairncross, ed, *The Robert Hall Diaries*, II: *1954–61* (1991), p. 260.

[128] A valuable source to read alongside the diary is F. T. Blackaby, 'Narrative, 1960–74', in idem, ed., *British Economic Policy, 1960–74* (Cambridge, 1978), esp. pp. 28–39.

[129] According to Brittan (Diary, 9 December 1964) it was Wilson who wanted the £800m figure included in the white paper; for the broader context, see R. Middleton, 'Struggling with the Impossible: Sterling, the Balance of Payments and British Economic Policy, 1949–72', in A. Arnon and W. L. Young, eds *The Open Economy Macromodel: Past, Present and Future* (Boston, MA, 2002), pp. 103–54; and Tomlinson, *Labour Government*, p. 14. Additionally, W. A. P. Manser, *Britain in the Balance: The Myth of Failure* (1971) remains the most important corrective, statistical and otherwise, to the orthodox story propagated in the 1960s about Britain's balance of payments problem.

[130] On the political economy of the balance of payments, and of the ideational construction of crises in particular, see B. Clift and J. D. Tomlinson, 'Whatever Happened to the Balance of Payments "Problem"?: The Contingent (Re)construction of British Economic Performance Assessment', *British Journal of Politics and International Relations*, 10.4 (2008), pp. 607–29 and J. D. Tomlinson, 'Balanced Accounts? Constructing the Balance of Payments Problem in Post-War Britain', *English Historical Review*, 124.4 (2009), pp. 863–84.

[131] Prime Minister's Office, *The Economic Situation* (1964). All of the triumvirate deal with the 26 October measures in their memoirs, but Jay, who on 17 October had sided with Wilson and Callaghan that immediate devaluation was not the correct course, is the most interesting and not just because he opposed the imposition of import controls (judging these illegal under GATT as against the alternative, quotas, which were not); *Change and Fortune*, pp. 298–9.

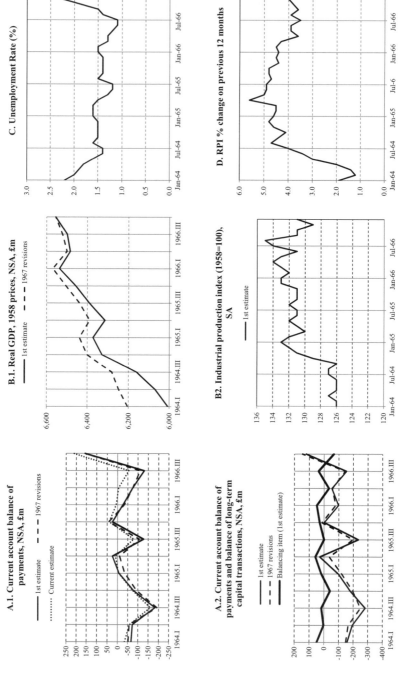

Figure 4. Key macroeconomic performance indicators. First estimates, 1967; revisions and current ONS estimates, 1964–66.

Secondly, there was preparation for an emergency budget (held 11 November):[132] this emphasised the importance of the 26 October measures to improve the balance of payments; it signalled both income tax rises and capital and corporate tax reform in prospect (in April); and in the interim raised both taxes on income and expenditure. Overall, it was designed to be broadly neutral with respect to demand and this was certainly the first judgement of the influential review (*NIER*) issued by the National Institute of Economic and Social Research (NIESR),[133] though the *Economist* was less sanguine, that it might be 'unwarrantably deflationary in relation to the current state of the economy.'[134] (Such was the uncertainty created by the budget that it was quickly followed up by an increase in Bank Rate from 5 to 7 per cent, a 200 basis point rise being highly unusual but nonetheless insufficient to calm the foreign exchange markets in particular so that pressure remained on the reserves.)[135] Although the DEA had no formal role in what was a Treasury-driven process of budget setting, it is clear from the diary the DEA was represented on the Budget Committee (12 November 1964) and that the emerging shape of subsequent budgets was a source of continual DEA interest/anxiety.

Thirdly, and here the DEA led the process, there were very detailed government discussions with the TUC and the CBI which led up to the publication on 16 December of the joint statement of intent on incomes and prices policy.[136] Achieving such a tripartite understanding was made all the more important by the decision not to devalue, for export competitiveness was seen as the key to improving the balance of payments and without restraint of inflation the pressure on sterling would not abate within a fixed exchange rate regime. What resulted was the first stage of the new government's (at this time voluntary, non-statutory) income and prices policy; it was also the first evidence of the coordinating role that the DEA was designed to play in economic policy.[137] Whatever the

---

[132] 'Budget Statement', *Parliamentary Debates* (House of Commons), 5th ser. 701 (11 November 1964), cols. 1023–45.

[133] 'Summary', *NIER*, 30 (November 1964), p. 20.

[134] 'Labour's Tanner', *Economist*, 14 November 1964, p. 669.

[135] 'Seven Days that Shook Sterling', *Economist*, 28 November 1964, p. 1041–4; see also Blackaby, 'Narrative', pp. 32–3.

[136] TNA EW 8/1, 'Joint Statement of Intent on Productivity, Prices and Incomes', 16 December 1964. This file contains drafts and there is evidence of Brittan's involvement (J. L. Clark to S. Brittan, 18 November 1964). The statement is reproduced in Brittan, *Steering the Economy* (1969 edn), p. 204.

[137] Although the thirty year rule precluded access to the public records at this time, a very good source for DEA involvement remains L. Panitch, *Social Democracy and Industrial Militancy: The Labour Party, the Trade Unions and Incomes Policy, 1945 to 1974* (Cambridge, 1976), ch. 3; see also on this

subsequent judgements about the DEA's effectiveness, most commentators were complimentary about the joint statement at the time and since.[138]
It was a good start for the DEA, and whilst it and the two other immediate
issues were not directly about the National Plan, it was important infra-
structure for that Plan.

Additionally, there was a fourth issue which did not have public
prominence but was absolutely vital: making operational the politician's
concordat of summer 1964 so that officials would know with clarity the
role of the new department and its relations with the Treasury and the
NEDC. Much of December was taken up with official discussions and
drafting, punctuated by interventions by Brown who, resistant to the clari-
fication sought by the officials, did 'not think it is necessary to spell out
all of the details, especially in a document which we intend to circulate to
other Departments.'[139] An agreed text was circulated on 10 December.[140]

By the first week of December the new department was bedding down
in Storey's Gate, 'installed at the backside of the Treasury' as Balogh had
warned Brown as a metaphor for what would become the DEA.[141] Brittan,
however, was already concerned about his role and now realising that
Brown had always intended to utilise him more as a journalist than as an
economist (Diary, undated [but early] December 1964).[142] Interestingly
there is no unambiguous mention of the National Plan until 9 December,
though the Diary is full of high level first- and second-hand reporting

---

element within the evolution of postwar incomes policies, R. Jones, *Wages and Employment Policy,
1936–1985* (1987), pp. 66–72.

[138] 'The Treaty on Incomes', *Economist*, 19 December 1964, p. 1325–6; O'Hara, *From Dreams to
Disillusionment*, p. 53; idem, '"Planned Growth of Incomes": or "Emergency Gimmick": The Labour
Party, the Social Partners and Incomes Policy, 1964–70', *Labour History Review*, 69.1 (2004), pp.
59–81.

[139] TNA PREM 13/2126, George Brown to Sir L. Helsby, 4 December 1964, p. 3.

[140] TNA PREM 13/2126, L. N. Helsby to Prime Minister, 10 December 1964; attached 'Co-operation
between the Department of Economic Affairs and the Treasury'. Within the DEA, Groves tried to
draft a concise statement of the DEA's work but this ran up against criticism from Allen that no simple
translation from a reading of the staff chart was possible for it 'fails to bring out the extent to which
the Department operates as a whole and can therefore lead to serious misunderstanding about the
responsibility for certain operations, notably DEA involvement in incomes policy: TNA EW 1/26, J.
D. Groves, 'Possible New Introduction for Draft Article on the Work of the DEA', 7 January 1965; D.
Allen to J. D. Groves, 8 January 1965. Some redrafting occurred but there is no final version on file.
See also D. A. V. Allen to Sir Eric Roll, 'Possible Changes in the Role of the Department', 28 March
1966, esp. pp. 3–4 on the 'boundary problem'.

[141] Brown, *In my Way*, p. 99.

[142] TNA EW 4/50, J. D. Groves to A. J. Wiggins, 1 February 1965 suggests that Brittan was very
quickly being swamped by requests to write speeches, some of which as 'political speeches' ought on
civil service conventions to have been produced by party headquarters.

of detailed economic issues and, pace Heclo and Wildavsky, the 'trial of personalities' (see p. 12) that is the bread-and-butter of civil service gossip. Throughout December and into the new year, Brittan is engaged on a huge range of issues, domestic and — with continuing trouble generated with the European Free Trade Association (EFTA) by the 26 October measures — foreign. Work on the Plan was the responsibility of the Economic Planning Division under the Deputy Director-General, Jukes.[143] With three Assistant Directors (John Grieve Smith*, Denys Munby* and Roger Opie), this Division mainly comprised much less senior staff who were mostly irregulars. Of these, seconded Oxford economists were in the ascendant,[144] many of whom would later write, directly or indirectly, about their experiences.[145]

---

[143] Extensive detail on the derivation of the Plan process, and of the operation of the DEA, was provided in 'Memorandum Submitted on Behalf of the Secretary of State for Economic Affairs' for the Estimates Committee Sub-Committee on Economic Affairs 1964–5, included in *Fourth Report from the Estimates Committee, Government Statistical Services*, HC 246 (1966–7), pp. 283–316; see also evidence by J. A. Jukes and B. C. Brown, 23 May 1966, pp. 317–22. NEDC evidence later that same day ('Memorandum Submitted by the National Economic Development Office', pp. 323–331) together with the questioning of NEDC officials (pp. 332–37) also provides a useful source on the DEA and its relations with adjunct departments. The Sub-Committee also examined Roll and Allen on the DEA, NEDC and government economic statistics on 11 July 1966 (pp. 431–8).

[144] *British Imperial Calendar and Civil Service List*, 1965 and 1966, has the following in that Division:

	1965	1966
Senior Economic Advisor:	Fred Jones	
Economic Consultants:	Wilfred Beckerman; H. H. Liesner	Wilfred Beckerman, H. H. Liesner; C. A. E. Goodhart; J. M. Marquand
Economic Advisor:	Brian Reading	Brian Reading
Economic Assistants:	R. M. Gibbs; Andrew Graham; J. R. C. Lecomber; Francis Stewart; A. P. Watson; E. G. Whybrew	
Chief Statistician	B. C. Brown	B. C. Brown; O. Nankivell

[145] Some are in Beckerman, ed., *Labour Government's Economic Record* (Graham, Goodhart, Opie); some published more extended accounts and analyses of the role and effectiveness of irregular economists in government (Opie, 'Making of Economic Policy'; Shanks, 'Irregular') and some have written memoirs in which their DEA years appear in passing (normally before proceeding on to more productive occupations): for example, W. Beckerman, 'Wilfred Beckerman (b. 1925)', in Backhouse and Middleton, eds, *Exemplary Economists*, II, pp. 165–9 and C. A. E. Goodhart, 'A Central Bank Economist', in P. Mizen, ed., *Central Banking, Monetary Theory and Practice: Essays in Honour of Charles Goodhart* (Cheltenham, 2003), p. 22. Extant Goodhart memoranda in the TNA make clear the dissonance between his creativity and the political realities of planning, and from this it is not difficult to see why his period as an irregular was so short-lived: TNA EW 24/93 C. A. E. Goodhart to Sir Donald MacDougall, 'The Future of Planning', undated but about 6 June 1965; C. A. E. Goodhart to Sir Donald MacDougall, 'The Strategy of Planning', undated but about 7 September 1965. Goodhart opposed 5-year rolling programmes, upon which Brittan was agreed: 'a rolling programme maximises

The following year for Brittan can be divided into pre-Plan and post-Plan publication (this being 16 September, though to all intents and purposes the Plan was finalised by the third week of August save for some last-minute minor redrafting to assuage objections on detail by some key parties).[146] To begin with there was continuing fallout with EFTA from the 26 October measures, frequent speculation about the exchange rate ('Everyone seems to be talking of the unmentionable'; Diary end of June 1965) but above all what strikes the reader is the extraordinary range of topics, individuals and institutions (domestic, European and international) that comprised Brittan's world for the calendar year 1965 and a month beyond. Amidst the hubbub, the 'First Secretary's Progress Meeting' provided a weekly structure, whilst preparation for Callaghan's second budget and the Plan provided a twin focus. These apart, the phrase 'A lot of frenzied and self-stultifying activity' (Diary, 13 January 1965) captures Brittan's frustration.

On the budget, the size of the 'budget judgment' (the amount of defla-tion, usually denominated in units of £50 million, which would comprise the change in fiscal stance in the budget statement) was a major preoc-cupation, made all the more so by the DEA having no formal involvement in what was a Treasury-driven process and Brown inevitably using the budget as a tool in the continuing internecine dispute with the Treasury. The diary abounds with rumours; there was a definite sense of contest with the Treasury ('If DEA wins over budget'; Diary 5 February 1965); and in the event Callaghan's April 1965 budget[147] did deliver a judgement of such a magnitude (some £250 million of additional taxation (with 6d (2.5p) on income tax having prominence) and public spending retrench-ment (including the cancellation of the high-profile TSR2 project) that the National Plan was already compromised on the demand side.[148]

---

the temptation to avoid difficult policy issues, by dangling the target a little further away each time round' (TNA EW 24/93, S. Brittan to Sir Donald MacDougall, 29 June 1965).

[146] TNA EW 25/100, K. F. J. Ennals, 'The National Plan', 19 August 1965. File contains last-minute redrafting and correspondence. It had been intended originally to publish an outline plan as a back-ground to the budget. This did not happen, but Brown circulated to the Cabinet (TNA CAB 129/121 'The Outline Plan', 30 March 1965) a progress report a week before the budget. This reaffirmed the 25 per cent growth target and expressed confidence that the measures taken to date to improve the balance of payments would not imperil that target.

[147] 'Budget Statement', *Parliamentary Debates* (House of Commons), 5th ser. 710 (6 April 1965), cols. 243–96; for respectively comment and detail: 'Is Virtue Enough?'; 'Budget: Changing Directions', *Economist*, 10 April 1965, pp. 147–9, 207–14; see also 'Assessment of the Effects of Government Measures', *NIER*, 32 (May 1965), pp. 20–2 for an assessment of the combined measures since autumn 1964 (but not including the monetary tightening) on a quarterly basis, 1964.IV to 1966.II.

[148] R. W. R. Price, 'Budgetary policy', in Blackaby, ed., *British Economic Policy*, pp. 199–200; see also chart 4.6 which (on a full employment corrected basis and using NIESR estimates) has the change

Brittan's position in the Information as against the Economic Planning Division meant that his involvement in drafting the National Plan was always piecemeal. He records (Diary, 14 July 1965) that he was drafting chapter one which when published ran to 21 pages, beginning with the plan in outline and concluding with a checklist for action. By the time of publication the growth target had been downgraded from the 4 per cent average set by NEDC for 1961–6 to 3.8 per cent for 1964–70 (still cumulatively 25 per cent but over six not five years),[149] and from the diary (25 January 1965) it seems this new target was set early in the new year. For the intervening six months Brittan mentions the Plan with variable frequency, but with the 27 July measures[150] — occasioned once more by concern with balance of payments weakness — it was finally clear that the Plan had been overtaken by events, recording (Diary, 28 July 1965):

> These latest measures mark the death of the NEDC Plan type of approach. They depend for their credibility on avoiding deflation. Something more mechanistic now required. Only regret toned down anti-D.E.A. stuff in book. Unrepentant believer in 'Planning' on original Neddy lines.

Interestingly, the diary does not mark publication day for the Plan, though his reflections on the Plan predate its publication by some measure. In June he had been lamenting that he might be 'About the only person left who believes in Conservative 1963–64 policies!' (Diary, 12 June 1965), while three months later he began more detailed reflections:

> Plan is:-
> (a) macro-target;
> (b) market research combined with growth rate;
> (c) programme of action linked with the above;
> (d) for purposes of government spending — in this respect not means of improving performance, but of housekeeping.

---

in fiscal stance between 1963/4 and 1964/5 as a move from mild expansion to neutrality and then subsequently to significant restraint for 1965/6.

[149] 'It was hard for Ministers to accept a substantially lower figure than this and there was indeed some pressure to adopt a growth target of more than 4 per cent' (TNA EW 24/93 D. J. Kirkness, 'The Growth Rate of the National plan', undated but probably 3 October 1966).

[150] Comprising cuts in public investment programmes, tighter exchange controls and restrictions on HP, Blackaby, 'Narrative', p. 35 agreed with contemporary commentators that this was a 'tough' package, designed to reduce demand by a further £200 million in a full year. However, there was an important lack of clarity about detail and timescale for effects when viewed in aggregate with the 6 April budget and intervening measures (especially credit restriction). That said, Blackaby, pp. 35–6 reported as important that the NIESR forecast for growth from mid-1965 was downgraded from 2½ to 1½ per cent between the May and August 1965 issues of the *NIER*.

Figure 5. Vicky cartoon on the publication of The National Plan, *Evening Standard*, 16 December 1965. Reproduced with permission of the British Cartoon Archive, University of Kent.

Absurd to make (a) and (b) centre of policy. Can only be adjunct. 'Category' mistake to think that "Plan" solves anything. Everything depends on its contents.

Why I believed in Planning: as expansionist Trojan horse. This route is now discredited. What is left is a capacity argument. [Roy] Harrod[*] has argued that getting economy to grow without demand bursting its seams is a very delicate operation. It is certainly difficult to combine with deflation.

Subsequent reflections on the Plan morphed into a personal reappraisal of his Treasury book and how it now needed to be revised in light of subsequent developments and his experience as an irregular (for example, two sets of reflections, 18 September 1965). Brittan's conversion to a managed floating exchange rate as a *sine qua non* for escaping 'Stop-Go' finds full expression in his published (with Political and Economic Policy, PEP) post-mortem on the Plan; it is here that for the first time he represents

The task ahead

This is a plan to make us more prosperous.

To succeed we have got to do two things:

—we have got to get out of the red quickly. It is no use running away from the fact that we are heavily in debt to the rest of the world, and our first job must be to pay our way;

—we have got to make sure that we do not get into this sort of mess again. This means big changes in the way we do things, so that we can get production up, costs down, and, at the same time sell enough abroad to pay our bills.

Our aim is to step up production so that by 1970 we are producing a quarter more than last year.

This 25 per cent increase will give us £8,000 millions more to use in 1970. It will enable us to pay our way in the world, raise our living standards and play a vigorous part in international affairs.

It will all be needed if pay rises are not to be largely cancelled out by higher prices, if we are to take proper care of the old and the sick and build the new houses, schools, hospitals and roads which we must have.

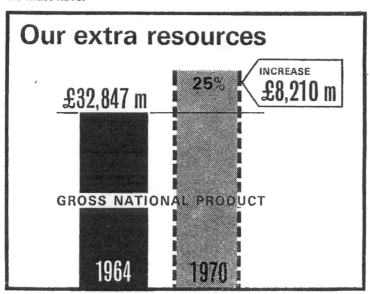

Figure 6. The 25 per cent extra resources. *Source:* Department of Economic Affairs, *Working for Prosperity: The National Plan in Brief* (1965).

the Plan as never having existed in any real sense, 'a confidence trick for inducing a favourable view of the future'.[151] This, of course, had been MacDougall's view all along.[152]

It would be too easy to see the post-Plan four months as a progressive disengagement by Brittan from the DEA. The last dated diary entry is 29 January 1966, a week before yet another set of deflationary monetary measures forced by continuing concerns about balance of payments weakness.[153] However, these were significantly different, and sufficiently so that the first *NIER* issue of the new year questioned whether the Plan output target could be maintained since:[154]

> In the first two years of the Plan, output is likely to have risen slightly less than 2½ per cent a year. For the 1970 target to be reached, it would have to grow in the remaining four years by an average of about 4½ per cent a year. This seems rather too ambitious an objective.

The NIESR refrained from saying that the Plan was 'too ambitious' given the unresolved 'great unmentionable', but the impasse now reached was even more a staple of economists' private conversations and soon, within the DEA, there would be discussion about whether a revised version of the Plan should be published and if so what ought to be the growth target.[155] By this point, Brittan had long departed to the job he had wanted for some time, that of Economics Editor at the *Financial Times*, for he had been in prolonged negotiations with Gordon Newton*, this newspaper's editor.[156] Even after his departure, and like so many economists inside but as well

---

[151] Brittan, 'Inquest on Planning', *Broadsheet*, 33.499 (January 1967), pp. 1–60.

[152] MacDougall, *Don and Mandarin*, p. 138; see also pp. 174–5 for his later reflections on the justification for the DEA, in which he emphasised the coordinating role.

[153] Blackaby, 'Narrative', p. 37.

[154] 'The Economic Situation: Annual review', *NIER*, 35 (February 1966), p. 12.

[155] TNA EW 24/96 contains extensive correspondence on whether to revise the published Plan, from which it is clear that there were at least thought experiments in terms of 18 per cent as against 25 per cent growth by 1970; F. Catherwood to D. Allen, 1 June 1966.

[156] D. Kynaston, *The Financial Times: A Centenary History* (1988), pp. 329–30 provides an account of Brittan's return to the *FT*, explaining his departure from the DEA 'partly on account of Britain's involvement in the Vietnam War'. Certainly, Vietnam features in the diary (21 December 1965: 'Mil[itary] vict[ory] impossible for either side'; 10 January 1966: 'If UK helps, he [President Johnson] would be more helpful in other things'), but Brittan (correspondence with author, 19 September 2010) is adamant that his departure had nothing to do with Vietnam: 'I merely used my physical proximity to express my opposition to the venture on separate occasions to Brown and Roll.' He continues: 'I did not think I was going to remain an irregular and I doubted if the Civil Service would have wanted to establish me; and I had to consider how to make a living. When George Cyriax[*], then chief economics writer there decided to leave an obvious opportunity occurred. I believe, although I have not checked[,] that Nigel Lawson reminded the editor of my availability.'

as outside of Whitehall, he maintained the self-denying ordnance about devaluation throughout 1966 and into 1967.[157]

Brittan recorded in the second edition of his Treasury book a day-by-day account of events in mid July 1966,[158] the point at which following a serious docks strike the run on the sterling reserves was met by a further, most severe to date, deflationary package (designed to reduce domestic demand by £500 million and overseas spending by £150 million),[159] this in effect — as Opie had judged it — the point at which the National Plan 'died (possibly murdered)'. What was not public knowledge at the time was that in July 1966 Brown, now finally convinced that devaluation was both desirable and unavoidable, made a last ditch stand to save the National Plan through an easing of the external constraint.[160] Had Brittan still been in the DEA his views on this idea would have made interesting reading indeed.

6. Postscript

As we have seen Brittan did not immediately launch into print on the DEA or the 'great unmentionable', and before briefly surveying his short-, medium- and longer-term reflections on this era it is appropriate to first remind ourselves quite why the National Plan, and thus the DEA, mattered.

In Figure 7, which uses the latest data to generate an updated version of the much reproduced chart by Leruez,[161] we model what might have happened to the British economy by 1973, the end of the so-called 'golden age', if the 1963 NEDC 4 per cent per annum or 1965 DEA 3.8 per cent per annum growth plans had come to fruition. Taking the NEDC target as the reference point the shortfall by 1973 was 14.4 per

---

[157] Middleton, *Charlatans or Saviours?*, p. 255; see also Kynaston, *Financial Times*, pp. 327–9.

[158] Brittan, *Steering the Economy* (1969 edn), pp. 214–15

[159] Blackaby, 'Narrative', pp. 37–9. The measures were announced by Wilson on 20 July 1966. Although Brown had threatened to resign he moved from the DEA to become Foreign Secretary on 11 August 1966.

[160] Brown, *In my Way*, pp. 114–115; MacDougall, *Don and Mandarin*, pp. 167–9. Fortunately, with TNA records now available, these memoirs can be supplemented by: Tomlinson, *Labour Governments*, pp. 53–4, 88; Newton, 'Two Sterling Crises'; and idem, 'The Defence of Sterling, 1964–67', unpublished paper (2010); see also M. D. Bordo, R. MacDonald and M. Oliver, 'Sterling in Crisis, 1964–1967', *European Review of Economic History*, 13.3 (2009), pp. 437–59 and C. R. Schenk, *The Decline of Sterling: Managing the Retreat of an International Currency, 1945–1992* (Cambridge, 2010), esp. ch. 5.

[161] Leruez, *Economic Planning*, figure 11.1.

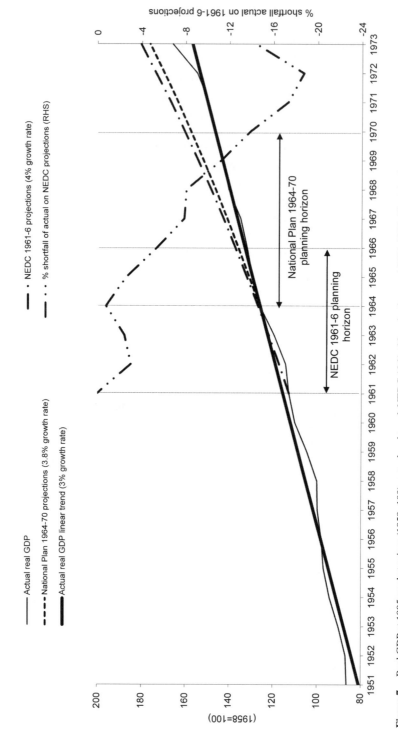

Figure 7. Real GDP at 1995 market prices (1958=100): actual and trend, NEDC 1961–66 projections and DEA 1965–70 projections.

Source: Middleton, 'Economists and Economic Growth', figure 8.1.

cent, and it is noteworthy that this would have been significantly larger had there not been the Barber boom following the infamous U-turn of 1971–2. Elsewhere I have argued that had the growth consciousness of the early 1960s been translated successfully into growth achievements in line with the NEDC/DEA targets 'then Britain would by 1973 have attained a standard of living so much closer to the leading OECD economies that the narrative of relative economic decline which now pervades the literature could not have developed.'[162] Disappointment with growth, planning and Labour were to set the tone of politics and economics for many years to come, though not all would go quite as far as one political economist, here reflecting on Crosland's legacy, that 'The consequences in the postponement of devaluation, the wrecking of planning targets and the dismemberment of the DEA constituted one of the greatest wasted opportunities of recent economic history.'[163]

For Brown:[164]

> The story of the D.E.A. … is the record of a social revolution that failed. The D.E.A. was meant to be — and it might have been — the greatest contribution of the Labour Party to the recasting of the machinery of government to meet the needs of the twentieth century. Its setting up was also the opening campaign of a major social revolution; its consequences — had it succeeded — more far reaching than anything else attempted by Labour since 1945….
>
> The revolution failed — partly because it was betrayed by some of those who were pledged to see it through, and partly because … fundamental changes in other policies were not carried out.

No doubt a high discount rate for Brownian rhetoric needs to be applied, but even so it is significant that the DEA experiment is still frequently invoked by the commentariat: for example, it surfaced when Michael Heseltine* (suitably equipped with a number of grandiose titles, including First Secretary) held the brief for competitiveness in the Major administration;[165] and it was sufficient of a live issue in the months before the 1997 election that one retired Treasury mandarin felt need to warn against 'repeating Harold Wilson's error in creating the DEA'.[166] It is unknown whether an

---

[162] Middleton, 'Economists and Economic Growth', p. 131.

[163] C. Crouch, 'The Place of Public Expenditure in Socialist Thought', in D. Lipsey and D. Leonard, eds, *The Socialist Agenda: Crosland's Legacy* (1981), p. 171.

[164] Brown, *In my Way*, p. 95.

[165] C. Brown, 'Heseltine Becomes a Lion to Roar in Whitehall's Jungle, *Independent*, 10 July 1995 <http://www.independent.co.uk/news/heseltine-becomes-a-lion-to-roar-in-whitehalls-jungle-1590707. html>, 23.07.10.

[166] L. Pliatzky, 'The Treasury's Mission under Gordon Brown', *Political Quarterly*, 68.1 (1997), p. 93.

interpretation of the DEA-Treasury relationship as more tension than creation informed Gordon Brown's decision not to hive off functions but to
transform the Treasury into an even more powerful department for domestic policy.[167] Interestingly, of course, in 1997 as in 1964 there was a third
man problem (in this case John Prescott). Finally, more recently the issue
of the DEA has featured in a Treasury seminar on the department's own
history, and in his contribution Brittan was able from very personal experience as well as the standpoint of over forty years of observation counsel
Treasury officials: 'The subject is of more than antiquarian interest, as
it uncovers some problems which are still very much with us.'[168] More
recently still, with the current Conservative-Liberal Democrat coalition
government, the example of the DEA has been cited by journalists ever
mindful (and no doubt hopeful) of tensions between the Treasury, with
its Conservative Chancellor, and the Department for Business, Innovation
and Skills, headed by a Liberal Democrat minister, an academic economist turned business economist and latterly politician.[169]

For Brittan, his early reflections are conveniently packaged in the
diary. They combine growing frustration with the 'absurdity of fixed
[exchange] rates' (Diary, 10 February 1965), such that Stop-Go and sub-
optimal growth would not cease without devaluation, with consideration of
a range of alternatives along with continued refinement of his strictures on
the ineffectiveness of British governments and bureaucracy. At this point
he did not favour the radical Frank Paish* option,[170] that of running the
economy at a higher average rate of unemployment to relieve inflationary

---

[167] Before the election, the influential W. Hutton, *The State We're In* (1995), pp. 287–90 had deliber-
ated on Treasury deficiencies but not recommended a counterweight such as a DEA. Within the New
Labour camp, there was some discussion of strengthening the Cabinet Office as a counterweight, but
this came to nought: R. Preston, *Brown's Britain* (2005), p. 75. However, when he became Chancellor
Brown wanted the Treasury to adopt a longer-term and supply-side perspective; indeed, one veteran
Treasury watcher argued that 'Gordon Brown made the Treasury into a kind of modern DEA with a
heavy emphasis on microeconomic policies, or the supply-side': W. Keegan, *The Prudence of Mr
Gordon Brown* (2003), p. 247.

[168] Brittan, 'The Moral of the Department of Economic Affairs', 22 October 2007 <http://www.
samuelbrittan.co.uk/spee52_p.html>, 22.07.10.

[169] For example, L. Elliott and J. Treanor, 'Cable and Osborne are the odd couple who could make
or break the coalition', *Guardian*, 13 May 2010 <http://www.guardian.co.uk/politics/2010/may/13/
cameron-cable-osborne-visit-banks/print>, 22.07.10.

[170] Paish, who had a deep understanding of the cyclical behaviour of the British economy, developed
early the thesis that the British economy needed to be operated at a lower average pressure of demand.
His major relevant writings for policy, often first appearing in the *Lloyd Banks Review*, are collected in
Studies in an Inflationary Economy: The United Kingdom, 1948–1961 (1962) and *How the Economy
Works and Other Essays* (1970).

and balance of payments pressures and thereby avoid sterling crises ('I objected to slow growth and the distortions of the fixed rate'; Diary, 16 August 1965). Indeed, Brittan never subsequently favoured the Paish analysis as the minimum unemployment level could not be estimated,[171] though of course by the 1970s his analysis of the determinants of unemployment and of the potential of discretionary demand management had changed considerably.[172] That said, relative to post-golden age unemployment, the unemployment rate was both very low and very stable during 1964 and 1965 (NSA it averaged 1.4 per cent for Brittan's fourteen months at the DEA) (Figure 4, panel C). At points in his diary reflections he is explicit that he is reading the current situation in relation to what he wrote in his Treasury book and beginning his mental redrafting for the second edition (Diary, 18 September 1965):

> *Reflections on Book* Re-reading page 268 — on Ministers doing the right thing, but too slowly and with too many delaying Committees, all seems terribly familiar!
>
> Labour Party continued the "New Conservative Policies" of 1964 — pushing them further in some directions, but making an appalling mess through their delighted screaming that all they inherited was awful.
>
> G[eorge] B[rown] vastly exaggerated how National Plan differed from NEDC exercise. R[eginald] M[audling] could have achieved same publicity effect if he had been more of an enthusiast for NEDC!

Brittan's medium-term reflections were published first in his PEP pamphlet (January 1967) and then much more substantially in the revised edition of his Treasury book (August 1969). The preliminary matter makes clear the intellectual journey since the first edition, including acknowledgement of the valuable time spent in the DEA; there is a new chapter on 'indicative planning, British style'; and an epilogue which complements his important *Left or Right* (1968) which marks an important stage in his reaction against contemporary trends in both economics and politics.[173] His epilogue was blunt and was much cited by reviewers:[174]

> part of the reason why Labour did not fulfil its promise to 'get Britain moving' after the 1964 election, but instead presided over the biggest series of economic crises in the postwar period, is that it spent far too much of its last years in Opposition on

---

[171] Brittan, 'A Backward Glance'.

[172] Brittan, *Second Thoughts*.

[173] Brittan, *Steering the Economy* (1969 edn), pp. xi, xv–xix, 276–89, 313–27; *Left or Right?: The Bogus Dilemma* (1968). On the importance of the bogus dilemma book, see Middleton, 'Brittan on Britain'.

[174] Brittan, *Steering the Economy* (1969 edn), pp. 314–15; cited in 'Treasury Under Both Sides', *Economist*, 23 August 1969. p. 48.

questions about departments and who was to run them and not nearly enough on matters of substance. If as much time had been devoted to a realistic analysis of the balance-of-payments constraint on policy as was in fact devoted to second-order issues of machinery, the result might have been very different.

He closed the 1969 edition thus:[175]

Almost every conceivable medicine has long ago been prescribed for the British economy, which must be among the most over-diagnosed in the world. The need is not for highly original measures but for the application of a consistent combination of those that are already known. Such an application could yet produce what passes for an economic miracle in the oratory of the subject.

Further perspective came with the final edition which included some new material but also an extended introduction which reflected on the first edition:[176]

The Treasury Under the Tories was regarded by some reviewers as strongly critical of the Treasury. But what I find most interesting, looking back on it now, is the extent to which it shared the Treasury outlook of the time.

My real policy error in 1964 was the institutional sphere ... the whole 'planning' movement was a bad tactical mistake which actively delayed the basic re-appraisal of the exchange rate and other priorities desired by its adherents. The moral I would emphasize is that it is better for critics and reformers to argue for their beliefs directly and avoid getting caught up in fashionable causes of doubtful validity.

---

[175] Brittan, *Steering the Economy* (1969 edn), p. 327.
[176] Brittan, *Steering the Economy* (1971 edn), pp. 13, 15–16.

Samuel Brittan
the Diary of an 'Irregular', 1964–6

Labour having won the general election on Thursday 15 October 1964, and Harold Wilson* having announced his Cabinet the following day, George Brown* (hereafter GB) became First Secretary of State, thereby de facto Deputy Prime Minister, and Secretary of State for Economic Affairs, in which capacity he was charged with establishing the new Department of Economic Affairs which would formulate and implement the National Plan which was the centrepiece of Labour's economic policy programme. Brittan joined the new department on 1 November. (* indicates an entry in Appendix I. Dramatis Personae; additionally, see also Appendix II. DEA Minister and Senior Officials; Appendix III. Calendar of Key Events; and Appendix IV. Contemporary Economic Statistics and Later Revisions.)

2 November 1964 Gloomy toilet with no soap or towel. I donated a piece of soap to the toilet, which afterwards vanished. Apparently suggestion of a modern type ticking roller towel has never got anywhere in Whitehall! One has to keep a horrible towel and soap in a drawer. A laundry then comes round with a fresh piece of soap and a towel every week, (or is it every fortnight?) if one is at one's desk at the time.

There were no telephone directories in the so-called 'suite' of offices in which I was or at the entrance to the Ministry. Directory enquiries took ages to reply. (Since got telephone directories!)

No tea was being provided. This was a privilege of the messengers, but there were no messengers allocated to our corridor. The messengers who served our rooms were not regarded as 'our' messengers, but 'served other men'. Therefore, John Groves'* [hereafter JG] secretary made the tea instead. I nearly jumped out of my seat when she asked me to bring a cup! (Have since found tea-making a huge industry. For hours in the morning and in the afternoon one sees secretaries walking about in corridors, carrying huge teapots or urns. They make tea, pour it out and then wash up. Seems a colossal waste of labour which ought to be centralised by a few people carrying a trolley.)

Found cupboard in my room which wouldn't open. Told about stringent security precautions. But there was no security cupboard in my room yet!

According to JG the measures (import levy etc.) were prepared by officials under previous Government.

[Chaim] Raphael* making a bid for high level co-ordinating job for Information side of both Treasury and DEA. Raphael's memo quoted all sorts of qualities required in this high level co-ordinating — could only be possessed by one man!

Before GB's television broadcast of October 29 on Thursday night he 'sacked' Raphael and JG for providing him with only a short two-page brief for television. ('you're no use to me at all'.) Apologised profusely next day.

Economic Secretary's[1] Weekly Progress Meeting of October 26th mentioned capital exports as possibility for investigation. [Donald] MacDougall* [hereafter MacD] suggested engineering enquiry.

Treasury's Balance of Payments briefing for new Government suggested that two thirds (or was it three quarters) of 1964 deficit was due to non-recurring factors. This was also true of half of the expected 1965 £450m deficit.

CEDC met on November 2. Agreed on future of NEDC. GB emphasised need in last resort to control work of 'little Neddies'. [Thomas] Fraser's* statement on railways also approved.

At CEDC meeting. Minister of Works presented paper on building. Offices represented £130m — about 5% of work load of £2,635m. Demand increasing at 7% per annum, supply by 5%. In 1964–5 excess demand was about £100m. Minister of Works would suggest a target for increase in brick production of 8% in 1965. Opposed building control or restriction of demand. He would prepare plan for expanding production and attracting more manpower. Wanted targets and financial incentives for completion time and sticking to targets for site labour.

EFTA.[2] Memo from [Douglas] Jay* arguing for complete unilateral abolition of UK tariffs on January 1, ahead of time. Small effects in UK import bill.

(Origin of this was at a meeting of officials where Foreign Office in panic, couldn't think what to do. [William] Nield [hereafter WAN]* said only possible thing was unilateral acceleration of EFTA tariff reductions. But proposed this as something that would happen after abolition of surcharge.[3] Thus there would be no discrimination in favour of EFTA.

[1] Tony Crosland* appointed as Minister of State, DEA was initially also Economic Secretary (Appendix II).

[2] European Free Trade Association, established 1960 and comprising Austria, Denmark, Norway, Portugal, Sweden, Switzerland and the UK (known throughout the 1960s as the 'outer seven' as against the 'inner six' founding members of the European Economic Community, EEC).

[3] As one of a series of palliative measures to ease the balance of payments problems facing the incoming government, on 26 October 1964 a temporary surcharge of 15 per cent on the value of most manufactured and semi-manufactured goods was introduced. Although not an unprecedented development within the international community, it was known to be in conflict with GATT regulations and thereafter strong representations were made — especially from EFTA member states — for the abolition of this surcharge, which was reduced subsequently to 10 per cent in April 1965 and,

FO and BoT leapt at the suggestion, but wanted this to happen now before abolition of surcharge. Thus effectively killed idea.)

3 November October 1964 Treasury Briefing: Treasury's long term growth model. Two projections for 1963–8 before any measures on assumption of 3% and 4% growth rate.

> Exports to rise by 5.3% per annum in 4% case. (Compared with previous increase of 3.4%)
> Private consumption by 3% in 4% case.
> > 2% in 3% case.
> (Population to go up by 0.7%. Therefore private consumption will increase by <1.5% in 3% case.)
> (Consumption had previously risen by 3.3%. Rate would be less in future because of capital formation, public expenditure and need to increase exports more than imports. Working population to increase by 0.5% per annum compared with 0.8% in previous periods.)
> In fact there would be a probable shortfall of £200m per annum, (Over average of period or at end of it?) in 3% case; £260m in 4% case.
> Earnings to go up 5½%–6½% per annum (depending on case chosen)
> Prices by ....2½% per annum
> Real Incomes by 3%–4% per annum
> Required increase in savings = 32%–38%
> Estimated increase in saving's ratio = 20%–25%
> *Therefore extra annual tax would be £490m–£875m*
> Increase in public expenditure is given at 5¼% per annum.
> Would have to be (I think) 3½%–4½% to avoid increase in tax??
> *Recommendations on growth.* Recommended:
> (a) discarding target, simply trying to get as rapid a rate as possible, or
> (b) reducing target
> (c) 4% as aim for unspecified date.

In 1961–64 not very far towards target.

Treasury warns that high target runs risk of inflating demand; or misallocating resources, e.g. for electricity, which might actually reduce growth.

5 November Raphael regards himself as over the two departments. GB hardly knows of this!

Have got own 'secretary' — an elderly audio-typist who is trying to cope!

---

following an announcement in May 1966 that the scheme would be terminated, their complete abolition in November 1966: see J. H. B. Tew, 'Policies Aimed at Improving the Balance of Payments', in
F. T. Blackaby, ed., *British Economic Policy, 1960–74* (Cambridge, 1978), p. 344.

GB wants me to know what is going on in Department, attend all meetings including 9.30am ones. [Tom] Caulcott* very difficult about this; makes clear this is not on.

Reflection. Weapon used for excluding people is 'no time'.

6 November 9.30am MacD dislikes idea of shadow rates of growth for Government expenditure and for private economy. He said the plan would have to be more detailed and better as the Government was committed to it. The last Government used NEDC whenever it suited it and not otherwise.

Reflection. MacD is interested in power as well as planning!

9 November Came in in the morning and found three telephones on my desk. Then one was put on the floor and started ringing! A grey-beige one was put in and then disconnected and then put in again.

Reflection. Machine works through Private Office.

10–11 F[red] Atkinson*: complained of new establishment versus old.

[Tony] Crosland:* Some sympathy with officials about 9.30 am. GB wants masses of people there, including Parliamentary Private Secretaries! Says point of maximum demoralisation reached in battle over rank and status. Chief difficulty is insiders versus outsiders.

Crosland: Devaluation ruled out within couple of hours of new Government. Those of us who are very unhappy about this must accept the issue has been shelved if we are to retain any influence at all. Export subsidies would have been a much greater breach in international trading rules than the levy. Officials and international bodies would then have displayed rabid hostility instead of just neutrality.

Atkinson. Old school not trusted. Two people from NE1 have come over with [Douglas] Allen* [hereafter DVA].[4] Brown only trusts MacD's people. Labour Party somehow associated [Alec] Cairncross*[5] with Selwyn Lloyd's* policy and does not trust him. Cairncross was away with pneumonia during transition. He said the Labour Party would have

---

[4] Allen provides a retrospective on economic policy during the 1960s; see Lord Croham, 'Were the Instruments of Control for Domestic Economic Policy Adequate?', in F. Cairncross and A. K. Cairncross, eds., *The Legacy of the Golden Age: the 1960s and Their Economic Consequences* (1992), pp. 81–93, and comments by academic economists, other officials (including MacDougall and Cairncross) and the then Chancellor.

[5] Whilst Head of the Government Economic Service, 1964–9, Cairncross kept a diary: *The Wilson Years: A Treasury Diary, 1964–1969* (1997); see also his *Managing the British Economy in the 1960s: A Treasury Perspective* (1996).

to make up its mind whether to sack him and introduce the spoil system. (Atkinson thought *I* was old friend of GB!)

Atkinson said the 1½% export incentive was considered about two years ago. Rejected because it was too small and might tempt other countries to similar things. Thinks that the effects of the surcharge are less than the effect it has had in reducing our effective borrowing powers.

Caulcott: outsiders believe that Ministers *originate* policy. Policy *originates* in departments, Ministers *decide* policy.

Caulcott complained that GB would like one great intellectual debate bringing everyone in, going on in his room all the time!

Reflections. A ministerial Cabinet might be better than having these extra Departments. The Wilson solution is no substitute for a thorough reform of the Civil Service to make it natural for people to go in and out at all stages.

The system operates through the Private Offices and through the Treasury control of establishments (e.g. Caulcott). It would have been better not to have had the Economics Ministry, but to have hived off the control of the Civil Service. It is Treasury control of establishments that determines the real loyalties of the civil servants.

12 November 9.30 am *GB on Frank Cousins**. At Durham Miners' Gala. Cousins announced at 2 am the night before, that *he* was having the economic planning job! GB has doubts about his physical and mental state. (GB and [Fred] Catherwood[6] would agree that [Austen] Albu* is no use) Catherwood says he contributed nothing to committee they were both on.)

At Transport House on October 15, Cousins said to Brown that he was sharing the job. Now wants his Ministry to sponsor engineering. DEA would prefer general brief on technological efficiency. Technology view supported by [Maurice] Dean* and [James] Dunnett*.

GB mentioned that at last week's EDC on EFTA, the Foreign Secretary and the President of the Board of Trade were 'terrible' but later [Denis] Rickett* 'phoned from Paris (saying French would not have discrimination) to Chancellor; and matter settled in five minutes! GB would not have minded to give in to general European pressure.

---

[6] Catherwood's* memoirs, *At the Cutting Edge* (1995), ch. 6 recount his DEA experiences; ch. 7 his NEDC service; see also his 'The National Economic Development Council: A View from Industry', *Contemporary British History*, 12.1 (1998), pp. 77–81.

GB very reluctant to lunch with Governor of Bank.[7] 'What have I got to discuss with him?'

[Bryan] Hopkin* says that Spanish export cancellations and effects of the higher National Insurance contributions and of fuel tax will cancel out the export rebates![8]

Eric Roll*[9] [hereafter ER] to be on Budget Committee. Need for Department to have budget view so it can be given in January to the Chancellor in good time. ER is to be Chairman of economic steering committee. DEA has taken over the chairmanship of the committee on the construction industries ([Evan] Maude)*.

13 November Fantastic row with [Jack] Diamond*, who wants to veto Ministry of Works' ruling on ministerial cars. (Old rules, not in practice enforced, said junior Ministers must use the pool and travel back by bus). The previous night Crosland 'phoned Diamond and said that he wouldn't speak to him again. This was the Wednesday. Crosland mentioned this to Brown on Thursday morning. Friday before lunch Crosland and Diamond were still arguing about it on the telephone.

Jay and [Patrick Gordon-Walker] GW* in panic over EFTA.

Crosland told GW about our liberal GATT list. GW was very excited and wanted Crosland to send him a memo. (This I did for Crosland. I don't know if it was ever sent. Surely would have been covered by normal FO briefing.)

18 November It was said that GB was not coming in until lunch. Believed to have hangover. (My speech was taken over by [Bill] Greig*, who thought it was not suitable for press gallery occasion).

DVA: In 25 years in the Civil Service never felt so dispirited. Good will of Treasury was evaporating. A split could work only if the two departments worked as a united team. If one told GB that the Treasury wanted Raphael for DEA job, then GB will say no and vice versa. DEA first insists

---

[7] George Baring* (later Lord Cromer), upon whom Brown had strong views, telling Wilson 'I find his speeches tedious, inappropriate and designed to create the maximum embarrassment for Ministers!': TNA PREM 13/275, George Brown to Prime Minister, 16 February 1965.

[8] This was a further element in the 26 October palliative measures, providing for the refund of certain indirect taxes on exports to an estimated value of approximately 2 per cent of total exports. It was repealed on 31 March 1968: see Tew, 'Policies Aimed at Improving', p. 344.

[9] For the first three months of his new DEA post he had also to continue with his previous Washington responsibilities, shuttling between the two: E. Roll, *Crowded Hours: An Autobiography* (1985), p. 155.

on complete division of functions and then puts finger in every pie. Brown could so easily get his way without insisting on being formally the top dog. ER and MacD are 'born meddlers'; will always be busy whatever the work. 'And they say [Robert] Shone* was worse'.

Crosland causing much of the trouble through ignorance of how Government machinery works. Forecasting still formally under DVA. Treasury will accept it coming under him but no one else. But the long-term forecasting has completely gone to pieces. Regarded as incompatible with what 'planners' are doing. On the external side the Treasury is very much on its own.

Michael [J.] Stewart:[10] He and [Thomas] Balogh* [hereafter Dr B] have great difficulty in seeing things as Wilson says they should see. Decisions and policy were made very early. Labour Party leaders were genuinely shaken by Balance of Payments figures. Probably only William Armstrong* [hereafter WA] there when decisions made.

Peter Jay: [Reginald] Maudling* [hereafter RM] didn't care about colleagues or about the Tory Party. One thing that interested him was breaking through into sustained growth. Wanted to delay any action on imports as long as possible — until clearly demonstrated that there was this trouble even though there was no case for deflationary action at home. Would in the end devalue if things did not come right. Labour Party could not bluff through in the same way but had to do something.

19 November Miss [Annabelle] Lee* speaks of jealousies against imported information officers. There is a ganging up against Trevor Lloyd[-]Hughes*.

There is now a farcical situation. Raphael and JG are both behaving as Head of Information Department, but Raphael is not getting the information.

Appears from a Paper that the Chancellor is not to be on NEDC.[11]

---

[10] Shortly after leaving the Cabinet Office Stewart participated in the series of exchanges in *Encounter* provoked by M. M. Postan's 'plague of economists' critique of contemporary economists and their culpability with respect to Britain's economic difficulties (*Encounter*, 30.1 (January 1968), pp. 42–7), being extremely critical of attacks upon the broad stance of policy since the Conservatives embraced planning with the establishment of the NEDC (*Encounter*, 31.5 (May 1968, pp. 54–6). Later, he published a much more critical assessment of British economic policy since 1964, the aptly entitled: *The Jekyll and Hyde Years: Politics and Economic Policy since 1964* (1977).

[11] Thus it was Brown not Callaghan who chaired the NEDC between 1964–6, an announcement made on 19 November 1964. According to K. Middlemas, *Industry, Unions and Government: Twenty-One Years of NEDC* (1983), p. 46 the Chancellor of the Exchequer's attendance until 1967 'was, at best, irregular.'

(When I raised this with Brown later, he said it was too late but that I should write a minute in case it came up again. Asked whether it was considered. Formula was simply that NEDC was concerned with physical not financial planning. Think this minute of mine went down quite well. Brown said he would rather have had the Chancellor than 'Minister of Technology'.)

Went to meeting of MacD's economists. Asked to do 'article'. Apparently Dr B wants to cut 'upper class' consumption. Thinks of progressive purchase tax like wartime D scheme.

Row over control of public expenditure. Export figures really quite good if dock troubles taken into account.

Otto [Clarke]*[12] has paper suggesting that Defence should be absolutely constant in real terms. [Roy] Jenkins* wants either to go ahead with a much smaller programme of two prototype Concordes, or would really prefer Anglo-French-US project.

Public expenditure: DVA says this involves going back on [Edwin] Plowden*. Instead of leaving things to Departments, they would have to insist on a regional and industrial breakdown. Said again that experience shows that split doesn't work — except with united team and divided surface.

MacD's people seem to be floundering around at that stage, without access to official information. E.g. [Hans] Liesner* said in paper, 'Judging by press reports'. (No access to Treasury information on overseas side!)

Reflection. Split can only work: *either if Economic Affairs reduced to NEDC floating in the air away from immediate policy, or if Treasury is reduced to supervision of public expenditure and details of tax system.* Why do other Departments follow Treasury on 4% growth rate? Is it Treasury's hold through promotions?

Caulcott: Power still with Treasury.

20 November [Robert] *Neild*: No chance of a 4% [growth rate] in the first couple of years. Danger of waste of electricity investment. Also 4%

---

[12] Clarke was the originator of the public expenditure control and management system, known as PESC, which had been recommended by the 1961 Plowden report: see A. Ringe, N. Rollings and R. Middleton, *Economic Policy under the Conservatives, 1951–64: A Guide to Documents in the National Archives of the UK* (2004), pp. 25, 42, 156–8. Clarke posthumously published an account of PESC and its evolution which includes a number of comments about the National Plan, the DEA and about its relations with the Treasury: see R. W. B. Clarke, *Public Expenditure Management and Control: The Development of the Public Expenditure Survey Committee (PESC)*, ed. A. K. Cairncross (1978), ch. 11.

average will imply 5% later on. On the other hand, 4% would be all right to give to little Neddies to aim at. DEA is byword for chaos and confusion. GB 'sacked' Caulcott a number of times.

Neild's tensions with Cairncross. Very suspicious over letter to Times on the [Per] Jacobsson*-Cairncross plan for Germany.[13]

[James] Callaghan*: Neild has to explain everything to Callaghan like to a first-year student. No refined policy on Budget Speech possible 'with these politicians', they must be at things the whole time: bogy of a hundred days.

Callaghan told Cyriax:[14] We believe in 4% but found it isn't there.

Vast numbers of people constantly coming to me about requirements. Vast delays in getting everything, but vast numbers of people seem concerned!

23 November Bank Rate Day[15] GB mentioned to industrial correspondents and trade unionists 'off record' that there had to be two lines on [B]ank [R]ate, the internal and the external one.

Reflection. Case for new Ministry, that persevering with internal expansion is stressed. If all were under Treasury the internal side would be suppressed, *but* will Bank Rate increase without other things do the trick?

---

[13] Letter from H. W. Auburn, 'Learning from the Past: Economic Recovery in Germany', *The Times*, 20 November 1964, p. 13. The Jacobsson-Cairncross Plan to resolve the liquidity and balance of payment crisis affecting Germany in 1950 was highly contentious at the time and since: see J. J. Kaplan and G. Schleiminger, *The European Payments Union: Financial Diplomacy in the 1950s* (1959), ch. 6 and A. K. Cairncross, *Economic Ideas and Government Policy: Contributions to Contemporary Economic History* (1995), ch. 7.

[14] Cyriax became Economics Correspondent at the *Financial Times* when Brittan moved over to the *Observer* in 1961, and in turn when Cyriax left the *FT* in 1966 (to pursue a career as a management consultant) it was Brittan who replaced him. Cyriax and Michael Shanks*, who was Industrial Editor until 1964 when he became another irregular in the DEA (Diary, 20 January 1965), have been credited with a key role in setting the *FT's* intellectual tone at the time that the paper was being transformed into a broad based business daily: see D. Kynaston, *The Financial Times: A Centenary History* (1988), pp. 304, 329.

Shanks' *The Stagnant Society: A Warning* (1961) was one of the triad of diagnoses of Britain's economic difficulties in the late 1950s and early 1960s which was a key propagator of the growing mood for modernisation of which Brittan's 'great re-appraisal' was part. The other works were A. Shonfield, *British Economic Policy since the War* (1958) and A. Sampson, *Anatomy of Britain.* (1962). Shanks published a critical but — by comparison with others of his contemporaries — balanced account on his time as an 'irregular' ('The Irregular in Whitehall', in P. Streeten, ed., *Unfashionable Economics: Essays in Honour of Lord Balogh* (1970), pp. 244–62) and a full length study for PEP of the planning experiment in Britain: *Planning and Politics: The British Experience, 1960–1976* (1977).

[15] Bank Rate was raised two percentage points to 7 per cent, the highest level since October 1961 and the largest increase since 24 August 1939.

DVA: Should have done Bank Rate immediately after the election. He wanted 6% Bank Rate even before!

Meeting with TUC. T[rade]U[nion]s muttering and grumbling; [George] Woodcock* inaudible. Asked: Why emphasis on wages? Why not other things? Difficult to pin down. Questions about effect of Bank Rate and production. Lionel Murray* to join unofficially in redraft of Statement of Intent.[16] Brown seems to understand the psychology of these people; rumbling appeals to help get country out of rut into which relying on the 'two sides' has landed us. 'Otherwise what do we do? 8% Bank Rate, 10% Bank rate? Do we devalue?' Says we have to be on the 'razor edge' between vagueness and too much precision in incomes policy draft.

Treasury and DEA seem to be at loggerheads on capital exports.

Callaghan: Brown said that Callaghan wanted to frighten foreigners. Wilson told Callaghan not to put in way that destroyed confidence at home. Armstrong seemed to agree.

Some officious person has removed my second waste paper basket!

24 November Spent from noon to 8 pm drafting case for Incomes Policy. Mostly re-written by Donald. Seemed endless process, with bits of paper all over the room; premature drafts retyping and then retyping again. Most of problem seemed to be typing one[s]. I see what DVA means by Donald's method of drafting. JG thinks Reserves lost £80m on Friday.

Told [Ian] Hudson* about book.

Reflection. Can waste vast amount of time on speeches which regurgitate all policies. Then on consulting Departments and people within own Ministry, clearing the whole time and constant retyping, and this is quite apart from all the committees.

Officials attend so many meetings with other officials at top and medium level that most of time taken up. Very little time to think. The sheer job of getting something out and agreed and (or clearly disagreed) exerts a great pressure for orthodoxy and following precedent. Any solution must involve more rugged edges, less co-ordination and more breaking up tasks into individual jobs. Different departmental policies should be allowed to emerge. Only high level questions at point of crucial decision should have

[16] A draft 'Statement of Intent' on the government's prices and incomes policies was delivered to the TUC and employers' organisations on 18 November. The TUC Economic Committee accepted the final draft on 9 December, and the 'Joint Statement of Intent on Prices, Productivity and Incomes' was signed by the three parties on 16 December: see pp. 35–6.

to involve agreed unified Government action. Too high a price is paid for the myth of Government unity.

24 November R[17] ...
Co-ordination on separate policies. But how much consideration to strategy as a whole? Link between different policies — e.g. NATO, ELDO, C[ommon] M[arket] & £.

25 November Asked to do pro-Sterling speech for Brown for Saturday, listing everything we have done.

26 November Speech cancelled. (International banking credits agreed!)
Study of Engineering Industry. Thought how much better it would be if one or two engineering directors were present. Conflicts between exports or import substitution, and investment? What exactly happens in this type of enquiry will depend entirely on the Board of Trade and Brian Hopkin. He thinks there will be a 6 or 7% increase in demand for plant and machinery; but capacity won't be there to meet both this and investment demand.

Reflection. One and half hour discussion does not help the engineering enquiry very much. These meetings are mostly an exercise in good will. The smaller group that was called will do all the work. Brian says that on the whole those who go to meetings don't write and vice versa. He only goes to about one meeting a day and some days pass without any meeting.

David Hancock* says *all* briefs have to be redone for new Government, for it would be intolerable to have parliamentary discussion on the lines of 'why wasn't official advice taken?'

DEA proposes to Treasury a tax committee. MacD's division is planning a paper on capital exports.

Crosland export promotion meeting. I was asked to write a paper on use of Honours' List and minute to First Secretary on speaking to export gatherings. Suggested that it should be televised question and answer marathon, with detailed questions from exporters about their difficulties.

GB wants me to keep up outside contacts and to go abroad sometimes.

27 November GB said Chancellor complained bitterly in Cabinet about 'undermining' of 7% Bank Rate by colleagues, — presumably GB's efforts

[17] Runs on from end of previous entry.

with trade unions and industrial lobby. GB would like to stop talk of being back to stop-go. Wanted me to go to OECD. Should see him occasionally and put views in writing.

Note of meeting where Chancellor asked his colleagues to announce plans (including steel nationalisation) in a way that would not only gain political support at home, but also gain confidence of overseas holders of sterling.

View was expressed in Cabinet that positive and rapid action to increase production and productivity was more important to industry than the more gradual elaboration of an incomes policy.

GB: Neild wanted more deflation. *Flexible rates* were considered in last few days. Argument against was that they would be disturbing to business.

[Nicholas] *Kaldor's* export recommendations:* Abolish Employers' National Insurance contributions (replace by more indirect taxation) or have differential regional payroll subsidy for manufacturing industry.

Minutes are put up not to Ministers or Permanent Secretaries but to their Private Secretaries. Added degree of impersonality.

Mr [S. T.] Charles* said he was shocked to think that my knowledge of the Civil Service started with the DEA. So very few professional staff—clerks and secretaries don't know their work. In the Treasury all this is automatic.

George Cyriax: Said to me that Cromer threatened to resign the previous Sunday unless Bank Rate was raised to 7%. On the previous Friday George Bolton[18] was telling his bank to 'sell everything you've got'. If bankers were not sabotaging the pound that Friday, they were certainly not supporting it.

First Week of December (Visit to OECD Ministerial Meeting) Learnt on way (I think from Atkinson) that GB is supposed to have toned down budget and pushed against a Bank Rate increase. (Afterwards heard from other sources that GB, advised by MacDougall, opposed the increase and got it postponed from Thursday to Monday). Government said to have made up its mind in its first few days and brushed aside any contrary advice. (This was meaning of GB's TV reference to solution 'buried under

---

[18] Bolton was a key figure in the 1960s in the new realism about sterling not being sustainable as a reserve currency and in need for City institutions to embrace current financial innovations; see R. Fry, ed., *A Banker's World: The Revival of the City, 1957–70; Speeches and Writings of Sir George Bolton* (1970).

load of bumph'.) Did not seriously try borrowing instead. Treasury, in fact, advised against the surcharge. BoT would have preferred quotas. FO against the surcharge and the Concord.

([James] Marjoribanks* said that [Harold] Macmillan* regretted Nassau[19] for ever afterwards, because of effect on Common Market. [Edward] Heath* was cross — had not even been informed about it. There was no real hurry.)

Reflection by WAN

DEA has the functions without the people.

Paris.

French (and others?) clearly think devaluation inevitable. Against it happening in panic.

Valiant Italian Rearguard Action against Deflationists.

Successfully insisted in adding sentence on increase in investment necessary for Italy in communiqué. Also got 'increasing' insistence on price stability changed to 'great'. [Thorkil] Kristensen* unhappy about these amendments. Kristensen ignominious role. Said to have said privately that after Bank Rate increase no longer thought UK should deflate more. But then nevertheless kept call for more deflation in his conference address.

Personally kept very much in dark by Treasury about what was going on in Paris.

? December Spoke to MacDougall about functions. Told me to speak to [John] Jukes* about taking part in economic work. Seemed that GB had me in mind for Information side from first. But he wanted me on inter-departmental committees. Told that this would cause resentment and didn't press it (although he does press some things). When I said felt 'frustrated', MacDougall mentioned 'like the rest of us'.

Finished a paper on the use of the Honours' system. (But did the export Honours in the New Year list have anything to do with this exchange of memoranda with Crosland and GB?)

Finished section of paper for Nield reviewing progress on various fronts. GB told MacDougall he would like to be a good European, but is prepared to go in for siege economy, if necessary.

---

[19] The Anglo-American summit at Nassau in December 1962 resulted in an agreement to form a multilateral NATO nuclear force, thereby permitting the US government to provide Polaris missiles as part of Britain's so-called independent nuclear deterrent; the latest scholarship would suggest that Macmillan was right to fear the adverse effects of this summit on Britain's first application to join the EEC (announced in the House of Commons on 31 July 1963): see G. Warner, 'Why the General said No', *International Affairs*, 78.4 (2002), pp. 869–82.

9 December DEA to be represented by MacDougall on Sir Richard Clarke's sub-committee examining the tax system in relation to exports, economic growth and regional development. Jukes taking over chairmanship of (a formerly Treasury) working party on long-range economic assessments. — WPLREA! (Name later changed to Working Party on Plan).

At Progress Meeting GB said he would like some agreement on stages two and three by NEDC meeting on February 3.

Reflection. Great pressure on Ministers to agree to official recommendations because of *time*. Estimates for 1964/5 show 9% increase (on usual meaningless basis).

Crosland said at the meeting that the assumption must be that we were going back on [Gordon] Richardson!*[20] [Siegmund] Warburg*[21] going round saying Richardson all nonsense! PM believes in importance of a[n] incentive in the form of a check! (Later on over the Christmas holiday GB summoned Catherwood and Richardson to see him. But Richardson succeeded in blinding GB and Catherwood with science — Crosland).

DVA, Treasury forecast (then 4% increase in GDP) too expansionary, because of effects of Bank Rate on confidence etc. Average loss of reserves was £10m in last few days. £20m in previous 24 hours. DVA says first reduction in Bank Rate will be in 'six weeks to two months'. (Early February). Second reduction will be in spring. Economy certainly does not require more deflation. Worst of volatile sterling balances now run down. Surcharge will probably go down to 12½% in spring and stay there the rest of the year. Perhaps 10% in December.

---

[20] Committee on Turnover Tax (Richardson Committee), BPP 1963–4 (2300), xix, 299, published in March 1964, recommended against the introduction of a tax similar to VAT/TVA as used in continental Europe. It also concluded 'that companies in this country are not more heavily taxed than companies in other countries examined' (p. 54), thereby paving some of the way to Labour's proposed corporation tax; see also Diary, 20 January 1966.

[21] Brown, *In My Way*, pp. 100–2 identifies Warburg — 'perhaps the most influential financier of his time in the City of London' (A. J. Sherman, 'Warburg, Sir Siegmund George (1902–82)', *Oxford Dictionary of National Biography*) — as part of the core of his 'unpublicized body of industrial advisers [which] had enormous influence on the apparatus we set up' for the DEA. The other members identified were Frank Kearton*, George Cole* and John Berkin*. Kearton was a NEDC member, 1965–71 and in 1966 became the first Chairman of the Industrial Reconstruction Corporation, a key institution in Labour's industrial policy, with Berkin also a member, 1966–8: see D. C. Hague and G. C. G. Wilkinson, *The IRC: An Experiment in Industrial Intervention. A History of the Industrial Reorganisation Corporation* (1983) and R. Coopey, 'Industrial Policy in the White Heat of the Scientific Revolution', in R. Coopey, D. Fielding and N. Tiratsoo, eds., *The Wilson Governments, 1964–1970* (1993), pp. 102–22.

DVA also said that Government's first economic White Paper was re-written by Wilson on Friday.[22] DVA managed to get into a room with GB and LJC to urge and got agreement to omission of £800m figure. Later saw Armstrong, found him in very curious mood. Took out all of DVA's corrections: 'The PM wants the figure'.

GB tried to stop some things on general economic front with unfortunate results. Has led to erosion of influence. Then rushes to other extreme. Apparently opposed Bank [R]ate increase (and PO charges — here some justification). Urged larger 'social' expenditure.

9 December LJC antagonised City according to W[ynne] Williams*. First told off city editors for putting interests of City before Nation. Following week apologised.

10 December [Michael J.] Stewart: Wednesday of credits, Wilson had showdown with Cromer. Did not accept his views on the need for further deflation. (Yet credit squeeze announced later! SB) Told him to get credits instead. Dr. B now believes in [devaluation]. Stewart advocates spring election and then deval[uation].

At Progress Meeting Nield says the biggest obstruction comes from BoT. Treasury is more subtle and keeps DEA short of staff.

At meeting immediately after the Election (was told this by Stewart or MacDougall) Armstrong said things would be easier with higher rate of unemployment. GB said: 'Not acceptable'.

Reflection. Officials continue to press old attitudes irrespective of declared views of Labour Party. (And perhaps their own Ministers), and one has to appease these official views. (Position varies from Ministry to Ministry. BoT very 'departmental'. DEA has new ethos of own. LJC to some extent going along with Treasury.)

11 December 'The Tea Ceremony at the Treasury' According to [John] Grieve Smith*, Atkinson and Hopkin led protest at way at which Cairncross was treated in early days of Government. Cairncross was supposed to have come back from illness and found Neild in room. Neild complained that he was shifted from one room [to another] four times in a week!

---

[22] Prime Minister's Office, *The Economic Situation* was issued on Monday 26 October 1964.

14 December Bryan Hopkin: Export rebate scheme was turned down in 1961. BoT urged international opposition etc.

Hopkin thinks that up to 1967 there should only be balance of payments' target. Cannot see how balance can be achieved without some deflation, with unemployment creeping up to nearer 1.2–2.0%. Moving from 1.5–1.8% would take 1½% off GNP.

15 December GB getting enormously excited over Incomes Policy. (PM wouldn't come for drink on the occasion). Was telling people on the phone most important event for years. Unfortunately clashed with Foreign Affairs Debate.

16 December At Progress Meeting it was said that a first report of the Tax Committee would be ready by mid-January. The export committee under [Richard] Powell* not yet set up! Crosland was furious. GB asked him to take over responsibility for export promotion. Nield was anxious to get postponement of EFTA meeting in February. First Secretary urged Chequers-type meeting on Economic Affairs. (One is to take place on 16.1.65.)

17 December Nield: DEA no impact at all on overseas finance. [David] Pitblado* taking lead in EFTA. Worked out that ratio of external to internal staff was 7 to 65![23]

GB said over drink in H[ouse] of C[ommons]: W[ilson] was PM 'for present'. W[ilson] seems to have gone to pieces altogether. GB was doing things PM should be doing. Would have to run whole show.

Reserves going out at rate varying from £1m to £4m a day. (Figure includes forward commitments). DVA predicts mass exodus of Civil Servants from Whitehall next year. (Nield put in train free trade area with Ireland). Was told (I think by GB) that GW and Jay panicking again over EFTA.

Plan Co-ordination Working Party. Treasury paper predicts a lowering of the pressure of demand. Says must be allowed to go some distance without being reversed. Would mean 12–24 months' period with production increasing less than capacity. Government must be free to let this happen. This is an argument against publication (of preliminary plan?).

---

[23] The ratio of 'irregulars' to established civil service members of the DEA.

DEA can go up to £8,000, in all, in recruiting men from outside.

In negotiations and background briefing on Incomes Policy, GB uses dates of church calendar! Also inclined to say: 'We are all white and over 21'.

GB complained bitterly that just as pressure on sterling was stopping, RM makes statement on taxation of Gilt Edged mentioning £.

DVA inclined to ask me: 'Still think things are so easy?'

Reflection. Callaghan said in Declaration of Intent ceremony that this demonstrated that one Minister couldn't do Incomes Policy and all the other things. But as against this there is a disadvantage that the Economics Minister is not centrally placed to control the taps. Could the No. 1 Man be at the Treasury and the No. 2 do the Incomes policy? (But would any man of lesser stature be able to get Incomes Policy through?)

Treasury now has no role but to be restrictive. But perhaps better to institutionalise conflict between two departments. Need for pressure group in favour of growth. DEA stronger than NEDC. Likely to build up strength.

The very same people, in e.g. the Bank, who are saying how right RM was in 1963 and 1964 to do less than economists thought, are now urging further deflation! If the pressure of demand is too high, why did authorities let it get there? (Norman Macrae* says the 'Treasury' were going round in summer saying that they urged RM to do more).

Macroeconomic questions do come up before GB [b]ut in the same sort of way as they would to the Prime Minister. Difficult to be effective this way. Difficulty similar to that of Cabinet in controlling tax change. GB lacks detailed day to day control over financial policy and detailed day to day contact with men running it.

DEA does not control financial policy; but GB has personal powers 'of last resort' over it at very top level; and MacDougall advises Brown.

17 December R[24] ...Whatever First Secretary's powers and involvement, can hardly have detailed day to day contact with financial policy and the men running it.

17 December Eric Roll terribly pessimistic. (Found out that 'figure' for that day was loss of £60m.) Discussed the effects of new taxes on Gilts and investment allowances. (Trade figures showing no fall in imports yet in November and not much change in exports. Published the same day as

[24] Follows on '...to do more).'

Declaration of Intent). Roll asked me whether I would pay more attention to the Incomes Policy statement or to the trade figures?

[Maurice] Laing*[25] made remark to me about Chairman of the TUC.[26] being a Peer and Chairman of Employers being 'Mr.'.[27] Passed it on to GB.

DVA: using regulator[28] would reassure foreign opinion. Might have to do it. (I was egging him on here). But danger of deflation being pressed too far. Laing reported to have said that 60 miles north of Birmingham no shortage of labour. No one placing any new contracts.

DVA, if anything happened *this* Government couldn't hold any rate! But 1961 was basically worse. Should be all right eventually. Real pressures would be in February — EFTA and WP3.[29] Complained not on Budget Committee any more.

Reflection. How far is there always a straight choice between deflation and exchange rate? How far could better handling of situation mitigate it? Might not short sharp deflation be less bad than a long protracted nagging one? Real argument against past deflationary measures was that Government acted too late and hung on too long.

Working Party on Plan: Compromise agreed in public expenditure. Existing estimates brought up to date in light of policy changes and extrapolated to 1970.

---

[25] Cairncross, *Diaries*, p. 154 reports Laing advising the Prime Minister in 1966.

[26] The TUC does not have a chairman, but instead a president, being for 1964–5: Lord Collison (1909–95): General Secretary, National Union of Agricultural and Allied Workers, 1953–69; TUC General Council, 1953–69; member, Royal Commission on Trade Unions and Employers' Associations, 1965–8.

[27] The formation of the CBI in April 1965 was agreed in principle in June 1963 by the leaders of the three main employers associations: the Federation of British Industry (FBI), the largest, the British Employers' Confederation (BEC) and the National Association of British Manufacturers (NABM). The merits of this amalgamation had emerged as part and parcel of employers' participation in NEDC activities, and was encouraged by government. For an insider's account, by the Director-General of the FBI between 1946–65, see N. Kipping, *Summing Up* (1972), pp. 99, 102, app. 6; also S. Blank, *Industry and Government in Britain: The Federation of British Industries, 1945–65* (1973), ch. 6. The FBI's president who brokered the amalgamation, was Peter Runge*.

[28] Introduced in the April 1961 budget, the regulator — strictly speaking, regulators — was an innovation to permit greater fine-tuning of demand between budgets through either variations in employers' National Insurance contributions or variations by ±10 per cent in Customs and Excise duties. The surcharge was never used, being dropped in 1962 in face of fierce opposition within government and from employers' organisations, whilst the tax regulator was activated in Selwyn Lloyd's* July 1961 measures: see Ringe, Rollings and Middleton, *Economic Policy*, pp. 150, 161.

[29] OECD Working Party no 3 on 'Policies for the Promotion of Better International Payments Equilibrium' was established on 30 September 1961 by the Economic Policy Committee and was chaired by Emile van Lennep*. The February 1965 meeting is discussed in R. Roy, 'No Secrets between "Special Friends": America's Involvement in British Economic Policy, October 1964–April 1965', *History*, 89.3 (2004), pp. 411, 412; the broader significance of WP3 in H. James, *International Monetary Cooperation since Bretton Woods* (1996), pp. 182–4.

Jukes in chair of Working Party; said the Treasury paper came close to saying: Planning was undesirable and present policies were leading to a considerable degree of deflation, which should be allowed to continue and this would lead to a reduction in output.

Hopkin apparently advocated no commitment to any particular level of demand, nor any commitment to steady growth of output. Said that plan should not make it impossible to allow deflation to continue. Opposed to too much emphasis on statistical model for 1970. (Hopkin basically right on latter point; wrong on earlier points, SB).

Public expenditure review would be ready in June.

Jukes did not accept the pressure of demand would be reduced and deliberately kept on to have balance of payments. In order that plan should be as imprecise as possible, said that two notes should be drafted outlining the two points of view for decision of higher authority. (Think that this was somehow avoided or done in different form).

Original version of Concordat by W. Armstrong. Passages on public expenditure by DVA.

21 December 'Figure' about tea-time was £38m. Was £10m before lunch.

Dinner with MacDougall. Told me that at Planning Meeting today both R. Neild and Treasury prepared to see down-turn in investments to make way for exports.

Received letter from [Arthur] Cockfield* showing sharp drop in sales in November and December, well below those budgeted. PM had economic dinner last Wednesday and the next one.

MacDougall was writing paper for GB (Did he read it?) NIF forecast was 3½% for 1965. But probably too optimistic. Unemployment likely to rise in winter of 1965–66. Investment levelling off and down-turn likely mid-1965 and after. Before having even touched the 1961 level. Very unsatisfactory. There was a basic deficit of £400m–£500m. The only way of getting the balance of payments right was a massive export subsidy:

(a) Subsidy to be paid to Engineering Producers, instead of investment allowances.
(b) Refund of Employers' National Insurance contributions (Payroll Tax instead? K[aldor] would argue for TVA).
(c) Regional payroll subsidy.

These things should be the No. 1 concern of the Committee; in addition to which long-term loan (in any case necessary) should be negotiated now to restore confidence. Believes in April election, in any case advocates election as early as possible.

23 December Roll complained that economists being used as private army to brief MacDougall. TV broadcast that GB planned stopped by PM, who wants to broadcast himself after publication of trade figures in mid-January.

Pre-Christmas week: Monday figure £60m, Tuesday not quite so bad; Wednesday was bad.

DVA: Treasury recommending £500m off 1968–69 public expenditure programmes. (These are £800m too high).

Mistakes of December 1963 White Paper:

> (a) Assumed 4% growth rate.
> (b) Simply stated that expenditure would grow by 4%. Not that it could be paid for without tax increases, even at 4% rate of national growth. (On these assumptions £200m too high?)
> (c) Conservative Government then added to it.
> (d) Some errors of forecasting.
> (e) Labour Government added to it — pensions etc.

Dinner of 23.12. PM says must be prepared to substitute import quotas for surcharge. Machine must be ready to make substitution in February. (PM later sent note saying 'not in favour'; simply suggests this as bargaining counter. GB sent round note he was strongly against quotas). Agreed that certain measures should be considered: Measures to make firms repatriate export proceeds more quickly; purchasers of forward exchange to deposit 50–100% of sterling equivalent; measures to close Hong Kong gap;[30] consider token call for ½% special deposits[31] (depending on state of sterling).

Additional measures to go in export statement for mid-January: new approaches to docks; partnership with selected industries for encouraging expansion of capacity. (Round robin sent round to departments on this. DEA exports task force thought it could simply create opposition and hostility; ou[ght] not to be announced yet. GB asks me to investigate [Joe] Hyman's* scheme).[32]

---

[30] A parallel foreign exchange market tolerated by the British government as it allowed greater flexibility within the formal fixed exchange rate regime for sterling; see C. R. Schenk, 'The Empire Strikes Back: Hong Kong and the Decline of Sterling in the 1960s', *Economic History Review*, 57.3 (2004), pp. 551–80.

[31] A monetary policy instrument, announced in July 1958 as a temporary arrangement pending the recommendations of the Radcliffe committee (Committee on the Workings of the Monetary System, *Report*, BPP 1958–9 (827), xvii, 389) which reported in August 1959, and first used in April 1960, whereby the Bank of England could call for special (compulsory) deposits from the clearing banks which, because they were non-interest bearing and non-liquid, diminished the banks' asset base and their ability to make advances within the then existing liquidity ratio; see J. C. R. Dow, *The Management of the British Economy, 1945–60* (Cambridge, 1964), pp. 111, 240–2.

[32] Hyman's scheme to rationalise and transform the British textile industries had entered a new phase in 1964–5 as he brokered a strategic alliance with ICI who were themselves engaged in a long-running

Other point to be mentioned: Government-industry consortium to build automated shipyard. December 23 meeting suggested that consideration be given to cheaper credit through an Ex-Im Bank;[33] long term review of investment allowances. (How could they help exporters more[?]). Agreed that public sector growth over next five years to be restricted to 4¼% per annum. Defence expenditure for 1965–66 not to exceed £2,000m. PM to broadcast on January 19.

There has been an import control alert ever since April 1964. (About two months to impose them after alert).

GB intends to get rid of private secretary who, among other misdeeds, informed Downing Street of intended T.V. broadcast. But on 8.1.65 looked as if Caulcott would succeed Caulcott!

4 January 1965 Heard from JG about fantastic events in prices battle.

GB 'sacked' Maude for contacting Ministry of Agriculture on grocery prices,[34] Mrs [P. B. M.] James* for obstruction on South East. Farcical scenes when Minister of Agriculture [Fred Peart]* arrived in fury at having been left out from statement about the letter to the grocers. GB agreed to his being mentioned and then made sure that it was already too late. PM seems to have found out same night. Apparently investigating all these activities and the affair of private secretary. GB apparently received a talking-to.

Reflection. GB's unpredictable and intolerable behaviour is the only way to stir things up in this country. GB works at extra rational level. Perhaps one has got to be a bit of a bastard to get anything done.

Where does power lie? At top seems to lie with 'experts'; at assistant secretary level in departments. But people at that level have to work in restricted policy framework which they are in no position to question. Policy is dictated by external events and general climate of opinion, which causes them; or are they 'statistically' determined? or even randomly? Tolstoy's theory of powerlessness.[35]

---

conflict with their rival Courtaulds whom they had failed to take over in 1961. For an insider account, see A. Knight, *Private Enterprise and Public Intervention: The Courtaulds Experience* (1974).

[33] An Export-Import Bank; this proposal did not come to fruition.

[34] Shortly after the joint statement of intent on incomes and prices policy was signed, Brown made contact with a number of trade associations and chairman of retail chains 'expressing [his] anxiety about prices increases' and how the new mechanisms would be brought to bear to contain inflationary pressures; see L. Panitch, *Social Democracy and Industrial Militancy: The Labour Party, the Trade Unions and Incomes Policy, 1945 to 1974* (Cambridge, 1976), pp. 69–70.

[35] See L. Tolstóy, *War and Peace: A Novel*, trans. L. and A. Maude (Oxford, 1932), pp. 489–537 (second epilogue).

Treasury's End Year BoP forecast. Deficit on current [account] and
... balance [of trade] of £230m (diminishing throughout year.) Assuming
12½% surcharge from April to end of year. Balancing item not significant.
Between 1964–5 exports to rise by 2½–3% on balance of payments basis.

Home Economic Forecast. GDP to rise at annual rate of 3¼%, from
Q.3 1964 to Q.4 1965 at annual rate. Total fixed investment by 5% (All
figures at annual rates). Manufacturing investment to reach peak by mid
1965 and then fall away, but fall-off will be very slow. Exports of goods to
rise by 2¼%; of goods and services to rise by 1½%. Personal consumption
to rise by 1½%, (Tax and price increases). Compared with 3–3½% averaged since 1958. Production potential rising by 3.4%. There will be a low
stock ratio at the end of 1965. There will be a heavy 'deficit' for stocks of
imports.

5 January GB has been against early election. No joke if unemployment to rise next winter. (GB evidently now knows MacDougall's view
of outlook). Said that Germans told Roll that if financial decisions to be
taken again would veto loan for UK. (Do they mean it?). GB seems to
favour price control. Received very dismal report on prospect of export
incentives. Nothing possible this budget. Looks as if Treasury vetoing it.
And FO and BoT again trying to weaken levy. Crosland received nasty
note from LJC for part in GB letter urging control on overseas capital
investment. Also received very severe talking to from GB for privately
advocating the unmentionable. (Privately thinks it ought to happen after
an election. Would only happen now as a result of crisis. Give us early
election and doing it in the autumn.)

6 January *Export Saga.* Catherwood asks me to do a draft of a part
of export statement, mentioning DEA ideas in non-committal form to
persuade Powell to agree to have them in statement. DVA asks me to write
paper on way in which export statement should be presented.

Reflection. Difficulty of the Treasury as an Economics Ministry. [Leo]
Pliatzky*[36] on P[ublic] E[xpenditure] side of Treasury trying to cut down
very small expenditures on market research. Wanted to narrow financial
commitment. Colleagues from OF not quite with him.

---

[36] In retirement, Pliatzky published a number of works on British economic policy, of which his
Getting and Spending: Public Expenditure, Employment and Inflation (2nd edn., Oxford, 1984), pp.
57–8, 73, 85–6, 97, 104, 118 made a number of pertinent observations about the DEA.

7 January Flesh creeping Treasury forecasts (very tentative and verbal) for 1966. Demand will rise substantially less than productive capacity, but balance of payments gap will widen; and may be excessively large (insupportable?) even with the surcharge!

8 January Very heavy loss on the day. Backwash of weakness of dollar caused by French conversion of dollars into gold.

Nield asked me to guess forward commitments. When I said $800m–$1,000m gave me a look (and confirmed) that I really had pitched it very low. Expect that it cannot be far from, or perhaps even over, $2,000m.

12 January MacDougall tried to stop increase in National Insurance contributions. Equivalent to effect of at least one year's incomes policy, on which GB is spending every hour of day and night.

Fantastic wastes of time: spent long time last week on draft of how export measures might be presented. Now PM insists on swallowing them in a lot of other measures, including defence, which will get all the publicity.

DVA says that PM is suggesting that 500–600 seater aircraft be developed to hold design teams together.

13 January A lot of frenzied and self-stultifying activity, e.g. hurried summoning of Ministers for a little 'Neddy' for docks (suggested by Catherwood); only to find there exists [Thomas] Padmore* Committee, [Patrick] Devlin*[37] and National Ports Council.[38] Decision deferred till April. (Eventually it was agreed that it should be set out but docks were not to be specifically mentioned. Title like 'Transport for Exports' but not quite!)

Official brief argued that an Ex-Im Bank or direct financing would inflate budget deficit, disturb existing banking and financial arrangements, and add to problems of monetary management. So much for Keynesian Revolution!

Reflection. Is Treasury becoming more balanced budget conscious and financially conservative because of DEA?[39]

---

[37] Committee of Inquiry into Certain Matters Concerning the Port Transport Industry (Devlin Committee), *First Report*, BPP 1964–5 (2523), xxi, 811; *Final Report*, BPP 1964–5 (2734), xxi, 827.
[38] The National Ports Council, an independent statutory body established by the Harbours Act, 1964, was empowered to prepare a long-term plan for the development of the ports, to consider major development schemes put forward by individual harbour authorities, and to coordinate government departments' policy towards the ports: National Ports Council, *Annual Report and Statement of Accounts, 1964*, HC 241 (1964–5), p. 1.
[39] R version: 'Danger of becoming more balanced budget conscious and financially conservative because part of Economists shifted towards DEA.'

Vast number of outside enquiries being set up. Thought that Labour Party had put an end to all this. Constant words like 'enquiry', 'consider', etc.

14 January Crosland said at weekly progress meeting that one must insist on discussing national economic strategy at forthcoming Chequers meeting and not get bogged down in gimmicks like atomic electricity! Postal charges postponed.

GB says that Ministry of Defence are very strongly against all three projects (including TSR2) but insist on US replacement.[40] GB thinks we ought not to give in because it puts the aircraft workers out of aircraft work. Would save £700m over ten years if US replacement bought. But GB thinks the Ministry of Defence cannot have as many TFXs as it likes. Terms of purchase important.

Governor of Bank of Sweden told GB that UK should be tough with Americans. US will not let pound go and will force Germans to come in to support it. [Douglas] Henley*: Moment of truth in aircraft industry. Has ceased to be technical front runner. Risk of waiting for Plowden Committee.[41] We will get further committed with more cancellation charges. Nothing serious if gap from 1968 to early 1970s. According to Kenneth Keith* the [C]ity view is that it is the crucial test of the government's intentions.

GB insisted on being present at TUC meeting with Chancellor. To show that budget no longer done just at the end of corridor. 'I don't decide tax policy; but am entitled to look at it in connection with your sort of thing.' (Looking at MacDougall).

Crosland refers to Cabinet as 'great gathering of leakers'! Crosland's memo for Chequers:

1.) Keep levy.
2.) Introduce at least two export incentive tax gimmicks.
3.) Need for action on capital exports.
4.) Long-term loan.

[40] The British Aircraft Corporation TSR2 (Tactical Strike Reconnaissance) fighter jet project ran from 1957 to its cancellation in the budget of 6 April 1965, it being announced that the TFX, the General Dynamics F111A, would instead be purchased (*Parliamentary Debates* (House of Commons), 5th ser. 710, cols. 299, 330–1). In fact, this decision was later rescinded, at considerable cost, and a Royal Navy aircraft (the Blackburn Buccaneer) was adapted to meet the RAF's needs. The TSR2 was one of two—in Labour's eyes—'prestige' aeronautical projects inherited from the Conservatives, the other being Concord (Diary, 19 November 1964, First Week of December 1964). Denis Healey*, then Secretary of State for Defence, provides a detailed account of the military projects that Labour inherited and the difficult decisions that had then to be made: *The Time of My Life* (1989), pp. 272–3.
[41] Committee of Inquiry into the Aircraft Industry (Plowden Committee), *Report*, BPP 1965–6 (2853), iv, 189 published 16 December 1965.

On the whole NIF forecast of 3¼ growth (as then was) does not suggest need for reflation. (MacDougall queried this). (But E[conomic] F[orecast] Committee thought that growth more likely to be less than 2½% than more than 4%).

15 January *Reflection*. How much of GB's influence is DEA's and how much is First Secretary's? DEA has little expertise and authority in many fields of economic policy, e.g. finding jobs for redeployed aircraft workers, or new contracts for their firms. But if instead accent were on strengthening existing Ministries, how could they be prevented from being spokesmen of their vested interests?

(Good trade figures and BoT investment survey showed no downward revision of intentions).

18 January PM's draft for export announcement. (Prevented by Churchill's illness).[42] Seemed hour-long statement full of wind and little matter. Announced grudgingly that Concord was staying and nothing on TSR2. No analytical framework whatever.

Relations between PM and GB very bad. Fighting for economic credit. Paragraph in the 'Evening Standard' accusing GB of always talking in first person — where did that come from? Wilson evidently jealous of GB's publicity.

At previous weekend Chequers meeting, in morning Wilson spoke all the time. In afternoon MacDougall and Crosland thought that economic forecasts might be too optimistic. Cairncross thought the other way round — might achieve 4% in 1965. GB wants 'selective reflation', e.g. loans or grants for firms in north east with export potential. Crosland urged restraint on capital exports of £100m.

19 January BoT and IR say that subsidy to engineering producers in place of investment allowances would be contrary to GATT. But seemed to favour subsidy for users.

At Plan meeting [Robert] Workman* of Treasury argued for £200m–£250 BoP *overall* surplus to repay debt. Effect of separation of departments is to break up departments into interest spokesmen. DEA members labelled 'growth optimists'.

---

[42] Churchill died on 24 January and received a state funeral on 30 January, the conduct of much government business having been adversely affected by these events: Cairncross, *Diary*, pp. 32–3, in an entry for 17 January!

20 January GB terribly depressed by Leyton.[43] Talks about 'Belper',[44] in on minority vote. Spent two hours, with [Michael] Shanks* and Percy Clark* also in the room. Percy Clark blamed and abused for Leyton in the most embarrassing way in front of everyone. (Would not have stayed in position for one second in Clark's place). Clark told to start working for election in first week in May. Told to regard everything from that point of view. Otherwise there would be a House of Lords defeat on steel in July, leading to an election. Thinks that PM has been persuaded of this and will bear this in mind in Budget. Asked for economic policy to be thought over in light of election.

GB says DEA being blocked on all sides.

2? January Ministers don't usually see *official* papers!

WA and Hopkin want statistical forecast for year ahead to be published. Plan will be list of issues for Ministers.

BoT doesn't know which of our exports has done best! (My experience with export winners' article).

22 January PM's reported remark: 'If GB misses any more meetings through 'morning sickness' will be wondering if he is going to give birth to a 'little Neddy'!'

---

[43] Leyton by-election in which Gordon Walker, who had failed to secure a Commons seat in October 1964, failed once more to get elected and Wilson was forced to replace him as Foreign Secretary with Michael Stewart* who would later be Secretary of State for Economic Affairs, 1966–7. See Stewart, *Life and Labour: An Autobiography* (1980), ch. VIII for his brief period at the DEA.

[44] Belper, Derbyshire was represented by Brown between 1945–70. As the following shows his position was far from precarious:

	Belper			UK		
	1959	1964	1966	1959	1964	1966
Turnout %	84.2	86.1	84.1	78.7	77.1	75.8
Conservative % of vote	46.3	37.5	46.7	49.4	43.4	41.9
Labour % of vote	53.7	47.3	53.3	43.8	44.1	47.9
Liberal % of vote	0.0	15.2	0.0	5.9	11.2	8.5
Two-party (Butler) Swing % points	1.9	−1.2	1.6	1.1	−2.9	−0.2

Sources: D. E. Butler and R. Rose, *The British General Election of 1959* (1960), p. 224; D. E. Butler and A. King, *The British General Election of 1964* (1965), p. 322; and D. E. Butler and A. King, *The British General Election of 1966* (1966), pp. 296, 318.

25 January MacDougall said there was a very firm directive from Ministers saying that devaluation was ruled out.

Plan Committee has 25% target for 1964–70. This will cover immediately productive capital investment. But other parts of public expenditure will be geared to 22½%.

3 February *GB Progress Meeting.* Difficult to get away. Some 200m tons coal target—could manage 192m–194m tons, but gradually get down to 165m tons without being too brutal now.

MacDougall wants ministerial Outline Plan to list decisions for Ministers. GB wants it to contain what *ought* to be done. This intervention has stiffening effect. E.g. capital exports need to be cut by x million pounds. These seem to be the ways of doing it. Some friction apparent between MacDougall and GB. Roll complained that PM went too far in telling the General [de Gaulle] that France's ideas on liquidity are the same as our own! PM doesn't want GB to see [Lyndon] Johnson* before him. (A visit of GB's was therefore cancelled).

GB complained that two great boxes kept him up until 2 am. Do I have to read them all! M[inister of] State apparently takes no boxes home at all. Reference to need for O&M book!

MacD suggested that labour costs per unit of output will go up by 1–2% less because of incomes policy. Working party on BoP not commissioned to look at policy!

Plan is supposed to be forcing-house for decisions! Toying about with all these BoP calculations for last three months. GB apparently doesn't read these documents about BoP problems!

Exchange Account[45] took in £1m yesterday. £28m day before.

4 February Shanks says that N[ei]ld and Kaldor entirely supporting Treasury deflationists. Callaghan bumped into Shanks in corridor and said: 'How can you say economy not suffering from excess pressure of demand?'

Letter from Armstrong calling for increased motor taxation—idea is to release labour for exports. Catherwood called meeting. Shanks wrote strong memo against this: (a) motor industry is good exporter; (b) regional

---

[45] The exchange stabilisation account through which the Bank of England, under the control of the Treasury, intervenes in foreign exchange markets to manage the sterling exchange rates: see Bank of England, 'The Exchange Equalisation Account: Its Origins and Development', *Bank of England Quarterly Bulletin*, 8.4 (December 1968), pp. 377–90.

effect; (c) not much expansion expected in any case in motor industry this year; (d) depressing effect throughout industry; (e) Treasury also wants to cut road programme.

[M.] Franck* said at dinner at Political Economy Club that views were expressed that devaluation would happen next year.

5 February *MacDougall's 'daydream' on balance of payments.* (First of many). Shows over £800m annual improvement in BoP by 1970. Over £300m from incomes policy and £200m from 'Catherwoodery'.

Caulcott: What has come in is only about 5% of what went out!

Nield says that levy to be reduced by 5% at budget time. But to be announced before EFTA meeting. If intervening trade figures really bad, wire EFTA and they will postpone meeting.

Jukes's first paper on decisions for Plan. Heavy emphasis on difficult choices and need to restrain consumer spending and raise taxes. Defence spending to be pegged at £2,000m in 1964 prices!

Reflection. I was right in book to emphasise interdepartmental co-ordination and disposition to agree. No Minister can order any another Minister. *If* DEA wins over budget, this will be due to (a) economically literate PM or (b) predominance of GB in Cabinet, (or DEA?). Could same influence be exerted by PM and/or deputy PM or by NEDC without DEA?

MacDougall's meeting. How can one have Outline Plan without the plan? MacDougall: the trouble is need to borrow. The lenders insist on our not growing — in which case we would not need to borrow!

Only export incentives which now look possible according to MacDougall are:

> (a) Payroll tax on non-manufacturing services in London and south and subsidy on manufacturing in north east, etc.
> (b) Merchant Bank or ICFC as regional weapon for developing north in export increasing and import saving direction. (doubtful).

7 February *Reflection.* Endless committee meetings and talk; then everything is done in an excessive hurry.

System of separate loyalties, such that it would be disloyal to send remarks on e.g. Outline Plan to people outside economic group.[46]

---

[46] R version ends: '... disloyal to send remarks on to people outside Department, or even section of Department.'

8 February My idea for redrafting Outline Plan to contain chapter on use of resources accepted.[47] Arguments at Roll's meeting about publishing short-term forecasts! GB furious at not being invited to Aviation Committee. Lost temper at CEDC meeting, which ended in shambles. (Later wrote letter of apology to Chancellor).

10 February *Reflection.* Labour on coal equals Conservatives on aircraft!

MoL still envisages for 1965 training centres for 12,000 men, increase of 38%! About one hundredth of Sweden in relation to population.

Abysmal quality of a lot of BoT and MoL stuff. E.g. labour costs and prices in UK and competitor countries.

At Progress Meeting it was mentioned that a Chancellor's note on the economic situation mentioned need for deflation. DVA forecast neutral budget.

Paper to Ministers on Plan suggests continuing deficit of £300m per annum after 1966. (Getting larger?) £400m if repayment of debt going on.

Reflections. Absurd to create large crisis over such a small proportion of GNP — shows absurdity of fixed rates. Nevertheless Plan ideas for bridging gap unconvincing.

Fantastic: PM talks of import substitution, but mustn't use it in Plan paper because Otto [Clarke] objects! Similarly mustn't mention 'less essential' in connection with offices, shops etc. because Ministers who still have 1945–51 mentality are liable to jump at it. For these reasons Ministers who allow officials to process papers, which are agreed as far as possible, are completely in the hands of the officials who process them. In my book I underestimated effect of inter-departmental co-ordination — pernicious.

On eng[ineering] and agriculture it was thought that DEA was protectionist. Result was a meaningless hash rather than a clear cut statement of alternatives. But does DEA really know what it is proposing on these subjects? (Working group set up later). Do verbal gestures for sake of Whitehall public relations really matter?

J. Grieve Smith: Why should other side make all the rules? E.g. it seems out of order to quote in one's support anything said by Wilson before election.

Some officials have very little idea of what has already been published.

Reflection. The target should be for personal consumption (per head, per worker) with time discount, rather than for physical output. This is where NEDC started off on the wrong foot.

---

[47] Subsequently published as ch. 15, 'The Use of Resources', *The National Plan*. BPP 1964–5 (2764), xxx, 1.

Regression since early 1950s. Then it was taken for granted that import controls were preferable to deflation.

Reflection. Levy is the best thing that the government has done. Saved full employment. Pity that the effect was entirely spoiled at the autumn EFTA meeting.[48]

Outline Plan indicates need for squeeze on consumption. Is this right?

DVA: Budget Committee has not been reconstituted. Brown has so bullied Callaghan that latter has retired into shell and is not telling anyone about the Budget. Chancellor feels that Brown is guided purely by politics. (Cairncross told DVA that he thought Plan White Paper was really about the Budget). Working Party 3 made it clear (letter from its chairman)[49] that international Bankers required some gesture towards deflation before we could have rest of IMF drawing. BoP forecasts (may be too pessimistic) show that we can't get through without deflation. If Callaghan overruled, as he probably will be (according to DVA) then there will be run on pound and choice really will be between deflation and devaluation. Economic Forecasts Committee set up under Armstrong (including Roll) as substitute for Budget Committee. Temptation for gesture like surtax increase. Would be regarded as deflationary at home and inflationary abroad. Industrial advisers said to be hopeless. One of them could not attend 4.30 pm meeting because he would miss normal train home. Assistant Secretary at a quarter the salary has to come with some of them to all meetings. Two best ones Shanks and Young*, not from industry! Seeing the people who get £12,000 a year tells one what is wrong with British industry! Great resentment in Civil Service at these industrial advisers' salaries. Grumbles come out through [Peter] Thornton*.

Preparing Outline Plan. Far too much time spent doing draft after draft.

DVA?: last traces of determination to hold Defence at £2,000m for 1970 withering away. (By end March looked as if it would be at least £2,200–£2,400M if nothing were done. But TSR2 decision suggests determination might be increasing.) Running away like most previous governments.

Dr B briefs Prime Minister on economic documents. Too many different sources of economic appraisal instead of one thorough one. WA says that post-1956 Generals were preparing to win the Suez-campaign!

Preparing Outline Plan. Fantastic problems of circulation! Should it go straight to ED(O)[50] or should First Secretary see paper? Meeting with

---

[48] R version ends: '... spoiled by way it was handled.'
[49] See Diary, 17 December 1964.
[50] Economic Development (Official) Committee.

ER. Little points made and then he is constantly running away to other meetings. Then going over his comments with others. Enormous waste of manpower. Stages:

  (a) Conferences.
  (b) J. Grieve Smith.
  (c) Amplification of my intro[duction].
  (d) Own draft.
  (e) Conference with Jukes.
  (f) Roll.

and then: GB, Treasury etc., ED(O), Ministers, PM.

Process to continue from February to end March!

Reflections. What is wrong:

  (a) Collective responsibility of Cabinet.
  (b) Idea of seeking agreement and that nothing is being put up without being cleared through every department.

Most doctrinaire nation in taking seriously idea of collective responsibility.

Fantastic team loyalties bind people together in common attitudes towards particular groups. These are shared by people who have only recently met each other. E.g. industrial group is contemptuous of Committees unless an industrial adviser happens to be on it. Then it is the real stuff. Take it for granted that if one of their members reports on something, e.g. British Productivity Council, then report will be all right. (In contrast to any previous reports!) Similar loyalties within planning group. Will only take seriously reports coming from their number.

Full 1965 NIF. GDP will rise from fourth quarter of 1964 to fourth quarter of 1965 by 3%. By fourth quarter of 1965 to fourth quarter of 1966 by 2%.

13 February *Reflection*. Treasury seems to be abandoning even *steady* growth (at lower pressure — objective). In favour of being free to apply brake at any time and blatantly subordinates growth of demand to state of balance of payments. Even long-term objective of 'capacity growth' abandoned in favour of balance of payments and sterling priorities. Adverse effect of division.

16 February There is to be Chequers weekend on the seventeenth, for Budget and Plan in place of Budget committee.

GB said that Chancellor said that he only wanted £100m. GB will accept this. (ER said the same later). But very great pressures from officials etc. for far more. Bank wants £200m. National Institute Review hints at £300m. GB wants official Plan paper sharpening argument against deflation. He wants only selective deflation to balance expansion elsewhere. Cairncross has sent round top secret memo asking for large deflation. Obsessed by balance of payments.

GB summonsed by P[rime] Minister because of Evening Standard's story over Budget row with Callaghan. GB previously wanted the Plan to look like a plan, now wants document with very few figures for publication in outline form.

17 February MacDougall suddenly found out that Outline Plan figures were too pessimistic. £1,000m improvement not needed by 1970 and extra £600m is available for personal consumption! Terms of trade expected to improve and not deteriorate as at first thought!

Sterling now OK, but only a little coming back.

Reflection. Real disaster was the handling of the surcharge. This was supposed to bear the brunt of the short-term gap and be a substitute for deflation.

DVA said no rows between officials, but between GB and LJC. (GB told people at TV studio previous week that LJC and Treasury Knights ought to be sacked!)

GB told lobby of 'selective deflation'.

PM apparently alleging, without mentioning names, that journalists who came to DEA are leaking to press.

NIF Forecast Brackets (prev[ious] y[ea]r)	Q.4 1964–65		Q.4 1965–66
Final Expenditure	2.2		2.3
Imports	–0.5		3.8
GDP	2.9	(3.7)	2.0
Wages rates	5.7	(5.3)	4.7
P[ersonal] D[isposable] I[ncome]	5.9		3.7
Consumer prices	3.9		2.2
R[eal] P[ersonal] D[isposable] I[ncome]	1.9		1.5
Cons[umers'] exp[enditure]	1.7	(2.2)	1.5
P[ublic] Auth[orities'] (Current) [Expenditure]	3.9		4.3
F[ixed] Inv[estment]	6.1	(11.2)	3.3
(Public)	6.9		6.9
(Private)	5.2		0.0

22 February Headlines now about there being no differences between departments, Budget going to be deflationary.

Everyone is saying DEA played hand badly. [Anthony] Wiggins*: not insisted on being in on little groups of officials; whole role of DEA in Budget delicate. Caulcott: all sides taking up position in advance. Wiggins: no one in Treasury want[ed] £300m! Cairncross not giving figures.

Ominous reference by MacDougall to tough Budget and monetary relaxation. Says if not for BoP DEA would actually want expansionist Budget and Treasury neutral one. School of thought if we have a tough Budget now and hang on in two years situation will be OK. (We've heard that before in 1957 and 1961!)

Reflection. 'Split' cuts off physical contacts and flow of information between expansionist elements and 'old' Treasury. The Plan to a large extent led by Treasury; because Treasury leads public spending and BoP—both in fact and in planning sub-groups. *No substitute for putting at No. 11 Chancellor who knows what to do including […?]—and on bringing in staff to do it.*

Last Friday First Secretary asked for plans to be prepared for building controls. (Shift controls […?])

Said that WA would accept £150m give or take a bit. Rickett (and Cairncross?) actually emphasised to WP3 that our deficit was larger than they thought!

Proposal for replacing investment allowance by user subsidy for 1966 Budget! Probably not in 1965.

Osbert Lancaster's* [*Daily Express*] cartoon on GB and surcharge.

Reflection. GB's historical function is to lay down incomes and prices machinery. This may not be permanently effective, but can be yanked into action in a crisis. For all blunders, hopelessness at Macroeconomics and international negotiation and in much else etc. this may be his contribution.

Statement on doubling expenditure made in terribly misleading way with emphasis on spurious increase in Estimates. JG thinks PM deliberately hardened Callaghan's statement and had it made when GB in Geneva. Also thinks that Wilson had come down in favour of Callaghan. Thinks GB being pushed out of Budget decision.

GB very drunk in Geneva. Scene with journalists one night 'Are you British?' Insulting Jay in front of everyone. Nield: Paradox was that he went down extremely well with the Swiss who were eating out of his hand.

25 February Treasury has built a wall round Budget proposals. Top secret memo from ER on [Tony] Vice* story [in *Sunday Times*]! 'Budget compromise of £100m agreed;' also on [Ian] Aitken* in Guardian saying that DEA lost on regional ingredient, which won't be in Budget. (In fact GB did the leaking). [Lawrence] Helsby* starting campaign to protect confidentiality of advice to Ministers. People are asked to say individually whether they had seen Vice or Aitken, and what they had said. McCarthyite atmosphere. Ministers asked never to see journalists without secretary or press adviser present. Everyone asked to urge utmost care in any contacts with the press. Minute of Cabinet meeting in which PM refuses to accept principle of 'Whitehall Correspondents'. Serious threat to normal procedure. Must not be given any special facilities.

26 February Plan paper for Ministers. Concludes: (a) press forward with effective incomes policy etc.; (b) adopt positive policy of increase in supply rather than negative one of decreasing demand.

BoP: (a) Major attack on overseas capital expenditure; (b) Review of defence commitments; (c) Reduction of defence spending (how adequate is all this?)

27 February Earlier on GB was going round complaining that Callaghan and Treasury deflationists spoiling his Plan. DEA was defeated on regions. Reconciliation meeting yesterday. Callaghan made Cardiff speech indicating that he would not be too deflationary.

Reflection. Reduction of surcharge may be price for surprisingly long period of keeping at 10%. Effect may have been underrated. Surcharge may have preserved full employment in UK.

Budget. Got impression that car licence duties may go up and that increase in car purchase tax from 25 to 33⅓% is being considered.

Surcharge. After GB came back from Sweden early in January, saying surcharge cut would have to be 5% and not 2½%, arguments over. Treasury did argue for 2½%, but weakly.

?28 February [Wynne] Godley*[51] tells story of [Paul] Chambers* hinting in letter that industrial support for National Institute will dry up if it published gloomy BoP forecasts of last summer.

Otto [Clarke]'s Plan E — for user subsidy to replace investment allowance.

Plan D — Regional payroll tax (on service employment) and subsidy.

Plan G is a sort of combination of the two.

1 March R *Reflection.* Civil Servants very good at drafting so as not to

---

[51] Godley had been seconded to the National Institute of Economic and Social Research (NIESR) for 1962–4, during which time he produced work with Shepherd which features in Diary, 29 January 1966. Although Chambers' presidency of the NIESR ended in 1962 he remained on the Executive Committee of the Council of Management (*NIER*, 31 (February 1965), inside back cover).

offend anyone. Very necessary because of possible shower from all sides if anything offensive in drafts. Keeping in touch with what everyone is doing, and writing so as to take in everything without offending anyone is a full time job, but can be a quiet life. No wonder lack of dynamism.

On March 1st, there was a Cabinet directive to study building controls.

In Plan documents, Treasury and Board of Trade don't like anything critical of past.

Outlook that emerged from Chequers meeting: 1965 output and capacity will increase in line; output would slow down in 1966 but balance of payments would be bad.

Plan D is a tax on services in the London and Birmingham area and manufacturing subsidy in north east, north west, Scotland and Wales. Manchester? (Presumably on pay rolls).

Security officers accusingly bring in bits of confidential paper from my wastepaper basket!

8 March Wilson written to GB saying he should not take any decisions while PM was away, or latter would see that he did not go to US! Said at airport: T[hank] G[od] that GB won't be around during Budget discussions.

GB not going to US.

11 March Plan D accepted by the Chancellor and PM. An appeal to firms on bringing back overseas profits etc. is also to go out. (Written by DVA). To be cleared by Chancellor before George sees it.

15 March Dr B made his great speech at official committee against Board of Trade paper pouring cold water on proposals for increasing Commonwealth trade.

Great flap on over US balance of payments measures. (Origin of more deflationary attitude towards Budget?)

Armstrong Report.[52]

This was report of a group of officials set up to consider ways of dealing with the balance of payments, which reported in September 1964, and on which new government based its decisions.

Armstrong's own introduction: £200m base BoP deficit.

Rejected deflation *by itself* as solution because of excessive cost — explicitly recognised that deflation would have to be multiple of improvement

---

[52] TNA T171/755, 'Balance of Payments Prospects and Policies', September 1964.

required. Devaluation dismissed as 'confession of failure'. Emphasis on absorption of advanced technical resources in defence.

Suggested new unemployment aim of 1.8–2%. Should work pragmatically towards it whenever opportunity affords.

Against import restraints etc., but they should be 'kept in readiness'. On the other hand the scale of deficit could exceed resources available for financing it. Main ideas:

> (a) Industrial efficiency.
> (b) Defence.
> (c) Lower pressure of demand.

So long as hope of international finance, keep import controls in reserve rather than use.

Officials' report. Group under chairmanship of WA, including Treasury, BoT, and BoE). Accepts need for import substitution, e.g. state loans for some purposes and savings in agriculture.

Against permanently higher long-term interest rates, for BoE type reasons — confidence and gilt edged.

Elimination of deficit through lower pressure of demand. Would require unemployment of 2–2½%. Objections, therefore compromise recommended.

If right steps not taken, or they prove inadequate, we may be 'forced into devaluation.'

Against this happening because (1) world trade conditions exceptionally favourable, (2) no clear evidence that costs and prices are out of line. (Then inconsistent to urge incomes policy or lower pressure of demand to control incomes). When adjustments not very formidable, overseas observers could regard it as excessive. Would be shock to confidence, strain relations with other countries, jeopardise sterling area and encourage capital outflow, would jeopardise BoP, cause uncertainty in exchange markets, disruption of world trade. Undermine reserve currency system; fraught with danger; relative costs would exceed temporary benefits and no fundamental effects in improving efficiency. (Fuller treatment of this subject available if required — no doubt).

Appendix on limitation of imports. Since levy involves breaking treaty obligations, increases likelihood of retaliation, may risk breaking up EFTA. Document hints that it is in favour of QRS. Appendices contain QRS and levy schemes under what GB called 'load of bumph'.

Overseas spending. In the 1961 crisis the aim was to hold overseas spending at £400m in 1962 instead of expanding to £480m–£500m. Did come to £475m!

Appendix 10. 2% unemployment would remove *half* deficit; 2¼% would remove all deficit.

Increase of unemployment from 1.8–2% would reduce increase in earnings by ½% a year. Labour costs are two thirds of export costs. Increase by 0.5 to 2.3%, would reduce earnings by 1.25%.

———

Great fuss about Plan. NEDC didn't like it because no figures. GB didn't like it because no plan. Afraid of DEA being discredited if convincing government document not produced. After all the fuss, he makes Minister of State responsible for it.

Latest MacDougall memo on Plan policies.

1964/5 growth by 3%; 1965/6 growth by 2½% (forecasts). This means 4¼% 1967–70, while working population hardly at all. (Very implausible even before Budget SB)

BoP deficit in 1965 £330m, in 1966 £420m. This equals £750m altogether.

Exchange control agreed at Chequers should save £60m a year. Treasury to propose other measures to save £50m a year. Determination to save £50m in two years. Surcharge of 5% or equivalent should continue next year, should save (£80m?) subsidising for coal export should save £50m in two years. This leaves gap of £350m, in 1965–66.

1967–70, deficit plus debt repayment of £550m a year. Investment and other to save £150m a year. Incomes policy effect rising from £50m in 1967 to £250m in 1970. Catherwoodery. £50m to £150m against £50m to £100m. (Many similar calculations).

16 March *Budget Prediction.* Judgement £100m–£200m. Basically £100m–£250m taken out. Perhaps 'made up' in some way, plus £50m of foreign exchange control, investment tightening up, etc. General statement on defence costs.

Car licences and purchase tax for cars and/or higher rates of P[urchase] tax. Alternatively part of regulator and/or lower rates by equivalent of regulator. Most probably car licences plus part of regulator.

17 March Progress Meeting. PM's minute. EEC should join EFTA! GB wants to be left out until serious possibility of joining EEC comes up.

Three Ministers to discuss Budget without officials this coming Friday.

Only two Treasury officials know full Budget plus Eric Roll. GB agrees not to be told; to be told later by ER.

Donald doesn't know, but will be told before absolutely finalised. Next Monday: meeting with PM over Europe.

Coal: Accept 180m tons over next year or two. Perhaps 165m tons by 1970. 'Jim' seems to be deciding NCB write-off.

TSR2 decision about to be taken.

GB: DEA would never be forgiven if Plan not in fact in useful shape by end of summer. PM never holds meeting without saying 'This must wait for Plan'.

Europe. BoT looked at all possible Commonwealth trade, poured water on all of them. Wilson very hurt. Committee looked at four different types of association. Came to conclusion only membership suitable. Review of kinds of functional co-operation. GB stands aside for time being.

23 March Had conversation with GB. PM wants US to support pound. Is bound on Vietnam; pressure to deflate at home. Wilson has a past to live down; rest of us can be more empirical! GB the only one to be against East of Suez.

DVA confirmed the US Treasury Representatives came to London with changed attitude to UK problems; plainly UK has inflationary problem and must deflate. (The real origin of the new attitude to Budget?)

GB says that PM came down on Callaghan's side and GB lost Budget battle. Deflationary injection would be outside my tolerable limit of £100m–£150m. Even DVA shocked by amount of it? GB sending minute to P.M; doesn't want to speak in Budget debate (but knows he will!) GB says only possibility left is pre-Budget Cabinet. Obvious course to combine there with Frank Cousins. But could hardly intrigue beforehand.

Amounts mostly being raised are indirect taxes. Only one specific thing like petrol tax to make GB cross (suppose it must be car licence duty). Previously agreed with Callaghan that it was to be a £130m–£150m deflation.

GB: More and more decisions going in favour of Treasury. Earlier decisions favoured DEA Perhaps was [sic] the less important ones.

TSR2 decision supposed to be taken today. But PM trying to postpone it till summer.

PM wants to manoeuvre between the two departments. Says given Treasury head now and do something about interest rates in the autumn.

Postal charges increase may be taken into account in Budget.

PM worried by attention DEA getting and is trying to reduce it.

PM against cancelling TSR2 because of European aircraft industry idea. Having been accused of being pro-American, he now (in the worst possible instance) doesn't want to get an American plane instead.

According to GB, PM asked Trevor [Lloyd-]Hughes* how to offset DEA press build up.

ER: Admitted OF-BoE link-up 'disaster'. Will talk to GB about governmental organisation after IMF. Weakness of government machine is there is no central directing organisation covering foreign and economic policy. Real criticism of PM is that he is indecisive. Relations between Ministers matter most. ER says GB won most of battles.

ER admits that in present set-up DEA can only come in when it can show that its interests are affected. Very little DEA stuff so far to impinge on Budget. Interests now are in matters difficult to prove. Effects of measures on confidence or regions — very intangible.

Roll queried whether devaluation would help. Asked but wouldn't everything be better off if Bank Rate had been raised to 6% straight away, and we had contacted Europeans as well as Americans on the levy.

25 March Jay still insisting on the black spots approach to unemployment districts.

26 March P. [Bob] Dixon's* last talk with the General. Regards C[ommon] M[arket] as just customs union — wants technical co-operation. Main revelation is how anti-German he is, spoke of need to keep atomic weapons out of German hands. Nassau was turning point that made him feel Britain not ready for Europe.

30 March Pressure of demand for 1970 assumed to be 1.5–1.7% now because of better regional adjustment. (Why didn't Treasury fight this harder? Doesn't take it seriously).

Plan predicts 3.7% growth for 1965/6. Hopkin points out that forecast is of 2.5% even without allowing for Budget.

Treasury Note on BoP debt

Assumes equilibrium by end of 1966. Policy will have taken £100m of forecast deficit from 1965 and £200m of forecast deficit from 1966.

Debt at end 1965:

IMF	£357m
Central Banks	*£215m*
Total	£572m

Forecast deficit for 1965	£380m
Forecast deficit for 1966	£450m
	£830m

Less balancing item	£100m	
	£730m	
less balance of payments 'savings'	£300m	£430m
Total financing		£1,002m

(S[easonal] A[djustment] expected to weaken in 1965/66)

Treasury queries whether we will be able to borrow this amount. Present IMF rights = £875m. (But is full quota available?) ?Rights under new quotas will be OK by $500m=£170m. Unused Ex-Im Bank=£90m.

Long-term borrowing in US and Europe on favourable assumptions could raise only £100m. And there is a Swiss credit of £28m for three years. Five bisques[53] = £60m each roughly.[54] Nothing else is known.

Assumes other means are used to reduce debt to £900m, e.g. sales of dollar portfolios. An IMF repayment will be required by 1967, but could be extended to 1969. Further drawings to be paid by 1970. May not be possible to secure agreement to have it 'rolled over'.

Suggested table of debt repayment.

1967	£100m
1968	£183m
1969	£183m
1970	£150m[55]
	£183m
1971	£150m
1972	£100m

The whole lot will involve moving from an overall deficit of £500m in 1966, to overall surplus of £100m in 1967. Difficult transition to imagine when Gov[ernmen]t will probably be reflating the economy to secure production target.

1 April Saw a public expenditure file. Estimates' increase in real terms was originally calculated 5½% but has now been recalculated at only 4.1%.

---

[53] A clause in a loan agreement that entitles a borrower to postpone payments of interest and/or principal for limited periods when experiencing balance of payments difficulties.

[54] The Anglo-American Financial Agreement of December 1945 permitted the UK, in certain circumstances and on a limited number of occasions, to suspend the annual interest and capital repayment due in December each year on its US war loans: L. S. Pressnell, *External Economic Policy since the War*, I: *The Post-War Financial Settlement* (1987). This was done in 1964 and again in 1965 (Cairncross, *Diaries*, p. 90). The final payment on this loan agreement was made in December 2006.

[55] The relationship between this and the next figure is unknown.

First Secretary originally opposed Chancellor on publication of 4¼% long-term figure on public expenditure. Uncertainty about whole picture and possibility of holding the figure. But Chancellor was worried how far opinion would react to publication of estimates. DEA suggested that Chancellor should play down Vote on Account.

Original spending proposals left by last government would have involved 5¼% annual increase in real terms (includes Local Govt. pension increases etc — without this about 4.6%). Would have meant tax increases from £800m–£1,200m over four successive budgets. Tax increases in November Budget would have provided £300m of this. (Surely £200m?).

Decision to reduce this to 4¼% involves defence staying at £2,000m instead of going to £2,400m. Social services going up by not much more than trends already going on. Incomes guarantee given low priority; wage related unemployment benefits preferred.

DEA criticises Chancellor's memo because it implies that all kinds of expenditure (including Purchases of Land Commission) imply pound for pound increase in taxation.

Basic programmes fixed for departments with a little leeway to be decided by government to extra programmes. This leeway amounts to about £200m over several years!

Chancellor said 4¼% choice [of annual average real GDP growth rate for 1964–70] would leave room for 1½%–2½% increase in personal consumption, taxes would have to go up by £500m .... 22½% [growth] assumption [over 1964–70] taken for planning and public expenditure.

Reflection. Treasury still has privileged position. Treasury asked to see GB Budget speech: But I haven't seen Chancellor's.

Fantastic that whole of overseas finance, fiscal and monetary policy completely outside Cabinet, interdepartmental Committees, or Cabinet Committees. A private mystique, an empire of its own. Like foreign policy before first world war.

Reflection. Funny that BoE unable to prevent weak pound: (a) Friday after no bank rate increase and (b) stopped supporting forwards a couple of weeks before Budget.

My latest Budget Forecast. Purchase tax on cars and possibly other high rates from 25% to 33⅓%. 'Regulator (10%)' increase in drink and tobacco (drink more likelier of two). Car licences. All this will give slightly larger package than required. Possible increase of 15% Purchase Tax rate to 20% might be in package.

Basis would be the regulator minus petrol with perhaps a bit more on cars and/or possibly car licences.

Package of £200m–£250m, unless something taken off.

If GB had any sense, would use TSR2 decision to get £50m taken off at pre Budget cabinet.

(Renewed weakness of sterling last few weeks because of US measure in response to De Gaulle's threats).

Own activities this year.

Export measures — didn't come off!

Outline Plan — Infinite variations, boiled down from presentation to Minister then blown up a bit for NEDDY. NEDDY didn't like it. Shone asked to prepare version. This was GB's favourite, it did contain some figures, but decided at end not to publish.

GB's speech for US bankers — abandoned, because he didn't deliver it. Then transformed into Albu speech.

Speech for [William] Rodgers*[56] — Planning Conference in Northern Ireland. Last two weeks on GB speech in Budget debate.[57]

4 April Draft letter from First Secretary to Chancellor, drafted by MacDougall. Chancellor evidently told IMF that he expected demand to increase by only 2½% per annum from the second half of 1964 to the second half of 1966, by which time the UK would be in balance. First Secretary's letter says that he understands that:

> (a) we must not be precluded from policies to secure balance of payments equilib-
> rium with faster growth of demand;
> (b) figures must be kept confidential because of effect on trade unions etc.

Chairman of Plan Co-ordinating Committee says that main conclusion of Balance of Payments Report is that BoP would not be viable in terms of a Plan even allowing for the Budget without other measures.

Telegrams show that *IMF* interested in Bank advances to Government sector. Asks for consultations on major changes of policy here. Huge gaps still in balance of payments in pre-Budget plan papers, even allowing for incomes policy. This makes a difference of about £400m to £500m.

13 April Met Chancellor in street. Setting up committee on international liquidity, 'Don't tell George!'

---

[56] His period at the DEA is covered in his memoirs, *Fourth Among Equals* (2000), ch. 4.
[57] Brown spoke in the budget resolution and economic situation debate the day following the budget: *Parliamentary Debates* (House of Commons), 5th ser. 710 (7 April 1965), cols. 519–43.

Suggested to him that he should not go further out on a limb than Prime Minister in defence of pound. Point taken.

14 April *TSR2*. April 1st Cabinet Meeting. PM suggests some sort of postponement of issue for further two or three months. Ministry of Aviation against cancellation if this involves purchase of TFX.

30 April *IMF Staff Appraisal* (from telegram dated April 30th). UK programme to restore balance by second half of 1966.

In its November appraisal Fund doubted whether measures were enough for balance of payments equilibrium by late 1965 or early 1966.

Programme to reduce pressure of demand (presumably UK Government's programme):

(a) 'make room' for higher exports;
(b) reduce wage drift and arrest 1964 slippage in competitive position (after one year of improvement).

There is expected to be gradual rise in 'difference between production and capacity' building up to an extra 2% by second half of 1966.

If programme works some basic deficit expected in 1965. Question of continued recourse to foreign exchange resources. In seasonally weak second half of 1965 the strength of sterling will have to depend heavily on market confidence that UK can continue to give external balance priority.

Moderate expansion of credit foreseen which is compatible with balance of payments objectives. But needs to watch monetary position carefully.

The 4¼% expenditure programme suggests some bias in favour of public expenditure, which is reinforced by the tax and credit changes. Frequent restriction of private demand may have adverse effects on savings and investment.

Because of uncertainty, it was stated that UK was determined to take such further action as may be necessary ... close contacts to be maintained — deserves Fund's support.

30 April *Fund Board* Doubts expressed by France on adequacy of measures and of likelihood of equilibrium. [Pierre-Paul] Schweitzer* emphasised UK's readiness to take further measures.

1 May Schweitzer would like to know factors behind recent increase in Bank advances. Forecast was that advances would rise by £230m and deposits by £400m in a year to March 1966.

11 May Outstanding forward commitments equals £1,146m.

Since beginning of May only £8m taken into reserve.

Chancellor's letter to First Secretary: not precluded from expanding demand by more than 2½% if balance of payments improves by more than expected, e.g. better trade figures or new Plan policies! *But not in position to embark independently on faster domestic expansion which would affect balance of payments.* Originally the IMF wanted month by month reports.

DVA advised First secretary to be satisfied with this reply.

12 May DVA at Progress meeting. Says will be pressed in October to get rid of all the surcharge by April 1966 at latest.

WP3 Speaking Note says that we aim to be in balance by second half of 1966 and following year have surplus for debt repayment. Predicts current surplus of £50m per annum by second half of 1966; capital outflow of £100m, making minus £50m — which will be offset by balancing items, giving balance. Expect 6% annual increase in exports by value (above the Plan). WP3 briefing also gave detailed account of borrowing requirement — how it arose and what it would be used for.

13 May *Report on meeting of WP3 and Group of Ten*[58]

The general tone was 'moderate' but sceptical. Germany, France, Belgium and one other country most critical.

'Limits of UK international credit will be reached with IMF drawings. Heavy repayment burden would be left. Might prove difficult to retain in confidence over so long a period.'

WP3 therefore preferred to rely on Chancellor's letter of intent to IMF.[59] (Further action if necessary). (Predict there will be 're-phasing of public expenditure'. SB) (Schweitzer originally wanted month to month UK banking position).

Next review will be on July 5–6 (and then in September).

Steel Debate. JG told us George Brown (after Evening News story of his apology to Cabinet) rings PM up at night saying that he will announce his resignation from the back benches. Spent a very long time with

[58] The Group of Ten (G10), a precursor of the Group of Seven (G7) nations, and comprising the current G7 members plus Belgium, the Netherlands and Sweden, was an informal and loosely organised institutional device operating from 1962 onwards which attempted to coordinate and cooperate on global and domestic economic policy issues.

[59] Correspondence and drafts in TNA PREM 13/3151.

PM following morning and hence the wording of the statement of the Parliamentary Labour Party.[60]

19 May *First Secretary's Progress Meeting*.

[Dean] Rusk* told by PM of 'total commitment' East of Suez. Therefore Germany only reducible commitment left ('will never do that' GB)

[Robert] McNamara* said he would support UK in very heavy run down of troops in Germany. Department has decided (PM knows of division in it) to press for Plan D for three regions — North, Scotland and Northern Ireland.[61]

On 30th May there would be Chequers Meeting on the Plan. It would be a sort of McCarthyite investigation! To investigate doubts raised and centrifugal tendencies which have been reported to the PM.

The morning would be on international liquidities.

GB: time coming for getting Bank Rate down. But Treasury thinking of credit squeeze reinforcements.

(Am still predicting public sector squeeze. SB)

GB getting concerned about situation. Civil engineering group told him they had never known fewer contracts. (Architects orders?)

GB very bitter about post-Budget rise in [C]ost of Living Index. Says warned Callaghan.

21 May MacDougall said that when WA and Rickett saw BoP projections for 1966 they were shocked and wanted further deflation. (Previous assurance that there would be balance in second half of year was not based on any real plan but simply on projections made to order!)

24 May *Planned Report on Savings and Taxation*

Balance will shift towards direct taxation unless deliberate increase of indirect taxation relative to it.

Large — hundreds of millions of pounds — reductions of taxation possible in 1970. But large increases necessary in 1967.

(Very peculiar path. SB)

Very wide variations from 1967 onwards. Wage related pension scheme might help when revenue required.

---

[60] *Parliamentary Debates* (House of Commons), 5th ser. 711 (6 May 1965), cols. 1571–1694; see cols 1685–94 for Brown's much interrupted contribution.

[61] See Diary, ?28 February 1965 for details of the regional payroll subsidy scheme

On 22½% growth assumptions taxation would have to be raised by £446m in 1967 and then would have to be reduced by £580m in 1969 and by £421m in 1970.

On the 25% growth taxation would have to be raised by £857m in 1967, reduced by £491m in 1968, similarly in 1969 and then down by £580m in 1970.

24 May *Conference on Chequers Meetings*

GB gave it a thorough doing over. Revealed astonishing gaps. ([Roger] Opie*[62] was asked to send GB minute, for Agricultural Committee.)

GB took the line it was inquisition imposed by one economist— Dr B—on another economist: MacDougall.

Brown and Roll believed that DEA should stick to its position. Any forcing of balance of payments issue would lead to Treasury victory.

Plan D. After arguments with both sides, Plan D accepted by GB for three regions only.

29 May Balance of Payments Sub-Group makes three projections:

(a) DEA Projection—output to be raised in 1966 above post-Budget level.
(b) Alternative Projection—keep 2.75% increase for 1965 and for 1966 but then catch up.
(c) Assumption of 22½% growth.

Effect of Budget overseas curbs on balance of payments rises to over £100m in 1966 and £116m in 1970.

DEA Growth Path gives overall deficit of £300m in 1965 and current deficit of £120m. Then goes on in complicated way. By 1970 still small deficit (£35m) after allowing for 'balance of payments debt'. By which time £700m of extra debt will have been incurred (from beginning of 1967).

PM trying to make take-over bid for Plan as a political platform 'now that things are moving'.

31 May ER says: GB fighting Cousins to death over incomes policy. Believes Cousins instructed TUC to vote against it. Is looking for excuse to resign.

---

[62] Opie reflected on his period as an 'irregular' in 'The Making of Economic Policy', in H. Thomas, ed., *Crisis in the Civil Service* (1968), pp. 53–82 and contributed the assessment of the National Plan for the Oxford economists' post-mortem on Labour in office: 'Economic Planning and Growth', in W. Beckerman, ed., *The Labour Government's Economic Record, 1964–1970* (1972), pp. 157–77.

3 June *Move to 6% Bank Rate. Stricter HP terms:* GB seems to have heard very late in day. 'Phoned Catherwood at 10 pm on HP restrictions.

MacDougall says GB very depressed.

16 June (*Post-Trade figures*) Nield: PM panicking. Only just managed to stop Dr B from pushing through prior deposits for imports. Dr B also wants to rush through import controls. Thornton and planners also favour this. DVA thinks that this is wrong but will happen. He thinks that this would work with delay and be bad for confidence. BoE talks of state controls on wages and prices?

DVA: BoE wants a bit of deflation plus wage pause. Argument against import controls is that other countries will think that UK has rejected deflation and devaluation will come next.

Lost another £20m today.

Previous day: £26m?

GB apparently against both deflation and devaluation. Wants import controls.

Most of Treasury want to sweat things out like DVA. WA inclined towards import controls. WA among those who wanted a direct device on the trade balance in 1964. DVA keeps on talking about 'economic consequences of MacDougall'.

July 1964 DVA: meeting of Chancellor, Cromer and officials asks whether anything should be done. RM asked round table whether anything should be done. Got answer he wanted. Did not get round to some of lesser people at the table? DVA wanted some check (6% Bank Rate).

18 June On Thursday 17th, £28m was lost.

Plan D looks pretty dead.

Plan E? PM forgot that [Plan] F was killed (subsidies to engineering producers) and trying to revive it on a regional basis. One idea was a group of officials under DVA should work for a fortnight full time.

F[red] Jones* arranged, through GB and Governor to get banks not to make award until after the Midland reference to the national incomes board.

Friday: some losses, but less than previously.

21 June *Industrial Meeting* Plan D no chance. Corporation tax used up all Treasury reforming zeal.

22 June *Reflection* Backward move from 1964. Then growth, planning, exchange rates, etc. — pressures were in radical direction. Now taken for granted that money — not real resources — limits; and exchange rate immutable; growth suspect.

About the only person left who believes in Conservative 1963–64 policies! Left wing plus part of the Conservatives kept up pressure for growth versus sterling — without absurd commitment to physical planning. NEDC, an outside body, had more effect inside as phoney planning organisation.

Cabinet decided to investigate ways of making incomes policy more effective with or without legislation, including temporary freeze — DVA pro-deflation, MacD thinks import controls will be necessary.

If short-term policy is restrictionist, plan will not work. If it is expansionist Plan elaborate planning mechanism not needed.

Reflection Most of civil servants' work is not policy *or* administration, but providing reading material for Minister so that he knows what to say. Ridiculous subordination to 'servicing' one man (although that man does not run policy!). Civil servants depend on others — executive officers, Inland Revenue, etc for practical know-how which they don't know themselves.

Would amalgamation of grades help?

Above leads to pressure to use existing machinery, and existing executive departments.

Fantastic meeting of high-powered economic policy information committee. Dr. B gives great address on 'Neo-classical economists'. Wanted to leave out of the list of outside writers of overseas information services, G[eorge] C. Allen*, B[enjamin] C. Roberts* and Paul Bareau!*[63]

Board of Trade very deflationary — shortage of capacity.

24 June DVA says Chancellor wants to deflate more.

Official view — if row with foreigners wanted, better to have it on surcharge and not have import controls.

DVA: Plan can have some policy elements — government expenditure, coal, agriculture. Investment stimulation won't be ready for Plan — Chancellor talking of simply withdrawing investment allowance and raising corporation tax.

---

[63] In the 1960s Bareau was a correspondent for *The Banker*, *Daily Mirror* and the *Economist*. An early supporter of the Institute of Economic Affairs, he was a long-standing critic of the conventional wisdom that growth could be promoted macroeconomically as against through supply-side reforms to raise productivity. He was also active in campaigning for the abolition of exchange controls.

Unfortunate incident of the industrial meeting on devising new set of indicators superior to Treasury ones!

Still talk of wage and price freeze.

Investment incentives held up because Ministers could not make up their mind which incentives they wanted. They would have to be very general for Treasury to consider — Catherwood. Callaghan sick and tired of being told that he was amending a half-baked scheme.

End of June? MacDougall: Committee will probably recommend keeping the surcharge in 1966.

Ministers beginning to realise balance of payments obstacle.

DVA: Chancellor still wants to deflate. Everyone seems to be talking of the unmentionable.

GB wants 'rolling plan' (shows misunderstanding) to keep Planners busy!

I have been seeing Plan this week — Ministers won't see it till late August!

2 July *Balance of Payments forecast*

	1964	1965	1966
Current	−374	−130	−180
L[ong]T[erm] Capital	−371	−200	−140
Overall	−745	−330	−320

Assumes import charge goes down to 5% in October and removed in April 1966. Import charge will reduce imports by £150m this year and add £50m in 1966. (Without the charge deficits would be £480m in 1965 and £270m in 1966).

Alternatively: charge reduced by 2½% in October and 2½% every six months — then in 1966 imports will be down by £100m. *Or, keep 10% charge in 1966*, then £170m off 1966 imports (unless other countries retaliate).

Assumes confidence neutral. Would be falsified if these deficits were allowed to happen. Deficit would increase and there would be adverse effect on the balancing item and in monetary movements.

Forecasts suggest that aim of restoring equilibrium *in 1966 would not be fulfilled on present policies*. Principally because of export forecasts. However, value of exports to growth by 4½% in 1965 and 3½% in 1966 (distorted by ships and aircraft). This compares with *trend of 5% slowdown in world trade.* Balance on portfolio expected to change from minus £57m in 1964 to plus £112m in 1965 and plus £144m in 1966.

Budget should save (c.£111m) in exchange control and £25m on corporation tax. Net private investment to change from –£251m in 1964 to –£66m in 1965 and –£8m in 1966.

If no unwinding of need of [...?] substantial negative balancing item possible in the second half of 1965; unwise then to count on positive one in 1966.

OSA balances may fall in second half of 1965 by £100m. *Unless strong reversals confidence movements, reserves could be falling by considerably more than the deficit.*

NB Very opinionated report ... Interesting how sometimes this sort of report steers clear of policy and pats itself on the back for so doing, and sometimes read like policy document!

Reflection Wonder when Ministers will see this. Late stage at which Ministers see all papers.

12 July Full Minutes of Permanent Secretaries on OGIP [Official Group on Incomes and Prices] on 30.6.65. Ministers might want crash programmes prepared. [P]erhaps pay freeze and statutory control of prices.

Domestic Economic Forecast

	GDP	Exports
Second half of 1965	+2.4%	+1.8%
First " " 1966	+1.8%	+1.3%
Second " " 1966	+1.8%	+1.3%

(Personal consumption rising 1½–2%)

Growth of production abruptly halted in second quarter of 1965.

Manufacturing investment expected to fall by 5% in the last quarter of 1966, compared with same quarter of previous year. Wage rates to go up by 6½%. During 1966 5%.

Retail prices in period up to May have gone up by 5% per annum. Two-thirds due to higher taxes, etc. Very little rise expected after June. But rate of increase in year up to second quarter of 1966 will be 3%.

GDP will increase by 1½% between first and second half of 1965.

Seasonally adjusted unemployment rates will reach 2% at the end of 1966.

13 July People (i.e. R. Neild) saying that it is 60:40 or 70:30 that we cannot hold parity over next few months. Therefore deflate now.

Chancellor all ready to hold up public buildings starts.

Wilson against further deflation — full of gimmicks, e.g. exporters' expenses — not worth much.

MacDougall against further deflation because devaluation may not happen. He mentioned it twice to GB without GB going through the ceiling. Climate seems to have turned against statutory price controls or wage freeze.

Mrs Aubrey Jones[64] says that road hauliers' statement worked out over lunch with them before GB saw them. But JG later said that statement was no good and that GB had had to substitute entirely different one.

Reflection Real 'flaw' in 'planning'. General programme of economic measures could be adopted without the 'Plan' elements. (That is without industrial survey and PESC.)

14 July Doing draft of chapter 1.

DVA says that trade figures are sufficiently reassuring for there to be no need of an immediate decision. Decisions will be ready before next trade figures.

Plans, such as D, E and F will not be ready in time for Plan printing. At a meeting of GB, Chancellor and the Foreign Secretary, it was decided that the surcharge would stay throughout 1966.

15 July Meeting with PM on economic situation next Sunday. Nield wants to amend a letter to banks on imports. Instead of prior deposits plus some small deflation, e.g. 5% regulator or ½% special deposits. He is arranging for 'non-leak' international consultations on continuation of surcharge.

15 July *Reflection* (Programme for Conservatives!) Said wrong things about economic policy, trying to be clever.

If non-dirigiste and pursues right policies towards demand and exchange rates, will be sufficiently different from present policies. No need to advocate high unemployment or retreat from expansion.

1. Gets balance of payments right by doing unmentionable.
2. Don't worry about inflation or unemployment, etc. [P]resent unemployment percentage is abnormally low for cyclical reasons. The average unemployment rate of past years would give tolerable rate of inflation.

   In any case labour shortages and rising demand are stimulus to productivity. If inflation still faster than in other countries, the answer is the adjustable peg.

---

[64] Aubrey Jones, NBPI chairman, published an insider's account in *The New Inflation: The Politics of Prices and Incomes* (Harmondsworth, 1973).

    3. Give figures for growth of demand based on long run productivity and small acceleration — will then be credible. And then don't have to dress up industrial survey to make it look like Plan.

    4. *The supply side.* Carry on with industrial training, labour market policy, competition, mergers, etc. — Orange Book[65] — last Government — this Government:

       (a) at moment all inhibited by balance of payments inhibitions and fears. Would be much more effective if balance of payments surgery were enacted.

       (b) Technological bias should be substituted for the Robbins idea.[66] Majority of students don't care what they study — could be led [more towards] eng[ineering &] science.

20 July Reserve drain again large in last few days. Ministers panicking.

Thornton: DVA given up hope on DEA! Minister of State wrote paper on Plan E. Revived in absence by the Secretariat of Committee and he endorsed it. It was full of qualifications and the need for some more enquiries. This reopened the whole question under Treasury auspices. Chancellor chief opponent. Afraid of fuss after Finance Bill.

Fear of mammoth crisis by Autumn.

21 July There was a PM's document — 28 points, not 20 pages!

DVA: was full of gimmicks — some people think that an actor has been substituted for Wilson! A half hour was spent on expenses for exporters — a good exporter seems to spend very little on expenses. Then scheme for selected list of firms which are good exporters to qualify for Plan E type grants to the value of £50m — possibilities of corruption. Impossibility of devising any list which will stand up. Assistant principal would get bad report for such ideas.

Before the Budget Wilson wanted 3d tax on the sort of literature soap firms put through the letter box!

DVA there would be a package next week (for the Censure Debate?)[67] aimed to hit at building immediately.

(L[abour] P[arty] liking for discrimination) Hold up new starts and all public work except houses, schools and hospitals, backed by licences for non-housing work in private sector above £10,000. Offices already controlled.

('Stop-go to end all stop-goes' — DVA)

---

[65] NEDC, *Conditions Favourable to Faster Growth* (1963).

[66] Committee on Higher Education (Robbins Committee), *Report*, BPP 1962–3 (2154), xi, 639.

[67] *Parliamentary Debates* (House of Commons), 5th ser. 717 (2 August 1965). The debate was opened by Heath with the reply by Callaghan (cols. 1087–1109), though it had been expected that it would have been Brown who withdrew very late in the proceedings (see col. 1134). The censure motion was defeated by 303 votes to 290.

26 July Very peculiar atmosphere about the unmentionable. (Wiggins asking me about it). Probably being discussed once more but rejected.

MacDougall says package mostly usual deflationary stuff.

DVA: PM's menagerie of advice.

27 July JG: GB did not appear in Teach-In really because of deflationary measures. ('was very good on them' MacDougall). PM made speech on measures to curb public sector spending over week-end to bounce GB.

MacDougall: ten days previously PM was asking how building controls would help BoP. Now supporting such measures. Callaghan apparently said what he did the previous week-end, reversing winding-up speech on Finance Bill, because new balance of payments estimates recently come up (out for weeks!)

Some of statements in Ch[ancellor]'s statement seem to describe what was happening in any case. SB.

Will foreigners be taken in by measures? Pound should last [...?] Friday! Cairncross apparently said they were worth £150m.

28 July *Reflection* Things *could* work out all right, after the pound storm has subsided — *if* competitive position is not too bad and policies on exchange controls, imports surcharge, overseas spending works. Might be all right — even though no early reflation possible.

Treasury less enlightened and less Keynesian under the Socialists, e.g. no purchase of land for town centre development by local authorities. Pure 'where will the money come from?' approach. Package in this and every other way very Conservative.

While all this 'stop-go' is being arranged, DEA is fiddling with the Plan.

28 July *Further Reflections* Unfashionable thing to say but control of demand and exchange rate more important than platitudes about change.

The control of demand is not something clever, but get it right. Principles are simple, but conflicting tokens –

1. below 1¾% unemployment is danger signal;
2. don't go above 2%;
3. avoid stops and unsustainable booms.

These latest measures mark the death of the NEDC Plan type of approach. They depend for their credibility on avoiding deflation. Something more mechanistic now required. Only regret toned down anti-DEA stuff in book. Unrepentant believer in 'Planning' on original Neddy lines.

Right back in 1957 position. Action depended not on real position, not even on balance of payments position, but on what foreigners thought. Mistakes of Labour Government:

1. £750m.
2. Handling of surcharge.
3. Increase in pensions.
4. Finance Bill stuff.

Instead of treating growth as delicate plant, knocked it around in ignorant fashion, claiming falsely to have something more scientific and better themselves.

29 July *Reflection.* Callaghan incident — saying no further measures would be required. How was he briefed? Thought maybe (a) Chancellor does not see real specialists, but only top brass; (b) how late in the day do Ministers see vital documents, e.g. balance of payments?

ER: measures were advanced from following week because of exchange situation.

30 July Nield 'take no notice of Jim'. Origin of measures: PM's gimmicky memo — not merely export gimmicks. Treasury took out some gimmicks and substituted others (although had itself been arguing for deflation for some time. Origin really the balance of payments forecast.)

GB worried and asking people what to do. PM's memo refers to 'fetishes' of overseas opinion.

G.B: Pay maximum attention to fetishes, while minimum of real deflation on economy. All decided in the absence of the Departmental Ministers involved.

Said to be £200m. In fact, very much less.

e.g. H.P. equals £65m — but only on assumption that everyone previously took up HP contracts for three years.

Reflection If not much extra deflation then, according to the forecast, there will be no balance of payments balance at the end of 1966 (except to some extent with aid of change in surcharge policy!)

Therefore either the measures are more deflationary than the DEA seem to think, or there will have to be another dose.

Outcome is race between bad trade figures inspiring unmentionable talk and recessionary forces bringing down import bills.

1958 situation all over again. World recession helps UK balance of payments through terms of trade. 1966 could, therefore, be a very good year on the balance of payments front, – all this is one possibility. This should start up the old cycle all over again.

Employers pressing for deflation.

F. Jones wanted First Secretary to intervene behind scenes in wage negotiations in the first six months of the Government.

At last meeting of fiscal incentive group, Treasury came up with point of 35% corporation tax not yielding as much as was hoped. There remained only £67m for putting back elsewhere what was gained from investment allowances.

1 August[68] George came back from Sweden on Sunday evening and 'phoned Callaghan in the Isle of Wight. Callaghan had to go long distance to 'phone. Asked him to speak in Censure Debate. Then GB telephoned Eric Roll, who advised against the switch. GB again brought Chancellor to 'phone but this time he would not change back. PM did not know of any of this until Monday morning.

On Monday morning GB wanted to issue Press statement denouncing the Press over some jocular remarks he was reported to have made in Sweden. British Ambassador — who was rung up over telephone — said that he *did* make quoted remarks.

According to JG, real reason GB didn't appear was domestic trouble. Wife[69] fed up with husband being a politician.

2 August *Industrial Division*: Danger of Plan E. being too complicated because of the difficulty of 'Bagritry'*[70] and selecting goods for export (Plan X). Industrial Division line was that there was a great danger of the baby being thrown out with the bath water; 'Bagritry' would cost £25m over narrow band.

At last Ministerial meeting PM kept on saying that there must be something for Bagritry and exports. On exports need to keep simple:

    (a) extra increase for exports under Plan E. Subsidies for investment new capacity in industries [in] which firms had good export record (Plan X).

---

[68] Between this entry and that for 9 August 1965, some entries are out of sequence in Coll. Misc. 745/3, pp. 24–7. Additionally, the entry for 5 August 1965 is not in this file but in Coll. Misc. 745/4, p. 2.

[69] Sophie Brown* (nee Levene) (1911–90).

[70] Leon Bagrit was a long-standing exponent and practitioner of automation in industry, this being the theme of his 1964 Reith Lectures, published as *The Age of Automation* (1965). There is a reference to Bagritry in Cairncross, *Diaries*, p. 79, but nothing in the other conventional sources.

(b) Companies would have certificates which they could pass on to component manufacturers to give them an incentive. Some industrial advisers think this is not workable.

4 August Employers decided not to endorse growth targets (too high) at tomorrow's Neddy.

Big loss of reserves following the Gold figures statement.

Tougher Incomes Policy seems more likely than new taxes, etc. At any rate this is what foreigners seem to want.

DVA: Plan E etc.—Papers to go to PM a couple of weeks after the holiday. There will then be discussions with industry. Nothing is likely to start before 1967.

Very ominous that Stock Exchange went *up* on devaluation talk. It will be noticed abroad.

5 August 1965[71] (*further note*) Yesterday employers were planning revolt against the Plan target, played 'hard to get'. Tracked down at Courtaulds country place with Mr. [Frank] Kearton*. GB drove down at 10.30 pm, stayed until 3 am—finally won them over. Car broke down. Thumbed a lift from a man with a beard in a Mini, who didn't give him away![72]

George Cyriax: anti-£ stuff from Lazards. City out to get the Government out!

6 August Nield: PM thought he could stop run on pound by an immediate imposition of QRS

(Forward figure less than £1,200m now).

(DVA: two days of heavy losses; then Thursday it was taken on the forward. Friday a bit less (there followed the week-end when people wondered whether the pound would last).

DVA: PM's hopeless reputation. Everything that has gone wrong his fault. (GB now very much out of it.)

PM says two things for two audiences. Personally responsible for paper on Aid coming out on the same day as the gold loss figure.

ER: told many things, but specifically told not to tell them to GB.

---

[71] Implies a prior entry, but non found in Coll. Misc. 745/1–5. The dating of this entry can be triangulated against G. D. A. MacDougall, *Don and Mandarin: Memoirs of an Economist* (1987), p. 159 and G. Brown, *In my Way* (1971), pp. 105–6.

[72] Brown, *In my Way*, pp. 104–6 recounts the episode, as does MacDougall, *Don and Mandarin*, pp. 158–60 who adds the important detail that Brown left the then only copy of the draft Plan in a mini which gave him a lift back (sans MacDougall, still trying to secure replacement transport) to London when his official car broke down in the middle of the night.

7 August *Reflection* Worst dis-service to Britain is lending us so much money — postpones the reckoning.

(Sense in which French, etc. are right about too much liquidity.)

Pseudo-Radicals — Reviewers of my [Treasury] book on the £. WRM

Those who are *obsessed* are those who are determined fanatically to keep the existing parity. Blockage here stops progress on every other subject.

Heath and Wilson show how little they understand it.

Reflections (2) Labour Party's greatest crime: suggesting that borrowing was a crime: rebounded on it.

Greatest mistake (perhaps it was necessary) in Election campaign — instead of starting from Conservative growth experiment, as a very fragile creature needing to be strengthened, they pushed it aside with a blast of ignorant impatience. They then came out with something similar, but overblown, having meanwhile blasted away confidence.

Better handled *might* just have just got through with surcharge.

DVA about only person who believed in the Conservative experiments of 1962–4 but very anti-Neddy + 4% per annum! Nevertheless they depended ultimately on willingness to devalue — otherwise would have been better not to embark on them.

Reflections (3) There could be a very sudden and rapid turn-round:

A. Effect of deflation on imports;

Rise in world trade may have been under-estimated (Common Market; US);

Benefits of terms of trade;

All measures on capital account, including saving on investment dollars and corporation tax, etc.

Then the same old thing starts again.

Race between better trade figures and US and international support on one hand, and factors that could cause pound to collapse on the other.

9 August *Reflection Election*. Both parties fought on growth platform. If Conservatives had won it could only have been on the assumption that public believed that they had turned their backs on old stop-go. Otherwise they would have won on a false prospectus and whole outside public and part of Conservatives too, would have been very sensitive to resumption of old ways.

These reactions would not have prevented RM from some deflation if necessary; but would have made sledge-hammer blows of the Callaghan kind politically almost impossible.

Ministry of Labour's proposal to have *seasonally adjusted unemployment figures* in Ministry of Labour Gazette, but not in Press Notice.

Callaghan says OK, contrary to advice.

GB does not understand the point. Scribbles against his advice 'does not answer Ministry of Labour's point'.

Both seem attracted by pathetic idea of concealing trend (even more conservative than the Conservatives about taking public into confidence).

Miss [A. D.] Stevens* was shown letter saying that July measures added up to £200m (Brian Reading* thinks they might do eventually — no-one seems really to know).

Stevens letter copied out for other purposes.

Miss Patricia Brown* has calculations showing GDP rising by 1% per annum between first and second half of this year; and by ½% during 1966.

Public investment up by 5% (instead of 8%) between 1965 and 1966.

Exports to rise by 1.9% instead of 1.3% (German support payment?)

	1964	1965 First Half	1965 Second Half	1966 First Half	1966 Second Half
Unemployment (Seasonally Adjusted)					
Wholly unemployed 000s	361	305	337	388	442
Percentage registered	1.6	1.6 (?1.4)	1.6	1.8	2.0

NB As seasonal element added 55,000 approximately, unemployment could well top 500,000 in second half of 1966 (could approach 700,000 in first quarter of 1967. SB)

Between 1965 and 1966 public authorities current expenditure to go up by 3.6% instead of 4.1%.

Imports to go up by 0.9% instead of 4.5% (£249m difference — presumably due to deflation and new surcharge assumption).

NIESR will publish calculations showing that enormous improvement in UK's competitive position will be required to reach lasting equilibrium and repay debts. This will be in the section on the long term balance of payments.[73]

---

[73] This was of the form of an appendix to the home economy section of its standard quarterly report on the economic situation: 'Arithmetic of the Long-Term Balance of Payments Problem', *NIER*, 33 (August 1965), pp. 18–21. The conclusion to its home economy forecast had been forthright: 'The Government has, in our judgement, sufficient resources to survive a run on sterling this autumn. It may also be successful now in getting a surplus on current and long-term capital account by the end of 1966, at the cost of virtually stopping the rise in output. Thereafter, there is — on present import and export trends [as detailed in the aforementioned appendix] — a choice between quasi-stagnation (2–2½ per cent growth of output, combined with rising unemployment), or an inability to repay by

10 August F. Atkinson: most thinking people in Treasury would favour devaluation if there were slack in the economy and still no evidence of solving balance of payments problem — rather than have serious deflation.
Reflection
Import Controls & Surcharge Case for them was to prevent deflation of production. But when imposed to supplement deflation (instead of substitute) […?] the evil day.

Atkinson: Measures have always been less than Treasury recommended, but by now they have added up to about same!

Atkinson: vast number of conflicting advisers. Too top heavy — one reason why Ministers badly briefed. Callaghan's unfortunate remark before the measures his own.

Reflection Ministers are like newspaper editors. They never understand anything interesting or important.

Reflection On the one hand Labour Government has done more to tackle trade balance and balance of payments directly — say £200m surcharge and £200m in other ways. On other hand, needed to do more — because of worse position than in 1961. (It is possible that competitive position has worsened, e.g. in export prices — but improvement may be in pipeline) and also because of hammer-blows to confidence. Net result is good old Tory stop-go.

Ambiguity of deflation. Deflation of demand; deflation of production.[74]

Reflection People really objected to crises, not to stop-go. In that case the answer to them should have been a [Frank] Paish*[75] policy.

I objected to slow growth and the distortions of the fixed rate.

Again, as previous crisis, it seems to be taken for granted that more belt tightening is required. Daily Mirror and other papers complaining that public don't *feel* it enough.

(Limited nature of what is really required).

1970 the debts incurred in the last year. So either import propensities or export competitiveness have to be changed' (p. 18).

[74] Handwritten marginal comment (which succinctly describes the problem of Stop-Go policies), part of a page (Coll Misc 745/3, p. 31) containing a number of alterations to the typescript. Repeated in R version.

[75] Frank Paish, who had a deep understanding of the cyclical behaviour of the British economy, developed early the thesis that the British economy needed to be operated at a lower average pressure of demand to lessen inflationary pressures and avoid major disturbances from the balance of payments. His major relevant writings for policy, often first appearing in the *Lloyd Banks Review*, are collected in *Studies in an Inflationary Economy: The United Kingdom, 1948–1961* (1962) and *How the Economy Works and Other Essays* (1970).

No change from 1931 mentality.

Indeed, worst of all is supine acceptance of slow growth by industry, even if this means lower profits.

Industry never thought through their earlier cry for growth.

Let them — and whole Neddy movement — off too lightly when wrote book; but made for more interesting book with information on conversion to planning, incomes policy, etc. None of this would have been available if had rejected third way uncompromisingly.

But ought to have insisted on facing exchange rate issue foursquare?

Should not advocate but explain and predict.

11 August *Reflection* Foreign travel restrictions to save the pound would be the last straw!

13 August Mythology that Wilson made mistake about pound on taking office (when could have blamed last Government) and 'cannot' rectify mistake. Never said about any other issue of policy.

Did take time to see how deep-seated deficit was.

Views very little account for career civil servant. Their views producing atmospheres that can influence the country — but that is different matter.

Quality required: ability to cope in a flap!

Policy makers in bodies like DEA or Treasury don't really know of practical difficulties.

Qualities required:

> (a) ability to inspire bodies like Board of Trade, Inland Revenue, or Customs and Excise to produce schemes of their own, e.g. Regulator.
> (b) Invent schemes to fit in with existing administrative requirements.

Much more difficult to change administrative methods.

Reflection (2) Transfer of Plan from NEDC to DEA did *not* strengthen expansionist voice of Government.

14 August Callaghan used to see Lombard[76] every fortnight until Bank stopped it! (Cyriax).

Reflection Not 'growth über alles but 'growth über £')

Difference between the two cycles:

No mistiming of internal situation. Simply bowed to prejudices of foreign creditors.

---

[76] Cyriax wrote the *Financial Times'* Lombard column.

Don't know if they could have been resisted (if public expenditure had been tackled first, a smaller overall amount of deflation would have been required). (But after so much had gone).

Further reflections Distinction between Foreign Office and Economic Ministry:

Minister in Economic Ministry hardly ever speaks to lower echelons and he hears the top level only at their Sunday best. Doesn't know what people who are doing the work are really thinking.

e.g. WRM on advice that will be given against devaluation.

(must deal in new edition with whether better to reflate and deflate in one swoop, or little by little approach.)

15 August *Reflection* More like 1957 than 1961.

1961 programme was supported by internal arguments on e.g., desirability of reducing level of pressure of demand.

1965 (like 1957) actions were either:

    (a) reducing demand as far as necessary to put balance of payments right;
    (b) doing whatever necessary to appease prejudices of holders of sterling funds.
    [...?]
    (a) probably determined size of packages;
    (b) determined their contents.

Extremely stupid to reduce roads, technical colleges, etc. What on earth happened to idea that DEA existed to give priority to growth? Is the culprit the DEA, or is it that Ministers, including Brown, don't really want to give priority to growth, but want to give priority to houses and schools (schools rather than technical colleges) in a simple-minded way.

16 August *Industrial Group Meeting*: Catherwood reports. Ministerial Meeting decided to abandon [Plans] D & F. Work should proceed in parallel with Budget of April 1966. Deadline of November for Ministerial and Industrial consultation.

Work on revised paper for Ministers. Stiff piece on timetable.
Hazards:

    (i) *Timetable* Plan E and Budget must go together. A list of investment allowances only palatable with Plan E.
          Legislation for Plan E being worked out by Board of Trade.
          CBI has said consultations with industry won't be ready before October.
    (ii) *Consultation with Industry* To get Plan E through, it was conceded that service industry should not be in it. Instead they will give uplifted initial allowances. Although majority of industry may welcome this, CBI won't give blanket

>   endorsement, (e.g. hotel trade!). Consultations should be aimed at smooth
>   introduction rather than general assent.
> (iii) *Size* Inland Revenue calculated at last moment that 35% corporation tax won't
>   bring in enough for 16% grant (previous grant would be worth 13%).

21% grant with 40% corporation tax. (old tax investment allowance was worth 20½%?)

Need for reasonable rate. Inland Revenue make much of theoretical reduction in tax yield on dividends if higher corporation tax. Real yield of a 5% increase in corporation tax is double, that is 10%; but they reduced it to parity.

37½% needed to get 21% grant? Assume [...?]

Government purchasing in last four months. Four months wasted in general approach. Now search for specific cases.

Company Bill Industrial Division having a go at getting exports separately reported. In recent survey 235 out of 300 British companies had refused to sell exports. An electrical EDC also suggested compulsory disclosure but Board of Trade has unhappy reaction to this suggestion.

DVA: neither the July measures nor the trade figures restored confidence. Last week was a bad one, (despite trade figures).

Ministers considering wage freeze accompanied by measures on unearned income.

DVA spent last week-end — Saturday — with GB in South of France and Sunday with Chancellor. Nearly had to go to Scillies!

17 August F. Atkinson: Crosland said to have converted GB to devaluation.
ER on Plan
Blames MacDougall for:

> (a) forcing through 25%;
> (b) forcing through September time-table;
> (c) continuing with Neddy macro-economic model.

Balance of Payments chapter just says: 'hope to attract short-term funds to London to pay off debt!'

Catherwood: 'mixed blessing'.

What to do about BoP (ER's view): $4 billion or $5 billion credit would help! One alternative would be to cut commitments drastically even if it means losing support for £ and devaluing. Go to country on anti-Bankers', anti-foreigner — platform. Would mean Labour Party going Left. Don't think the floating and the younger voter would want this.

Alternatively muddle through making overseas cuts where possible.

Reflection: National Institute, etc. neglecting duty and behaving like subjects of totalitarian State. Saying that action on the Exchange Rate is politically excluded. Whole point of commentators should be to argue for sensible political decisions (especially when these decisions are also technical).

Such bodies don't say that deflation is ruled out politically. Political decisions can be wrong and can change.

Further reflection: the great myth of 'industry'. Government discusses with 'industry'.

'Industry' has decided. These are 'Industry's own estimates'.

No such entity; Heaven forbid that there should be!

Sorry that I encouraged this way of speaking, when 'industry' seemed to be going the way I wanted it to.

It is one thing to find out through the CBI how majority of companies may be feeling. But CBI cannot make commitments.

18 August DVA: PM to make special broadcast on incomes and productivity before Plan (didn't seem to come off!) Ministers still to agree how far it is necessary for legislation to form part of new approach to this.

Daily Telegraph-Daily Worker incident, when reference to shorter working hours in my article in DEA Progress Report was given headlines as 'Brown's threat to workers' leisure'!

ER complains that everyone still has aggregative approach:

MacDougall: devaluation substitute for deflation;

Dr B: if we devalue, doesn't matter what we do internally;

Nield: devaluation plus savage deflation;

Cairncross: Everything O.K. with a little deflation.

Real trouble: a majority of three; and personal animosities of top Ministers emerge as policy difficulties!

Reflection: 1965 differs from 1957 and 1961 in existence of real balance of payments deficit (despite underlying improvement in balance of payments).

Real complaint is Labour Party — discredited expansionists.

23 August ER going to Washington.

7 September *Reflection:* how much of present strands of economic policy date back to [Selwyn] Lloyd-Plowden days? (see list of accomplishments in book).[77]

---

[77] Brittan, *Treasury under the Tories*, pp 211–12.

Is there in Foreign Office or elsewhere attempt to look ahead or foresee threats to peace, e.g. India-Pakistan? Contingency planning. This would be analogous to type of planning required in economic policy.

JG: when ER went to US, two or three weeks ago, told of need for strengthening the statutory controls on prices and incomes. Strengthened Treasury hand. (This all started with a minute from the Prime Minister that any Thursday could start a catastrophic run on the pound.)

GB threatened to resign. (This seems to be constant refrain.) Spoke to Woodcock who suggested statutory early warning system, may not have to be enforced.

Basle last week-end went badly.[78] ER off to US again this week-end!

Plan E. No Bagritry, exports or regional discrimination. Industry being offered £67m. CBI Questionnaire to be sent out on 10.9.65. Answers back by end of year. But CBI will be asked to hurry them up by end of October.

9 September [Henry] Fowler's* German visit. Blessing. Germans emphasise it will be a long job. Economics Ministry sceptical about need for extra world reserves. At Basle, Bank of England proposed support for Sterling. Blessing: too big for Central Bank. 'Time for Governments to stand and be counted'.

Views of Fowler, [Fred] Deming, [Ludwig] Erhard* and [Hermann] Abs*.* (Telegrams or did ER say this?)

Erhard very gloomy about UK: 'precarious'. Exchange guarantee would be 'counter-productive'. German attitude to UK one of bewilderment. Erhard was more precise in talks with US Delegation. Not disclosed.

Reflection For all that is said about opportunities for different viewpoints, papers to Ministers are in practice unanimous, e.g. paper on implications for Common Market signed 'HM Treasury' and therefore often anaemic.

11 September *Reflection WA* tells Estimates Committee[79] that outsiders underrate contributions to discussion and differences of opinion far down the line. In fact, agreed documents muddle everyone up. Ministers (First Secretary and Chancellor) tend only to see people near top of Department.

---

[78] 4–5 September, one of the regular meetings of central bankers held at the Bank for International Settlements (BIS).

[79] In fact, Armstrong gave his evidence on 3 May 1965; see *Sixth Report from the Estimates Committee together with the Minutes of Evidence taken before Sub-Committee E and Appendices*, HC 308 (1964–5), pp. 152–60. The previous witness, on 27 April 1965, had been Roll (accompanied by Hudson) answering questions on the DEA and recruitment thereto, pp. 146–51.

People do watch their superiors ('helpful') and ('unhelpful'). Happens all the way up to Permanent Secretary. Can't be human otherwise. Top people meet in Top Secret and no contribution possible from lower down!

Further Reflections: Interesting how everyone, e.g. ER, impressed by long-term National Institute analysis in the latest Review.[80] But took no notice of similar analysis in Plan Working Party.

12 September *Reflection on Plan*
Plan is:

   (a) macro-target;
   (b) market research combined with growth rate;
   (c) programme of action linked with the above;
   (d) for purposes of government spending — in this respect not means of improving performance, but of housekeeping.

Absurd to make (a) and (b) centre of policy. Can only be adjunct. 'Category' mistake to think that 'Plan' solves anything. Everything depends on its contents.

Why I believed in Planning: as expansionist Trojan horse. This route is now discredited. What is left is a capacity argument. [Roy] Harrod*[81] has argued that getting economy to grow without demand bursting its seams is a very delicate operation. It is certainly difficult to combine with deflation.

13 September 1965[82] Talks with Fowler and Deming (took place on 11.9.65). Change in US thinking on liquidity. Want to keep about present total of dollars in world reserves, while any addition to world reserves should be through supplementary assets. No decision on how.

US would like:

   1. Deputies to report in 6 months;
   2. To merge the Deputies with the IMF Board!
   3. World Monetary Conference.

---

[80] The then current issue's quarterly economic situation, home economy section, included an appendix: 'Arithmetic of the Long-Term Balance of Payments Problem', *NIER*, 33 (August 1965), pp. 18–21; see Diary, 9 August 1965.

[81] Harrod was a persistent and occasionally somewhat extreme advocate of demand expansion in the 1950s and 1960s, and an elasticity pessimist in the devaluation debate, frequently offering his advice to Prime Ministers and Chancellors of the time. For his views on the damage wrought by 'Stop-Go' and other errors in contemporary policy, see his *Towards a New Economic Policy* (1967).

[82] Coll Misc 745/4. This entry is followed by a photocopy of 'French Veto Casts Shadow over IMF', *The Times*, 13 September 1965, p. 14, being a review of F. Hirsch, *The Pound Sterling: A Polemic* (1965); see Diary, 15 September 1965.

2 and 3, if ever reached, depend on 1. Europeans would not agree to a communiqué mentioning all three stages. But continentals would not support French plan as it stood.

14 September *Reflection Fixed exchange rate makes mismanagement of stabilisation policy inevitable*

Because of a run on the £, deflationary action has to be taken, irrespective of domestic outlook; that is why more knowledge of fluctuations and more figures or expertise would not be the answer. Then reflation cannot be taken in time because of fears of upsetting confidence.

Only hope of this school is that we will avoid reflating too much. If one mis-judgement or political postponement; and off we go again!

All sorts of clever things about high or low level of demand have been said. Have subscribed to them myself. But in UK wide measure of agreement that demand should be in 1½%–2¼% unemployment range. 1½% dangerous until shift in working of UK economy; and 2¼% dangerous. Practical range of 1¾–2%.

Yet for much of time economy threatening to burst outside these limits.

Thing to do is to get demand *right*—both level and rate of increase. Never been done before (right and not destabilise). This is connected with the fixed exchange rate, which prevents foreign demand from being brought into picture and makes destabilisation inevitable.

First task of Government is to get demand right—including foreign demand, or, better, relationship between demand for home and foreign output. Never yet happened because exchange rate out of play.

15 September *Reflections* Fantastic how people can think Callaghan a good Chancellor:

    a.   who started Press talk of relaxations? Friday afternoon: Chancellor's briefing and Downing Street optimism.
    b.   The effrontery of the Express:
        i.   Sunday Express has headline about 'lower mortgage rates';
        ii.   rebuked by Callaghan, makes another headline 'Wait for it' (facile optimism). Pathetically Callaghan appeals to newspapers not to predict early end of squeeze.

Labour Ministers do not realise how many times they have been here before.

Comment on Times cutting [no comment inserted].

Supine way in which Bank of England line accepted.

Nothing has happened to make it so. (Said the issue was dead often before.)

Gullibility of Press in accepting further stand-by as gesture of strength.

16 September[83] *Reflection* Regret giving credit to S[elwyn] L[loyd] in book for special reason.[84] He did open up a lot of problems; basically opened way for 'Third Way'.

Reflection Naive idea of reports on the Plan that it will mean more cars, houses, etc. Such a 'plan' could have been generated from any national income projection.

Conversation with Maudling* [RM] (16.9.65)

1. Heath[85] wanted to launch attack on plan as Socialist plan. Can't do this with a Neddy-type exercise.
2. Macleod*, [Keith] Joseph*, [Peter] Thorneycroft* etc. all entranced with idea of working economy at lower pressure of demand. They don't understand why it is unworkable.
3. Resignation of [Alec Douglas] Home* came as a complete shock. RM thought he would win.
4. 1964 Election:
    a. didn't much mind who would win. Parties take it in turn. Doesn't matter when!
    b. 'Colleagues' wanted to say Socialists responsible for run on the pound. Was against it.
    c. Thought there would be a blow-up in the Autumn; but couldn't be sure. (What he told his colleagues).
5. a. Repayment of debt in time neither necessary nor possible. The IMF Loan was exchange of one debt for another.
    b. Took great credit (too much) for improvement in second quarter balance of payments.
6. Agreed that in office should ask for definite portfolio in the Government 'Foreign Office or Treasury — probably Foreign Office' I argued strongly for Treasury.

At this point in Coll. Misc. 745/4 the following letter (carbon copy) from Brittan to Neild has been inserted. Since it is of both considerable contemporary interest and relates to research that Brittan pursued when he left the DEA,[86] it is here reproduced in full.

---

[83] Publication day for the National Plan.

[84] 'The Results of Selwyn Lloyd', *Treasury under the Tories*, pp. 210–12.

[85] Confirmed as Leader of the Conservative Party, 2 August 1965.

[86] For example, the first econometric specification of a UK political-business cycle (C. A. E. Goodhart and R. J. Bhansali, 'Political Economy', *Political Studies*, 18.1 (1970), pp. 43–106) acknowledges (p. 45 n.2) Brittan's prior work in this field as an inspiration to their work.

PRIVATE AND CONFIDENTIAL

Mr. Robert Nield [sic] o.r.

UNEMPLOYMENT AND POLITICAL POPULARITY

I have unearthed some material which goes fairly fully into the relationship between unemployment and political popularity. The Sunday Telegraph articles in the graphs plot Gallup Poll figures against unemployment. I was unable to use the Gallup Poll figures in my own diagrams in the Observer because the Telegraph had the copyright, but I did look at the same figures.

I think the articles show pretty conclusively that during the Conservative period on office there was a very strong connection indeed between the *movement* of unemployment and the shifts in the Government's political popularity. The relationship with the absolute level of unemployment was very much weaker and only really became apparent during crisis periods. In my article of December 2nd I threw out a number of hares on consumers' expenditure, the Bank Rate and the electorate's ability to sense the way unemployment would move. But I am afraid that these remain speculations which were not properly followed up. The only relationship in which I would express confidence (up to the last election) would be that between political popularity and the trend of unemployment.

Unfortunately, I do not have the time, nor the access to the material, to bring these studies up-to-date. But I am sure that all political party headquarters have the Gallup poll figures and it should be quite an easy exercise to do. The Gallup poll has, I understand, a monthly publication (called, I believe, Political Index) which shows very clearly the trend of the polls and a large number of interesting relationships. The National Opinion Poll started very much later and was not, therefore, very useful when the articles were written. But for the last few years there may be something to be said for using some measure which would average out the two polls.

I hope this is of some use. Sorry I cannot take it any further.

    S.BRITTAN
    27th September, 1965

18 September *Reflection* Question to ask about any manifesto, etc.: translated into set of proposals for Department and imagined objections. Very valuable discipline.

Mistake for, e.g. Conservative Party, to put all its economic policy making into hands of people with no experience of this sort of objection. This is not a radical fresh look, but is just riding for a fall — especially when experience is ready to hand.

Industry's undistinguished role

Industry 'calls for' entry into Common Market. Won't say how, or indicate changes in foreign policy that would make it possible. If 'industry' had been quicker off the mark and not so long bogged down in old free-trade area approach, we could have been in.

Planning has given 'industry' much bigger role. Can see now how temporary and spurious the radical phase of 1960–61 was.

Secrecy

Labour Party less frank than even the previous Government in publishing short-term forecasts and objectives. (No unemployment percentage in Plan). This is the real stuff of economic policy.

Balance of payments chapter, even in Plan, shrouded in Treasury secrecy. Monthly movements even more hidden.

Often think myself how disastrous it would be to publish certain figures, but have not changed my views. Better to have principle of publication, e.g. Milton Friedman* for example of Free Speech in US. A purely empirical approach would not, say, allow Communists in McCarthyite America much say! But if principle is established it is much more difficult to stop them.

'Broken Promises' Debate[87] Incompetence of Opposition. Conservatives retrogressed away from anything they have ever learnt to platitudes about enterprise of the early 1950s. Very little hope can be rested in them. In practice they have largely accepted Wilson's charges against RM.

Generally known that RM did not act in the summer of 1964 against Treasury advice (but see section [of Treasury book] on way in which advice is conveyed). He says figure of deficit was steadily put up throughout year. See if this is confirmed in successive issues of National Institute Review.

(Deal with Conservative manifesto in any new edition.)

18 September *Reflection* Would Tories have been any better in 1964–65 crisis?

i. Crisis has always followed BoP deficit.
ii. Would not have made such a mess of economic management.
iii Might have got Surcharge off to a better start and working as alternative to deflation.
iv. But all this would have been counteracted by the size of the deficit.
v. If Tories had resorted to stop-go, there would have been screams about 'confidence trick'. On the other hand the real pressure on the Labour Government is to behave in orthodox way. The real crime of the Labour Government was to discredit idea of alternatives to orthodoxy.
vi. Always thought two economics ministers [would] be disaster. Sorry did not say it more vigorously in the book.

---

[87] Labour Party (Election Pledges) debate: the Opposition motion, 'That this House deplores the Government's failure to honour their election pledges', was defeated by 306 to 285 votes; *Parliamentary Debates* (House of Commons), 5th ser. 717 (29 July 1965), cols. 713–832. The government's response was made by Wilson, and Brown did not participate.

Conclusion With the Tories it would have only been a slightly worse mess than the 1957 or 1961; with a Labour Government it was much bigger. But improvement on the supply side.

Tory economic policy falling into hands of ignoramuses.[88] Idiotically ignorant, as all they advocate has been tried before.

Reflections on Book Re-reading page 268 — on Ministers doing the right thing, but too slowly and with too many delaying Committees, all seems terribly familiar!

Labour Party continued the 'New Conservative Policies' of 1964 — pushing them further in some directions, but making an appalling mess through their delighted screaming that all they inherited was awful.

GB vastly exaggerated how National Plan differed from NEDC exercise. RM could have achieved same publicity effect if he had been more of an enthusiast for NEDC!

Reference in previous paragraph of book to 'number of other worth-while reforms', Industrial Training Boards, Little Neddies etc. All in Plan — although referring to Conservative activities! It is true that the Labour party is *keener* on these things.

Every critic of RM (including his own Cabinet) must ask what he was recommending *before* the summer of 1964.

Conservatives already planning, in a welter of pseudo-liberal plati-tudes, to repeat the 1951–64 journey.

Real inadequacies of the book:

Sterling balances if £ went;

What would happen if price of gold stuck midway between present and final equilibrium level.

Should have kept in phrase about 'one ounce of financial radicalism worth one ton of physical planning'.

Even more sceptical about expertise now. There is no salvation in [Edward] Bridges'*[89] amateurs. Need is for economic types who will think things through and press policy dilemmas.

---

[88] The new leader appointed as Shadow Chancellor, Iain Macleod, described as follows by D. Goldsworthy ('Macleod, Iain Norman (1913–1970)', *Oxford Dictionary of National Biography*, <www.oxforddnb.com/view/article/34788>, 18.11.04): 'Macleod was no economist, did not propose to become one, and did not see much point in trying to construct macroeconomic policy in opposition. His favoured project was tax reform, and on this he did do a great deal of preparatory work. Otherwise he concentrated on attacking a government that was in fairly continuous economic difficulty'.

[89] E. Bridges, *The Treasury* (1964; 2nd edn. 1966), published as part of the New Whitehall series, provides a unique description and evaluation of this central department at that time, while his Rede lectures, published as *Portrait of a Profession: The Civil Service Tradition* (1950), remains the *locus*

Define two types of deflation:
Deflation of home demand — may be necessary;
deflation of production — much less desirable.

20 September *Reflections on the Plan* How many of *decisions* in Plan arose *out of* Plan calculations and how many were embodied in the Plan?

No suggestion that bits of policy *added up* to no more or no less than what was required.

Nearly all the items in it were obviously sensible without an elaborate plan. Did not need elaborate calculations to see need for more investment, better use of labour, more exports and import savings, or crucial role of balance of payments.

What is needed is long-term look at demand management and balance of payments à la National Institute. Greatest mistakes arise from calling these short-term policies. These are instrument[s] of economic control which can be managed from a short-term or a long-term perspective.

In 1964 Election the Labour Party did enormous harm to the country. It ran a *reactionary* campaign suggesting that borrowing was always bad; and that living within one's means was over-riding priority. Any fool can get balance of payments equilibrium with sufficient unemployment. The Labour Party was taking the reactionary line; RM the radical one. Unpleasing role of Socialist economists. One would certainly expect them to campaign for a Socialist approach to economics. I certainly don't believe in 'value-free economics' but perversion to act as party propagandist while retaining academic status, and twisting facts. Unforgivable when this involves taking reactionary views on borrowing & on using liquidity to finance temporary deficits — opposite of line they would have taken if Labour Government had been in power. Compare [Richard] Kahn*[90]

---

classicus of the generalist administrator in the civil service and in the responses it generated, some extreme, not least from Thomas Balogh ('The Apotheosis of the Dilettante: The Establishment of Mandarins', in H. Thomas, ed., *The Establishment* (1959), pp. 83–126), was important in establishing the momentum for civil service reform which resulted in the Fulton Commission appointed by the Labour government in 1966. Brittan devoted the first chapter of *The Treasury under the Tories* to the higher civil service, being critical in part but also appreciative of the steps being taken by the Treasury in particular to recruit more economists. There is no specific mention of Balogh's famous essay.

[90] Kahn's evidence before the Radcliffe committee was cited in its *Report*, para 394 as decisive in their conclusion that it was 'the structure of interest rates rather than some notion of the "supply of money" ... [that was] the centre-piece of monetary action.' For his evidence, see *Minutes of Evidence*, 25 October 1958, Qns. 10938–11024; *Memorandum of Evidence*, vol. 3, pp. 138–46. For the then nascent group of British monetarists, the Kahn-Kaldor view that the money supply was incidental to interest rate policy marked the high watermark of neo-Keynesianism in British demand management

in 1957 and 1964. A lot of the stuff sounded like Right-Wing Bankers castigating a profligate Labour Government; and indeed these Right-Wing Bankers were impressed by the 'legacy' and afterwards turned against RM.

20 September *Reflection* Spectacle of Party leaders — Brown and Heath — shrieking away on Regional Policy as if unaware of the fact that the other man was saying the same thing and really believing that he was offering a rival policy.

22 September Ministry of Public Building and Works say that July measures will lead to a reduction in demand in construction industry next year in excess of the overheating. Demand for construction work in 1966 will be down by 10%. [.../][91] more influential in a Labour Government, which tends to take the economy too seriously.

24 September *Reflection* If the City had any sense, it would advocate a floating rate as the best way of allowing free capital movement and continuing international business. Under present state of affairs international financial role will inevitably sink.

25 September *'Factory Production Committees'* These were just an idea in a Wilson speech. There was no work on them and Industrial Division is sceptical. (Heard nothing more on 6.12.65!)

One newspaper commentator says (approvingly) that National Plan could have been issued by last Conservative Government, but not by the next — precisely what is wrong with trend of Conservative thinking.

Reflection A toast to Hilson and Weath whose mindless pseudo-radicalism should keep economic writers in business for many years to come.

25 September *Reflection* [Christopher] Layton* at Liberal Conference: Conservatives want to abolish DEA — only Ministry with new ideas. Needs strengthening. Quite right.

In 1962 Tories sacked Selwyn [Lloyd]. Today they are saying that if he ought to have been sacked it was for not being deflationary enough & for

---

(A. A. Walters, 'The Radcliffe Report — Ten Years After: A Review of the Empirical Evidence', in D. R. Croome and H. G. Johnson, eds, *Money in Britain, 1959–1969* (Oxford, 1970), p. 40).

For Kahn's views on inflation, see W. Fellner *et al.*, *The Problem of Rising Prices* (Paris, 1961) for the OEEC, this being the report of an expert study group established in 1959 of which Kahn was a member. Kahn and Kenneth Berrill* were commissioned by the DEA to write a report on a prices and incomes policy in 1966.

[91] Coll Misc 745/4, p. 25: some evidence that some text may be missing due to photocopying.

relying too much on incomes policy. (Incidentally, on incomes policy the Labour Government initially let through many public sector claims that the previous Government would not — DVA.)

26 September *Reflection* How supinely both the Patriotic Right and the anti-US Left accepts subordination to the United States because of debts. No one dreams of asking whether we have to accept their terms or can come to terms with Europe. Still less whether it is too expensive to protect the £ at any price.

Growth Rates 4% — or any other rate — much better than 25% over X years. With an annual rate one can keep a running check; a rough moving average. Good years can then make up for the bad or a gradual move can be made towards a 4% objective. But the 25% target throws everything to the end of the period by which time another Plan would be in force.

28 September At *Copenhagen* [for EFTA meeting] the Danes were wanting Surcharge to go by April 1966 (the Swiss were also difficult) but would be prepared to yield if concessions made on bridge-building, agricultural integration and preferences for the less developed countries.

1 October (telegram) *WP3-Washington* Neild stated that unemployment might approach 2% by next Spring. Measures might have cumulatively bigger effect than predicted.

Rickett underlined deficit in second quarter, one third of 1964 rate. But the crude figures, because of special factors, might show deterioration between the second and third quarters.

Would be balance of payments surplus in second half of 1966 with the Surcharge. Without the Surcharge we would be in balance, except for abnormal stock rebuilding.

UK deficit in five quarters, from Q.4 1965 to end 1966 inclusive, might be £75m–125m. Total financing requirement would be £200m–£250m (over which period — why?)

[Maurice] *Parsons** major change in foreign exchange market after announcement for support of £ on September 10.

[Emile] *Van Lennep*:[92] understood the objective to be one of balance by the end of 1966 without the Surcharge. Hoped a high priority would be given to removing it. Recommended approaching reflation with caution. Should consult with WP3 before any change of policy.

---

[92] Chairman, WP3: see Diary, 17 December 1964.

Rickett: WP3 would be informed but no prior commitment to consult.

World Trade Definite slowing down to be expected — perhaps even more than earlier.

5 October *Reflection* The two parties are nearer to each other than to what either of them believed a little while ago: e.g. Expansion versus 2% unemployment. Extreme ungenerous Party politics which puts every issue in its own terms and does not give any credit to opponents, is combined with less and less real differences. The dissentients are written off as Left-wingers or 'Powellites'. Both led by conventional men never far from the Establishment fashion.

Macleod uninterested in economic affairs — using Shadow Office to re-establish his orthodoxy.

6 October *Reflection. Scarcest commodity in the Civil Service is information.* Like all scarce commodities it is not freely exchanged. Quite wrong to think that someone in another Department (or even in one's own) will give freely of knowledge. Therefore there is a premium on those with the knack of finding out.

Despite over-elaborate Committee structure, real, urgent decisions go on outside, leaving many of those affected, and with contributions to make, in the cold. High-level haggles.

Conservatives are relegating Lloyd and Thorneycroft because they are bad for the image, while adopting policies which if anything imply that the real criticism of them is that they did not go further.

7 October DVA's minute to Reading. *Bank wants to remove exchange control measures of last July at early date!*

Tells him to assume no change in Bank Rate before forecasting exercise.

It takes 2 plus 4 = 6 weeks to implement import controls (?)

Bank of England was against any mention of imports in the letter from Bank Governors. Said Banks would refuse to accept instructions.

A scheme for prior deposits has been worked out and is on the files. Arrangements made to draft legislation if necessary.

9 October *Reflection* In 1964 the Conservative Government was going, or about to do, all the things about industrial efficiency, mobility of labour, etc. which were in the Labour Party manifesto. No one believed them.

In 1965 the Labour Government committed: e.g. National Plan, to most of things about industrial incentives in Conservative manifesto, people won't believe them. In fact all these things started in the great appraisal 1960–61.[93]

The Economist: 'Business Efficiency' drives now overplayed.

11 October *Reflection* Much time spent in discussion, on arrangements for meetings, discussions on which Ministers will go where, briefings, etc.

Officials do notes and letters for P[arliamentary]U[nder] S[ecretaries] as well as Ministers.

B. Reading: minute on credit squeeze and investment: 6% Bank Rate has a smaller effect on investment now because of slower growth of manpower, therefore less unemployment, more investment.

Squeeze is also at earlier stage of the cycle when companies have more liquidity.

Reflux of short term funds helps to ease the squeeze, which is therefore wearing off at an earlier state of cycle.

Fund and Bank Brief (for September Meetings) Quota increases should come to about $1,450m in Fund's usable currencies and $1,200m (?) (in gold, before making special arrangements). UK originally wanted 50% increase in quotas and larger special increases, and more efficient mitigation of gold effects. France refused the special increase.

Total voting power of the Six[94] could easily have been raised (to 50%?) yet they criticise IMF for being Anglo-Saxon dominated.

UK Commitments to Fund:

1. *Letter of Intent*

    (a) [K]eep Fund fully informed of outcome of monetary situation — discuss it with Fund at frequent intervals.

    (b) Consult with Fund if advances rise by more than 5% per annum (equals £230m) or deposits rise in similar proportion (£400m).

    (c) Inform Fund on and discuss if necessary the balance of payments.

    (d) Take action if existing policies not fulfilling aim.

    (e) If any major shift in UK policy as outlined in Letter of Intent (while Fund is holding more than 125% of UK quota) inform Fund, and at request of Managing Director, consult.

---

[93] In *Treasury under the Tories*, ch. 7 the great reappraisal.

[94] Original six EEC member states.

2. *UK Executive Director [John Stevens*] said UK willing:*

> (a) [T]o provide seasonally adjusted Banking data;
> (b) Exchequer financial statistics;
> (c) Monthly Monetary Commentary.

Although no special conditions limiting future policy, UK was compelled to go further than wished. Desirable level of advances and deposits are regarded by Fund as targets.

Consultation on changes in policy — first occasion in which borrowing Member has given such undertakings for more than a year ahead.

In emergency we still retain the right to be first, but Fund has not agreed to written understanding on this, but has accepted principle. Fund to visit us every three months.

Fund Brief Call for tighter Fund discipline and suggested Fund should issue policy statement including a policy of continuing to insist on repayment within five years in all cases and only re-finance if Members pursue right policies.

Reflection Book was not strict enough on Bank and Overseas Finance Divisions of Treasury!

12 October *WEP*[95] US suggests continued rapid expansion.

US GDP Percentage change on previous year

	1964	1965	1966
Present Forecast	+4½%	+4½%	+4.2%
Previous WEP		+3½%	+3%

Due to Vietnam (addition of $5½bn defence spending). Underlying US growth rate was 3¾%. Unemployment is 4½%. During 1966 will fall towards 4%.

16 October *Reflection* Labour Party leaders, and so-called practical men who emphasise specifics, fact seekers, etc. don't realise that:
Macro-economic target has higher status than industrial figures
Detailed figures derived from global target and not other way round.
Figures are *consequence* of achieving target and not a cause of it. Therefore industrial figures cannot be heart of the exercise.

---

[95] World Economic Prospects, a regular internal report that preceded the Treasury's economic forecasts.

Profoundly unhistorical young men, who think that the latest thought which occurs to them in the bar is 'new thinking' ('incentive' and 'competition' were a staple diet of Conservative propaganda in the early 1950s — and had the same amount of moderate validity all the way through) but Press is now biased against Conservatives and pro-Labour. Near majorities for platform at Labour Party Conference were treated as great victories. Whereas any division in Conservatives was treated as 'split'. Reverses the bias of a few years ago.

Typical encomium on *Harold Wilson* is that of a conservative. They would say that he was fumbling early on, but is now following orthodox advice, e.g. 'statesmanlike broadcast' on Rhodesia.[96] Oddly enough the more radical Tories are more anti-Wilson than the City and the Right, who admire him for putting the £ first.

What I have against Wilson is not his being a clever politician, but the way in which the public are hoodwinked by his statesmanlike acts.

Arguments against the Plan like those against *Quantity Theory*. You are telling the Plan, it's not the Plan telling you;

e.g. fuel policy and housing policy brought into Plan. Little feed back. 25% assumption and 4¼% limit for public expenditure given very early on.

Plan therefore is literally document — but none the worse for that.

Both Incomes Policy and indicative planning are too small issues for expansionists to divide about.

The Tory young men emphasise action on the supply side, which is outside the jurisdiction of the Treasury. Yet they want to abolish DEA, which alone pushes such action!

There is a genuinely difficult problem of pressure group for growth. NEDC (with Press following) was such a pressure group but now castrated and not what it was.

BoT couldn't be such a pressure group.

Do we want a Planning Section of Treasury; or a PM's office?

The whole expression 'short-term' (with all its connotations) is misleading. Policy towards the Surcharge now must be based on a view of balance of payments in 1967 and beyond and the ways of influencing it.

The myth of 'researched decisions' (WRM on Conservative policy document) substitute for thought.

Heath and those follow in the so-called modern fashion:

---

[96] Southern Rhodesia had introduced import controls on all goods on 4 November and made its unilateral declaration of independence on 11 November.

Generalities of awful banality and mixed bags of unimportant proposals viewed without sense of proportion.

'Kennedy type' image Listened to all sorts of proposals. Distrust generalised or theoretical solutions. Over-developed appetite for detail. Is a substitute for real thought which must be individual.

Chancellor's three tasks:

> Managing economy;
> tax law;
> public expenditure.

Related but essentially different. Need they be done by the same man?

9 November Industrial Reorganisation Finance Corporation,[97] to come after Bill on Industrial Grants in February, but before the Finance Bill.

IRFC's idea came from [Alcon] Copisarow* to [Patrick] Blackett* to Dr B to PM (M. J. S[tewart]) DEA will be responsible for pushing it through. Will have £100m–£200m capital. Like a UK IRI.[98] Purpose is:

(a) to fill gap in existing institutions;
(b) a reconstruction catalyst — look for mergers, etc. should turn over its capital quickly.
(c) 'Uneconomic activities', e.g. investment to speed up exports — new type of vehicles or containers.

GB: Roll and MacDougall disappointing. Department getting into hands of civil servants. Insists on continuing to have 'irregulars'.

Minute from WA asking for economic forecasts to be kept particularly confidential.

Summary of Economic Forecasts (EPC and WP3 briefs?)

BoP forecasts for 1965–£385m deficit instead of £300m (actually it was something like £285m).

1966 forecast: Deficit of £150m evenly throughout year.

Reasons:

(a) net invisibles recalculated
(b) imports scaled up more than exports

due both to changed view of imports prices (expected not to fall any more) and higher import demand.

---

[97] See Diary, 9 December 1964.
[98] Istituto Ricostruzione Industriale (of Italy), currently still in existence as a state industrial holding company.

1966 worse off because of:

(a)[99]
(b)

Adverse balance of monetary movement in the third quarter of 1965 was £150m–£200m.

10 November WA: at a conversation Chancellor came out with balance of payments forecast — shouldn't have done because this was too early stage. GB flared up — saying 'Department is keeping something from him.' W. Nield had statement about margin of error put in.

ER: Note to First Secretary: Chancellor (being informed *ambulando* by officials) will want to circulate some version of forecast to PM. GDP to rise from 2nd half 1964 to 2nd half 1966 by 4½%.

Last June's forecast was 4¼%. After announcement of July measures 3½% was calculated.

DEA expects exports in relation to imports may be better. Study is being made.

The Chancellor will stress commitment of balance by end of year. Does not know whether he will suggest early measures on demand front!

WAN: levy dead after March.

Meeting of the Economic Forecast Committee. DEA members got reservations on exports written in. Impression that battle stage-managed. Criticisms came from DEA, Kaldor and M.[J.] Stewart. Treasury in unbroken ranks backed BoT.

DVA foretold large Budget deficit.

Reflection: Similar events in November 1961. After the electricity settlement, which broke the pay pause, City editors have given hint of tough Budget.

EF (BoP) forecast[100]

		Imports	Exports	Gap
		£m	£m	£m
1965	Q.3	1293	1211	−30
1965	Q.4	1272	1235	−37
1966	Q.1	1270	1236	−34

[99] No text provided for (a) or (b).
[100] 1965 Q3 exports less imports do not sum to figures recorded (−£30m).

1966	Q.2	1278	1233	−45
1966	Q.3	1278	1241	−37
1966	Q.4	1280	1248	−32

Top secret Memo for WAN on HP.

T. Davies[101] never sees the Chancellor, for whom his speeches are written!

12 November Chancellor's minute to PM: Will ask colleagues next week for further deflationary action.

The Economic Forecast Unemployment to reach 1.8% by end of 1966. Exports of goods and services. To rise by second half of 1965 by 5.3%; second half of 1966 by 1.1%!

Main reason for 1% upward revision of GDP over two years: higher exports and higher wage rates (not balanced by prices).

Much of increase of exports expected in first part of 1965 and early months of 1966 when heavy deliveries of ships and aircraft are due.

Volume of exports to go up by 2% during 1966 — excluding ships and aircraft by 2½%.

Balance of Payments - £m

	1965	*1966*
Visibles	−279	−148
Invisibles	+76	+103
Current Balance	−203	−45
Long-term capital	−181	−110
Total	−384	−155

Previous forecast was £300m (in fact £288m) for 1965 and balance for 1966. Difference is due to the fact:

- (a) imports to increase because
  - i. import prices to go down by less
  - ii. demand for imports higher because of greater activity.
  - exports also higher but not enough to balance.
- (b) net invisibles revised downwards for previous years. In 1964 there were offsetting other credit items of a once-for-all character.

---

[101] Unable to identify this person. After extensive enquiries, Scott Newton thinks this may be Tom Davies, journalist and Labour Party activist. Callaghan's memoirs do not record a T. Davies.

BoP forecast

Imports

Surcharge From now on effects of stocks less. The forecast assumes that the rise in imports in Q.3, 1965 was largely but not entirely forestalling, e.g. import controls.

Effects of Surcharge are on consumer goods, not capital goods.

World Trade to rise by:

14% during 1964;

10% " 1965;

8% " 1966 (near average of decade).

Deliveries of *ships and aircraft* relatively high 1965/66.

Export prices will rise about average next year, partly because of rebate.

	Export Increases %	
	Value	*Volume*
Trend rate of growth	+5	+3
Second half 1965 per annum	+7½	+6
" " 1966 " "	+3½	+2
Year 1965	+6½	+4½
Year 1966	+4½	+3

Excluding ships, etc. and non-manufactures, exports of manufactures to rise:

in 1965 by 7% value and 4½% volume;

1966 by 4%   "   2½%   "

Metals to US, etc. expected to fall back (remarkable rise of about 20% in 1965).

Further fall in UK share of trade in manufactures:

1964 – 13.7%

1965 – 13.1%

1966 – 12.6%

Private investment

1964 – +£228m

1965 – +£56m

1966 – –£40m

Effects of April and July measures worth about £135m

Net outward portfolio

To show *disinvestment* of £70m in 1965; more in 1966. Substantial overseas borrowing expected by oil companies.

OSA balances to fall by about £50m–£100m in the second half of this year, and again in 1966.

Export Credit to rise by £75m in 1965, and by less in 1966.
Central Bank Assistance and Swaps to cope with.
Balancing item estimated at £50m
Uncertainties:
  i. Effects exchange control measures,
  ii. meaning of recent high import figures?
  iii. confidence.

Flows of £8,000m in either direction. 1% variation in imports would affect balance by £70m. Scope for more than 1% variation on both imports and exports, etc.

Comparison with August forecast:

Visible balance for 1966	–	£93m	worse
Invisible " " "	–	£47m	"
Current balance		£140m	"
L.T. Capital		£15m	"

For 1965 main deterioration –
   in Invisibles (£70m?) and:
   Imports up by £166m; but exports by only £73m
   Invisibles: more revisions on travel balances, profits, and profits and dividends (oil)
   Imports: One-third of difference on import prices. Estimate of effect of import charge - £30m (?)
   Higher level of activity for domestic economy.

Domestic Economic Forecast
Assumes 35% Capital Gains Tax and Building Licenses.

Biggest Changes:
Hourly Wage Rates in the second ½ of 1965 will be up by 7% instead of 5.8%.
GDP for second ½ 1965 raised by 0.4%; for second ½ 1966 by 1.1%.
Result of:

  (a) Higher exports;
  (b) although money incomes are rising faster, prices not rising in proportion.

  Partly because of seasonal foodstuffs rose abnormally and should now fall back; and partly because of divergences of recent price behaviour from what would be expected from costs.

Public Consumption to rise at 4% rate: 1964–66. Central Government in Financial Year 1966–7 by 2¾%.

Investment: 1966 surveys suggest 5% increase in value, 3% in volume. *Official forecast is constancy.*

Surcharge reduces *stocks* by £85m to 1965 and nothing in 1966.

Wage Rates

In 1st Qtr. 1966 wage index likely to be 7½% higher. From then much less; timing of claims, pressure of demand, and incomes policy; also end of hours round.

Second ½ of 1966 0– +6%per annum

(Q.2–Q.4 1966 up by 7½ % per annum)

By second ½ of 1966, wage and salary bills should be *rising by 5¾% per annum* (compared with 7½% in the second ½ of 1965).

Average wages and salaries to rise by 6% assuming slight fall in employment.

P[ersonal] D[isposable] I[ncome] to increase by 4.3% in 1966 (compared with 5.5% in 1965).

Non-food prices are low in relation to costs. May be due to prices policy or ending of RPM.[102] Part of this relative reduction allowed to be maintained in the forecast.

Nationalised Industries' price increases foreseen to be less than in the past and low in relation to costs.

Seasonal food prices very high — will revert to trend.

Finally, rates not expected to increase so much next April.

2nd ½ 1965–66: *retail price index* to rise by 2½%; *consumer prices* by 2¼%.

Savings ratio. Fell from 8.7% to 8.2% in 1964–5.

Final expenditure to rise by 1¾% in 1966.

Imports by 1¼%.

---

[102] The Resale Prices Act, 1964, abolished the practice of horizontal price fixing by manufacturers known as Resale Price Maintenance, save in cases where it could be shown to be in the public interest not to do so: see H. Mercer, *Constructing a Competitive Order: The Hidden History of British Antitrust Policies* (Cambridge, 1995), pp. 18–21, 149–69 and 'The Abolition of Resale Price Maintenance in Britain in 1964: A Turning Point for British Manufacturers?', *LSE Working Paper in Economic History* no. 39/98 (1998). In *The Treasury under the Tories*, p. 268, Brittan identified Heath's RPM Bill as part of a wider package of measures designed to strengthen competitive market forces which themselves were part of the modernising programme which resulted from the 'great reappraisal'. In the event, the proposed abolition of RPM proved acutely controversial within the Conservative Party, and for many it was seen as a contributory factor in the Conservative's narrow defeat in the 1964 election: see R. Findley, 'The Conservative Party and Defeat: The Significance of Resale Price Maintenance for the General Election of 1964', *Twentieth Century British History*, 12.3 (2001), pp. 327–53.

Employment

(a) large inflow of school leavers may be upsetting seasonal pattern;
(b) either acceleration in productivity not continued or smaller than expected growth in the working population (assumption now 12.12.65 — no increase at all between June 1964 and 1965).

From Q.3 1965 onwards, *unemployment* to rise by 15,000 a quarter. *From Q.4 1966 to reach 390,000, that is 1.8%*

In 1962 it was rising by 35,000 per quarter. But output in 1962 was only 1½% up and there was a larger rise in the working population. (It was then rising exceptionally fast).

WEP

	% CHANGES DURING YEAR		
	1964	1965	1966
US GDP	5	4¼	4¼
EEC GDP	4½	4	4¼
WORLD IND[USTRIAL] PROD[UCTION]	6½	4½	5
TRADE IN MAN[UFACTURE]S	14	10	8
(IN VOLUME)			

US will be importing less and primary countries — In 1965 US imports high in relation to GDP.

Primary prices — slight fall.

Primary earnings — up by 4½–5% Better than June forecast.

(Half increase due to oil states).

Reserves will continue to move to *Western Europe*.

France and Italy to have large surpluses.

Outflow of reserves from primary producing countries to Continental Europe.

US and UK will get into balance.

Squeeze on liquidity postponed.

15 November *Chancellor's minute to PM*: economy not being deflated as hoped. Will be presenting further measures.

PM's minute:

i.   […?] of October trade figures.
ii.   Need for searching look at capital balance and invisibles before presenting new deflationary measures. (Seemed to assume that reasons for deterioration there).
iii. Information on Budget out-turn 1965–6.

Reflection Devaluation may not be buried after all. If devaluation comes, it will be surprising how much else will go on as before and how little of the incalculable consequences will have taken place!

Things to watch:

Rhodesia, triggering off something;

National Institute;

third quarter BoP;

next (November) trade figures.

16 November FO wants to declare that we are willing to join the Treaty of Rome in suitable circumstances. (WAN opposing).

17 November SGLN[103] told by M. J. S[tewart] that cable manufacturers are negotiating vast reduction in varieties of wire and cables.

Local Defence Expenditure 1965–6	£m
West Germany	87½
Far East	81½
Mediterranean (and Jordan?)	40
Aden	27
Rest of World	17
East Africa	1

18 November *Revised Summary Note to Economic Forecast* (this has very few tables — is that all Ministers see?) This gives alternative views [...?] But has £100m higher exports (in whole year [...?] at 1966 rate) gives only £40m improvement in BoP due to effect on GDP and import requirements.

20 November GB Another flaming row with ER. Previously had one with J[ohn] Burgh*.

Then, on recommended OECD delegation, wrote 'no need' for ER, SB or JG (Callaghan withdrew desire to go when found out that Fowler was not going).

24 November *COMPARISON OF AUGUST AND OCTOBER BoP FORECASTS FOR 1966*

	£m
Increase in value of imports	+166
Increase in value of exports	+73

---

[103] Unable to identify this person.

Deterioration in visible trade balance	−93
Deterioration in invisibles	−47
Deterioration in official capital	−20
Deterioration in private capital	+5
Total deterioration	−155

Gilbert and Sullivan performance over OECD. After First Secretary announced he wouldn't go, Callaghan wouldn't touch it — minor meeting.

President of Board of Trade to lead delegation (not going till Thursday afternoon).

When I came in this morning, first heard that President of Board of Trade to make main speech. Then both Diamond and Albu were going. Chancellor says Diamond must speak — was preparing to split speech.

Then told 'don't split it': President wants to make the main economic speech too.

Then [A. C.] Russell* rings up — Diamond refused to go if not speaking himself. Albu prepares to take on DEA part of speech, if [Douglas] J[ay] agrees, which he admits is unlikely.

Therefore, made extracts of DEA speech in a form that Albu could deliver as contingency plan, in addition to full speech J[ay] had!

25 November WAN: great deal work going on on Rhodesia. Fifteen inter-departmental committees. Work on economic effects of sanctions, and on their effects on UK BoP only now being done now! Trying to decide everything in 24 hours!

MacDougall worked out that effects of full sanctions and cutting off of copper on UK BoP to be £200m (MacDougall later says rather less).

WAN: action can only work if all countries co-operate.

HW call to 'sharpen swords'.

GB last night 'not Ministry of Economics any more but Ministry of Economic warfare'.

ER and WAN told to drop everything else.

GB determined to bring Rhodesia to knees. Said will not allow obstacles to be put up by reactionary officials. Two or three rival networks: PM at one time wanted Cledwyn Hughes* Committee to meet twice a day.[104]

Copper allocation scheme in existence.

GB determined to get in before Chancellor. WAN thinks 'Knight Errantry'!

---

[104] On Rhodesian UDI. Earlier Hughes had visited Rhodesia to try to prevent UDI (TNA DO 121/273; DO 183/778).

Rhodesian Economy: DEA Paper
GDP well spread.

Speed up of slow acting measures could be obtained if agricultural exports and oil imports could be completely stopped.

Would require full cooperation of other countries.

Tobacco would take some months to bite.

60% energy from local coal. Domestic agriculture provides nearly all food except £10m or so, – dispensable.

Tobacco 33% of exports.

No other single product more than 3%.

Much of manufacturing belongs to subsidiaries of European or US firms — financing of subsidiaries.

Manufacturing accounts for 30% of exports — half go to Zambia.

Very high percentage of Whites work in transport, commerce and services.

30% of imports from UK – £33m

South Africa £27m

The rest well spread.

Exports: Tobacco £39m. Asbestos £10m.

40% of exports to six neighbouring African countries — South Africa, Mozambique and Angola, Zambia, Malawi and Bechuanaland. UK and Zambia each take about 20% of exports. Rest well distributed.

Effective action would require wide measure of international cooperation over many commodities.

Reserves of £23m — half outside UK control.

Considerable part of imports could be dispensed with.

Imports

Final consumption   22%.

Capital equipment   12%

UK ban on transport, on sugar and tobacco accounts for 18% of exports.

Rhodesia seeking to cut import bill from £120m to £90m.

Of external payments of £181m, £39m are for service. (Travel accounts for £13m.) Investment income accounts for £23m.

Conclusions: South Africa and Portuguese Africa could provide considerable relief from an import ban. But could not replace cut off export markets more than marginally. Need for cooperation of other countries.

Note on Import Charge Renewal
Effect of charge in 1965 – £150m–£200m.

Due to both stocks and immediate use. In 1966 direct effect would be £150m.

Substitution of other imports would take this down to £100m or £110m; and there would be no stock effects.

Because of stock effects, etc., if surcharge were removed at end of 1966, imports would be £150m higher.

DVA: once EF figures are agreed, difficult to budge people. Views of DEA different, if DEA economists not properly taken into account. The views of the 'irregulars' regarded as not respectable. Although in the past there was always someone to raise a query.

DVA: memo from Chancellor:

Prospective budget deficit next year of £1,200m. Estimates of current prices up by 10%. Suggested:

    a. cut estimates and

    b. could not action be taken now? — More scope for affecting imports in 1966.

DVA: advising GB to wait until February forecasts.

Incomes Policy

GB and [Ray] Gunter* at meeting at House [of Commons] last night. Worked themselves up to decision to refer Bakers to NBPI. Couldn't get hold of PM, who was with the Queen and went ahead.

DVA: asked if sure they would see it through. If not, Court of Enquiry in a few days might provide a way out. Woodcock[105] said same thing.

Great row over Forces pay with Secretary of Defence. PM would not make statement. One reason why GB stayed in London, instead of OECD to make it.

Reflection Government (Wilson) will give in to Bakers. Willingness to see a strike through will make or break Incomes Policy.

Summary Note on Economic Forecasts-Final Revise

Alternative view of exports would be £110m or would leave a deficit of £110m; but with deficit narrowing throughout the year.

Bakers: according to JG, PM wants to give in to Bakers.[106] Give them £1 and let price of bread go up.

---

[105] George Woodcock (1904–79): General Secretary, TUC, 1960–9.

[106] See Appendix III, Calendar of Key Events, for the development of this industrial dispute which began on 24 October 1965; see also Panitch, *Social Democracy and Industrial Militancy*, pp. 98–100 for the broader context of the bakery industry dispute in relation to the evolution of the NBPI and Labour's income and prices policy.

Frank Cassell*: some modified version of MCA[107] ('next step') being prepared.

Basically true about UK indifference to Italian idea about Sterling balances.

Cassell wrote note to Cairncross. Taken up. Rickett: sorry if gave impression not interested. But nothing put forward to consider.

Best paper on future of Sterling area from [John] Fforde*[108] of BoE. But generally, 'thinking' still assumes continuation of SA.

When Cairncross was asked about Italian initiatives, said: 'in any case isn't it the private balances that are volatile?'.

26 November Incredible Treasury paper on Public Procurement. Assumes any import saving will increase the load on the economy and therefore divert goods from exports! (Therefore nothing can help BoP except deflation; and only obstacle to BoP availability of resources.)

(Real fallacy is that if such diversion occurs, this could be avoided by deflation, thus preventing the improvements. Whole process only unnecessary if deflation could lead to desired improvement by itself).

DVA: Callaghan thinks HW will want Spring election. Therefore get deflation out of way now.

29 November *Reflection: Opposition* Hoped at first Opposition would expose Government economic bungling, especially as I was not unsympathetic to last Government's policy last year. (Although this presupposed readiness to devalue).

Did not realise Conservatives would abandon own position so quickly.

They have missed the real points of criticism; attack on all the wrong fronts and — although without the responsibility for Government — present a posture much less attractive; e.g. dividing the House on renewal of surcharge; worried by thought that they may not be entirely hypocritical.

Prices and Incomes

Opposition making precisely wrong criticism that Brown interfered with Ministry of Labour.

Heath and Macleod have learnt nothing and forgotten nothing — advocate system of Peace at any price. In fact GB deserves criticism for

---

[107] Monetary Compensatory Amounts, part of the EEC CAP, a subsidy designed to compensate farmers for exchange rate variations.

[108] After a career in the Bank was appointed official historian in 1984, producing *The Bank of England and Public Policy, 1941–1958* (Cambridge, 1992).

being so afraid of 'bread queues' and letting in the Ministry of Labour conciliation!

Testing point of Incomes Policy always has been readiness to see strike through.

If terms of reference to NBPI toned down, or interim increase granted, whole point of pegging bread would have vanished.

Policy could deteriorate to shouting a lot to stay where we are (indeed reference had giveaway hint of Scottish bakers).

JG: Gunter's talks with Bakers Union for information; real decision today:

    a.   to carry on with reference [to NBPI] hoping that strikes will peter out (F. Jones); or

    b.   set MoL conciliation machinery to work (PM's inclination).

30 November A[nne] Muller*: Cabinet decided that Minister of Labour 'conciliate without breaking norm' (but Bakers have already had 7% in hours!)

JG: GB was in chair for decision!

W. Rogers will try to get him to get this decision reversed on Thursday morning.

3 December Fantastic meeting at Treasury on IMF briefing. They wanted to 'come clean' on 1965/6. Words such as 'not delude', 'deceive', etc.

Abject attitude.

Seem to want IMF to criticise us for not doing enough.

Imagine the French behaving in this way.

MacD: GB interested in

    a.   beating down [Ian] Smith* and

    b.   Callaghan not using this as excuse for further deflation.

1967 Outlook

Paper suggests;–

Either 3¼% growth throughout the year and BoP deficit of about £140m (including balancing item);

or surplus of £200m with output dropping by ½% over year (equals 2% during year).

Meeting of EF Committee: Meeting agreed whole range of possibilities was intolerable, even including better export assumption and no BoP surplus.

DVA asked any of those who thought that we could pull through in 1967 to be counted. None came forward (although well attended meeting).

DVA said that 1967 forecast overseas expenditure assumed Economic Departments got all they were fighting for. Not feasible to assume anything more. Very much gave the impression he did not think regulation of demand alone could not do job (although said earlier in the morning to Miss J[enifer] F[orsyth]* on the 'phone that he thought demand was too high.

F. Atkinson agreed unemployment in 1967 would not be in tolerable range.

Agreed paper would not be submitted to Ministers; but discussion would be reported to 'appropriate quarters'.

Seemed to be Snow-like atmosphere in which tacit change of attitude to certain long-established assumptions became apparent. Could be turning-point occasion.

Reflections

1. Election in March and then devalue?
2. Despite everything can see perhaps 20–25% possibility of pulling through in 1967 if exports rise more than forecast, if forecast is on right side of range and satisfactory outcome on invisibles, miscellaneous, etc. Could combine miserable growth but reasonable unemployment if labour force fairly stagnant, etc.
3. Wilson protected from frank discussion of devaluation by:
   a. positive correlation between advocates of devaluation and sympathy for Labour Government.
   b. playing game and 'not rocking the boat' (F[inancial] T[imes] etc).

6 December BoP deficit for year now up again from £385m to £445m.

Taking the bisque reduces this to £375m.

How far due to spurious accounting? e.g. transfer funds from Local Authorities to Gilt Edged?

Rather good memo from Callaghan over the week-end asking for 'more confidence presentation' to IMF.

Last Thursday night was Gunter's triumph. Bakers had agreed on reference to Board without any immediate major wage increase.

Then ER spoilt it all by telling GB that DEA must get a look in. Greig was told to tell one or two Lobby Correspondents about GB's meeting with Bakers and Employers — that Bakers holding price of bread a little while longer. — Caused a lot of bad feeling with MoL.

7 December ER has gone to Washington at a couple of hours' notice to fix support in relation to Rhodesia.

ER minute of November 30th on economic outlook (rather weak).

Chancellor says 1966/7 borrowing requirement will be £1,200m compared with £750m forecast for 1965/6 and realised £400m in 1964/5.

Partly because 'Supply' up by more than 10%. 'We have not succeeded in course we have set ourselves in July.'

On DEA forecast, we would be very near to balance by end of 1966.

BoP difficulties to continue into 1967. Will be difficult to expand demand in accordance with Plan — although much better on DEA forecast. (But 1967 study suggests very unsatisfactory).[109]

If shortfall in BoP target in 1966 due to IDI,[110] Unlikely to be regarded by creditors as falling back on commitments.

IDI therefore not argument for deflationary action unless external confidence affected and no other means available.

But does need reinforce to cut down overseas expenditure wherever possible.

GB should support getting 'Supply' Estimates down.

Should also support examination of capital accounts.

Deflating economy further might undermine confidence in National Plan.

Industrial investment keeping up but precariously poised. Might not take much deflationary action to cause major downturn.

Nevertheless heavy commitment to balance by end of 1966.

If exports unfavourable and no alternative effective measures are available, would have no option but to deflate further.

DEA wanted to defer judgement to February.

Also because confidence in £ is good, unless it is disturbed by Rhodesia, better not to have to argue that there has been a severe deterioration in order to justify further deflationary measures.

Only argument against deferment of decision on all this, would be need to get unpopular actions over now for electoral reasons.

H.P. — some industries already badly affected by it.

Regulator — would affect prices and incomes policy.

Tobacco — no real relevance, except psychological, revenue might go down.

Henley's minute on public expenditure
10% in money terms equals 5% in real terms approximately.

---

[109] See Diary, 3 December 1965 for paper on 1967 outlook.
[110] Illegal Declaration of Independence, the precursor of the now accepted acronym UDI, Unilateral Declaration of Independence.

Chancellor's Public Expenditure Committee will find scope for reduction limited to 'Category B'.

More difficult to get money rise below the 8.9% which was defended as inheritance from previous Government!

WAN—GB 'going back on everything accomplished in past year'. WAN would rather have 'prior deposits'. 'Worst run Government ever saw'.

Gleanings from Friday's Misc. Meeting

Chancellor:

A. HP

B. Ask oil companies to reduce overseas investment by 10%.

C. 'Check-point' on travel allowance, £100 instead of £250.

PM wants to emphasise reduction of public (capital?) expenditure.

8 December *IMF visit*

[Alan] Whittome* asked why 'Mecca' was always postponed. Said that in April £150m–£200m deficit was predicted for 1965.

UK Deputy Financial Representative in Washington ([Douglas] Wass)* thinks Whittome is full of goodwill but will have to send back critical report to Schweitzer, leading to salvo in January asking for further action (what Treasury wants—DVA).

DVA started off very frankly explaining difficulty of prices and incomes policy. Enabled him to end up on many things which are now being done and thus an optimistic note.

At lunch brought conversation to new and reduced status of forecast as just the views of a Working Group!

Wass: 'touch and go' (in August or early September).

Stand-by originally arranged by GB and Fowler. ER had critical times in Washington.

DVA agrees Cromer more likely to stay as result of speculation (although on balance probably would have stayed in any case).

DVA: transfer of engineering to Technology means that Whitehall shake-up is much more likely. A sort of Ministry of Industry.

Conservatives now cannot just abolish Technology. Previously DEA might have been able to dig in. Now much more difficult.

9 December Chancellor getting cold feet on financing of Plan E. Now wants free depreciation in stages. GB won't be at meeting with CBI in January.

10 December Industrial Division now no longer confident of investments holding up.

At cocktail meeting of senior Treasury and DEA Advisers, Treasury felt very passionately about reducing pressure of demand.

All talk is, if worst comes to worst, moving to another *fixed* rate.

'Rake's Progress' etc.

Economic Forecast Report for Ministers will not be finalised until PM holds another meeting in first week of New Year.

Meanwhile Committee of all five Economic Advisers to draw up report on 1967, etc.[111]

Kaldor apparently saying: 'Told you to devalue. Now no alternative but to deflate.'

Overseas Defence Review Brief for PM for Visit to Washington, December 1965

Intend to give up Aden. Committed to S. Arabian independence.

To be balanced by retaining and slightly strengthening position in Persian Gulf.

To retain position as world-wide power. (More than half defence spending East of Suez).

Similarly Singapore unmaintainable. Base in Australia instead.

Cannot unilaterally maintain defence of areas East of Suez, but would continue to do so jointly with US? Australia and NZ.

Obsession in brief with dangers of Chinese Communism.

15 December *Cabled summary of US BoP proposals*

Stiffening of direct investment curbs:

Dir[ect] inv[estment] $4.9bn in 1965; to be $4.1bn in 1966.

US overall BoP deficit:

1964 $3.1bn approx.

1965 less than $1.5bn

1966 ±$0.25bn, approx

Fantastic old-fashioned salvo from Con O'Neill* on ELDO.[112] In first person: 'could not rest easily if ...' etc.

---

[111] Namely, Balogh, Cairncross, Kaldor, MacDougall and Neild.

[112] In the wake of the cancellation of the Blue Streak ICBM project in 1960, the European Launcher Development Organisation was established in 1964 to develop a satellite launch vehicle for Europe. The designated site was Woomera, South Australia, from which ten launches were made, but no successful satellite launch was achieved and the programme was terminated in 1970. European satellite launch activities then shifted to Kourou, French Guiana, the home of the Ariane launcher now managed by the European Space Agency.

20 December R. Opie only found out about *WPTIC* when Planning Div[ision] was asked for technical information on effect of surcharge; then continued to turn up.

(When he suggested selling of quotas, BoE and [...?] generally spoke of getting down to level of hucksters — so much for vaunted belief in price mechanism).

WAN's paper on poss[ible] procedures:

    a. How to keep import charge on in 1966. Perhaps announce in spring power will not be renewed in November; and announce reduction to 5%?

    b. Foreign exchange controls and deposits — previously rejected (large part of goods invoiced in sterling).

    c. QRS. Earlier decided better to keep surcharge and

    d. Credit controls via banks.

    e. Prior deposits.

Previous Friday n[igh]t GB in terrible mood over Fairfields.[113] Had consortium of t[rade] u[nion]'s to put up £50,000 plus [Robert] Maxwell* and Leyton. Then vetoed by PM.

GB blamed Callaghan. Rang him up abusively. LJC pointed out that with two Labour MP's involved (who therefore couldn't vote) majority gone. GB saw point and then picked row with [Harold] Lever* in order to kill project.

1 am Greig told to announce resignation (told: too late for morning papers!) Earlier rang PM's office to do this. Reply was 'Good'!

Fairfields originally picked up by Callaghan! GB cross with Dept. for not finding it first!

21 December *QRS* Detailed preparations two weeks. Plus four weeks setting up organisation. Therefore *six weeks* from full final decision.

R. Opie: Draft from the committee of the *ec[onomic] advisers*. Several alternatives listed including deval[uation], defl[ation] direct measures (inc: export subsidies?), attack on cap[ital] acc[oun]t, etc.[114]

Run on £ likely well before Budget. (So much for Treasury's sense of timing. SB) Anything could trigger it off — Q3 BoP or backwash of Johnson's BoP message. Therefore need to act first thing in January.

---

[113] A rescue attempt for Fairfield Shipbuilding & Engineering Co. Ltd on the River Clyde which went into receivership in October 1965; became, with government guarantee, Fairfields in 1966 and the following year, with mergers of other Govan yards, the Upper Clyde Shipbuilders; L. Johnman and H. Murphy, *British Shipbuilding and the State since 1918: A Political Economy of Decline* (Exeter, 2002), pp. 163–5, 168.

[114] Cairncross, *Diary*, pp. 104–5.

Conversation with GB

Rhodesia: Force could be much cheaper! PM sometimes vehemently opposed.

If he was Chancellor would want force — cheaper than ec[onomic] sanctions.

    a.   Smith will collapse — may take time.
    b.   They all say this. Will he?

Knows that ec[onomic] outlook is 'bloody'.

Chancellor begrudges £1¾m for Fairfields; but won't fight Cab[inet] on Rhodesia.

Incomes policy collapsing around me. Fairfields in trouble. Only thing going well: 'Little Neddies'; Catherwoodery.

Brief for PM's visit to Washington

    FO Brief

Russians genuinely concerned about proliferation; wrong to give impression we are not.

Effects of De Gaulle's actions: 'loyal allies'. Hope that 5 [EEC states] will stand firm.

Ready and willing to neg[otiate] with Community provided essential interests safeguarded.

Meeting of Cassell and Mesmer; Germans to take strong stand against anti-NATO action in Paris in March.[115]

    V[IET]NAM

Objective to remind Pres. Johnson that US readiness for negotiations will facilitate British support (and if nec[essary] expl[ain] why no mil[itary] support).

    Backgr[oun]d Note (Better — SB)

Better mil[itary] situation in V[iet]Nam. But heavy price exacted — US sacrificed chance of improved relations with USSR.

Mil[itary] vict[ory] impossible for either side. *But this is probably not accepted in Hanoi or Washington.*

Washington wants S. Viet to be non-C. Hanoi wants it to be C.

Two dangers:

    a.   May become harder for Rus[sia] and China to resist N. Viet[namese] appeals for assistance.
    b.   Harder for US to neg[otiate] for less than total victory.

---

[115] The lead up to the March 1966 announcement of the end of French assignment of troops to NATO and withdrawal from NATO's command structure.

Latter is the greater danger.

'During the months ahead the main dip[lomatic] and pol[itical] prob[lem] in V[iet]Nam, and one of the greatest concerns [t]o HMG, may well be that the readiness for neg[otiation]s will decline in Washington just as it is beginning to grow in [...?].'

Moment (may come?) for Brit[ish] dip[lomatic] pres[ence] in Wash[ington]. Not yet. See US knows limits of support; and contin[ues] need for info[rmation] and where poss[ible]. Consultation.

21 December GB on BoE, Probably 'no' to Cromer.[116] Roll and Armstrong lead field, with Roll ahead — age, etc. [Nugget] Coombs* in it, but behind.

22 December *WPTIC*

[John] Owen*: 'Not too much theory'.

DVA: Ministers will not want to be left with no direct measures by the end of 1966.

BoP position.
Last forecast:
1965   –£385m
1966   –£150m

Import-saving from surcharge in 1966 is £100m.

These forecasts took no acct. of Rhodesia or latest US measures or new outturn for Q.3 1965. Revised figures for all quarters of 1965 now a good deal worse. Action to make it not appear too obvious. These reasons not too likely to affect 1966 outturn. (E.g. confidence or rephasing of inv[isibles])

Best forecast for 1966 is –£150m–£250m taking into acc[oun]t. Rhodesia, better exports and US measures. This assumes Rhodesia does not become worse. Could hit BoP considerably. (Say –£100m)

DVA If Rh[odesia] hits BoP, would it be easier to switch to QRS., or surcharge at higher rate?

Import deposits: Invite Ec[onomic] Advisers' c[ommi]ttee under Neild to report.

Rewritten WPTIC need by end January.

C[ommi]ttee view: if figures correct no arg[umen]t for QRS or higher surcharge.

---

[116] The conflict between Wilson and Cromer was semi-public knowledge and is now well documented, most recently in J. D. Tomlinson, *The Labour Governments, 1964*–1970, III: *Economic Policy* (2004), pp. 50, 53, 230 and F. H. Capie, *The Bank of England, 1950s to 1979* (Cambridge, 2010), pp. 225–6. Accordingly, when Cromer's term ended he was replaced by the then Deputy Governor, Leslie O'Brien*, on 1 July 1966.

But if more spectacular figures — say if copper adds £100m or more to payments deficit, then diff[icul]t. Apply QRS and carry through 1967.

QRS worth £140m–240m per annum.

2?8 December 1965 (cont.) Saw GB vomiting on stairs.

At WPTIC, Dep[uty] Ch[ief] Cashier[117] of Bank sympathetic to QRS. Confidence affected by people looking at 'gap'. (BoE later forced him to change view).

External peo[p]le seemed to think foreigners would get impatient even with Rhodesia effect on BoP.

WAN: last night Zambia wanted to cut official relations with Rhodesia — coal, copper. 1 am minute to [Kenneth] Kaunda* fighting it off.

Thinks sanctions could bring Smith down February or March. Full effect on BoP if copper goes £150m–£250m.

30 December DVA: *Import controls* probably out. After 18 months of surcharge they would lead to great international outcry. Seemed to think nec[essary] to raise surcharge to prevent forestalling (afterwards WPTIC members thought there would be better ways).

Prior deposits May be possible to phase out surcharge with them. Some impact effect, although not much continuing effect.

GB has lost everything that matters except investment cash grants, where PM on side.

J.W[iggins] showed me *Note by J. J[ukes] on first sketch of Report by Econ[omic] Advisers*.

Agreed there was choice between risking sterling crisis and forced devaluation, and measures which would demonstrate beyond all dispute that Plan could not be achieved. Dilemma not only for 1966 and 1967 but as far ahead as we can see. In any case not much growth expected in 1966 or 1967.

Choices include (and/or):

   a.   Import controls — risking confidence.
   b.   Illegal export subsidies.
   c.   Deflation.

---

[117] Unable to identify this person, but Capie, *Bank of England,* pp. 296, 365 has Richard Balfour* appointed to the post in April 1965 and Jim Keogh* as Deputy Chief Cashier in July 1965. There may well have been a hiatus following Alan Whittome's move to the IMF from the Deputy Cashier position in 1964 and this perhaps propelled Keogh into the job.

All three *Treasury advisers* agree:

  a. Need for further defl[ationary] measures in Jan[uary] — HP.
  b. If not, defl[ationary] Budget partly to reinforce incomes policy.
  c. Ag[ain]st further int[ernational] borrowing or attempts to realise private portfolio.
  d. Study further measures on capital acc[oun]t. (Incl. remission of earnings and incl[uding] £ area in exch[ange] con[cession]s).

Dr B's position uncertain.

Jukes opposed defl[ationary] recommendations because of 1967 outlook, effect on inv[isibles] etc.

Sterling difficulties could be sparked off by Q3 BoP, Rhodesia etc. (Visible trade estimate for Q4 now £20m down Sept[ember]–Nov[ember] reserve gain of £270m of which £80m repay[men]ts and –? approx. similar sum off forward commitment).

ER will send to GB comments on Report later. Asked for GB's prelim[inary] reactions:

Reflection

Fantastic contrast between relative optimism of City bus[iness'] N[ew] Y[ear] messages and Whitehall gloom.

C[ustoms] & Ex[cise] Report on Import Deposits

Six months required between Ministerial authorisation for planning and preparations and implementation. Assumes it replaces TIC and has approx. same coverage. Scheme covering all imports completely impracticable.

Report of P[arliamentary]U[nder] S[ecretaries]'s *Departmental meeting, Dec. 22*

Even if wage rate increase could be kept to 4½% in 'unaffected sector' in 1966, no prospect that overall average increase in 1966 will be less than 6%. 1967 is less committed.

Exp[erience] of DEA so far demonstrated that selective measures for tackling inflation in particular sectors of economy, for which DEA stood, not in themselves sufficient to overcome country's ec[onomic] diff[icultie]s when press[ure] of demand at pres[e]nt v[ery] high.

Dep[artmen]t attaches much importance to inv[estment] incentives, as best prospect when all indications suggest need for further deflation.

31 December [...?] 1968–9 bad fiscal y[ea]r for inv[estment] scheme (would be). Staggering had to be accepted to get it through.

Henley: All commitments gone into carefully at ODC [Cabinet Committee on Overseas Defence]. Persian Gulf commitment argued out.

Majority ag[ain]st. But Ministers decided to reinforce Kuwait for overall political reasons.

US surprised at moderation of Defence Review!

PM asked for enq[uiry] into possibilities if Kennedy R[oun]d fails.[118]

Jay: 2 possibilities:

    a.   deal with non-EEC world.
    b.   some sort of FTA with EEC.

a. w[ou]ld involve really only US & Japan as additional markets. Real place we want to get into is EEC.

b. But Jay regards b. as politically and morally wrong, when Fr[ance] and EEC would be cause of Kennedy r[oun]d breakdown.

Has personal pref[erence] for less spectacular moves such as FTA with Australia and N. Zealand.

1 January 1966 *Schweitzer's letter*

[John] Stevens summoned to see Schweitzer.

Worried by BoP outlook for 1965. Seems much worse than earlier in year or in Sept[ember]. Irregularities cannot explain away Q3. Outlook also worse for 1966. Diff[icult] to see balance in 1966 even with surcharge on. Or to see repayment of debt.

Could have grave consequences for UK IMF relationship.

Recommends action to curtail demand before Budget. Several weapons available although Reg[ulator] no help [...?] Pol[itical] Budget would have to be 'good one'. Public expenditure the greatest scope.

Miss P. B[rown]: UK *BoP for 1966* likely to be worse than thought because:

    1.   Higher import prices—not only copper—will not be completely offset by faster growth of ind[ustrial] markets.
    2.   'Fat' in imports does not seem to have been removed in Q4 1965.
    3.   Not all factors pushing up 1965 deficit temporary. 1965 deficit now expected to be £450m (Excl[uding] bisque?)
    4.   SA expected to have v. little import gr[owth]. Imports to go up more in non-£ primary producers.

---

[118] The Kennedy round of multilateral trade negotiations held under GATT began in 1964 and was concluded in 1967. This was the first round to be concerned with non-tariff barriers (NTBs); it also resulted in an average tariff reduction of 35 per cent for industrial products: B. Hoekman and M. Kostecki, *The Political Economy of the World Trading System: From GATT to WTO* (Oxford, 1995), p. 18.

Miss J. M. F[orsyth] not time to read liq[uidity] papers, etc. because of days and days of work in e.g. preparing procedures for ER's Lyons visit. Briefing on every conceivable subject, etc.

[Paul] Spaak's* call for Brit[ish] action on C[ommon] M[arket].

9 January *IRC ('Irk')* Memo by 1st Sec.:

Govt. should make it clear in conf[erence] to chairman that [Industrial Reconstruction] Corp[oration] expected to u[s]e its po[w]ers to assist exports directly 'to the max. extent consisten[t] with[out] open breach of international obligations'.

Para 4 of Chairman's (Roll's) covering note: In disch[arge] of its main function, opportunities may arise for the corp. to use its power to give fin[ancial] asst[istance] to ind[ustries] in ways which would bring subst[antial] returns in terms of export increase. Would involve provision of funds on spec[ial] fav[ourable] terms and should not be highlighted in White Paper.

[Hartley] Shawcross*, Laing, Kearton, [Reay] Geddes*,[119] Keith and [Andrew] Carnwath* all agreed on need for further institution to help rationalisation.

(Went through w[ith]out a word from Treasury because Armstrong in favour).

Inv[estment] grants.

Original scheme would have cost £250m in 1967–8 and extra £100m in following years and v[ery] little in 1970–71. Therefore 18 month lag in payment in 1967–8; reduced by three months in each of following years, reaching six months by end of 1971–72.

(Acceleration or deceleration timetable could provide cyclical weapon. SB)

10 January *WEP EEC Forecasts*

	% Change on Previous Years		
	GDP	Exports	Imports
1961	5.4	6.0	8.5
1962	5.4	5.4	10.3
1963	3.8	7.8	11.3
1964	5.5	10.5	8.8
1965	3.6	9.7	7.0

---

[119] Geddes chaired the Shipbuilding Inquiry Committee, 1965–1966, *Report*, BPP 1965–6 (2937), vii, 45; see J. R. Parkinson, 'The Financial Prospects of Shipbuilding after Geddes', *Journal of Industrial Economics*, 17.1 (1968), pp. 1–17.

	GDP	Exports	Imports
1965 2	4.1	10.1	7.9
1966 2	4.3	7.7	
1967 2	4.8	8.7	8.6

Wage costs per Unit of Output
1960=100

	UK	Five Main Competitors§
1963	106	109
1964	107	108
1965	112	110
1966	116	114
1967	119	115

§ US, Germany, Japan, Fr[ance], Italy. US costs changing from slow fall to slow rise.
[R. M.] Gibbs* 16.11.65

Elasticity of Demand for Exports
Ratio of UK export prices to competitors:
1954–8   =   0.978
1960–4   =   1.022
Taking into acc[oun]t falling share of world exports and price changes, elasticity = 4.96½.

Policy on Miscellaneous Trade Matters ([T. U.] Meyer* Note for [Eugene] Melville* discussion)

1. *Australia–NZ FTA*

   Waiver asked under XXIV of GATT ([…?] FTAs).

   FTA covers 60% of trade.

   No schedule for FTA within reasonable time.

   GATT Working P[ar]ty. Feb, 21–25.

   UK does not wish to acquiesce. Hopes UK keeps in the running.

   NZ increasing some of tariffs to match Australians.

   UK complaining this in breach of trade agr[eemen]t.

2. *Australian Disc[retionary] Pref[erence]s for LDCs*

   Have to accept Australian proposal in some form. But want to avoid precedent for e.g. France.

3. *Cotton Textiles*.

   Previous UK scheme expire end of 1965.

   Scheme for 1965–70 is global quota plus separate ones for India, Pak[istan] and H[ong] K[ong].

   (Interim scheme involving half quotas).

   Imports from LDCs are one third of UK consumption. GATT requires 5% per annum incr[ease] in quotas. But since 1962 UK under no obligation to increase quotas.

   UK new scheme allows 1½% per annum incr[ease] in global quotas.

10 January[120] Schweitzer to be in UK Feb. 15 (After seeing Van Lennep?) Pres. J[ohnson] personally involved in bid to stabilise (and revoke increase in) world copper prices — because of V[iet]Nam. If UK helps, he would be more helpful in other things.

(But judging by subsequent telegrams, UK still sceptical).

UK Paper for IMF (dated 7.1.66). CRU[121] plus MCA. Wanted to bring in LDCs in dist[ribution]. Ag[ain]st incr[ease] in the gold price.

11 January J.W[iggins]. Inconclusive Min[isterial] disc[ussion] of ec[onomic] advisers' report. Some package likely; but probably not before end of month. Probably early Feb (JG? Hull on 27th!)

12 January *WPTIC* Import Control scheme basically devised by Arnold France* in 1959!

Choice between continuing charge and negotiating change of commitment.

Bank repudiates itself on QRS to close gap!

Concl[usion] seems to be: keep or incr[ease] surcharge if nec[essary]

Dec. Trade Figures

For both exports and imports, Q4 in excess of forecasts by £5m. Exports partly due to ships and aircraft above forecast.

CSO Paper on Confidence Outflows (on BoP only)

Influences:

Inward direct   ) Affected in outflows

Outward direct   )

Inward portfolio — affected in outflows only

Confidence outflow estimated at £45m in Q4 1964 and Q? 1965.

Larger or smaller outflows possible.

Volatile elements, e.g. intra-company balances. Unwound fairly quickly once confidence restored.

Inflows more permanent (because of Exch[ange] Control?)

13 January *Public Sector Income Committee*

First Prog[ramme] Report, 3rd Feb. 1965

---

[120] In Coll. Misc. 745/4, p. 91 this and the 11 January 1966 entry out of sequence in file.

[121] Proposals for Composite Reserve Units had been ongoing within the IMF since 1963: M. G. de Vries, *The International Monetary Fund, 1966–1971: The System under Stress* (Washington, DC, 1976), I, pp. 53–73.

Plan A. TVA[122] replacing Corp[oration] or Purchase Tax. Rejected by Richardson.

B. Replacing N[ational] Ins[urance] contributions by TVA or other indirect tax. Would infringe contrib[utory] prin[ciple] and would be imposs[ible] to predict effect on wages, prices and exports.

C. Payroll subsidy financed by TVA. 'Artificial'; 'international difficulties'.

D. Payroll tax in London, etc. to finance subsidies in underemployed regions.

E. (The inv[estment] incentive scheme!)

F. Replace inv[estment] allowances by prod[uction] subsidies. Would conflict with int[ernational] obligations. Redist[ribution] of help; diff[icult] to ensure passed on.

Agreed there should be further study of D and E.

Second Prog[ress] Report in March.—Setting up of 'Mixed' (Min[ister]s and officials) fiscal incentives c[ommi]ttee.

May 20, 1965.

PM most likely bet—payroll tax on all service empl[oymen]t [and] payroll subsidy to eng[ineering] (or m[anu]f[acturing]) ind[ustry] outside London.

Ministers' Report on D & E, 14 June.

D rejected—subsidy absorbed by higher wages.

E recommended.

GB not happy that report embodied Ministerial recommendations.

Plan Z. Inv[estment] grants to depend on export records?)

11th July 1965.

Clarke's C[ommi]ttee Report.[123]

D, E and F rejected.

Came up with 'Northern Regulator'.

Multiple of employer's N[ational] Ins[urance] contrib[ution]s = 4% of payrolls to be returned to employers in regions when *national* unemp[loyment] above certain level. To apply to all empl[oymen]t.

Kaldor describes scheme as 'emasculated'.

DEA planners say it is to make defl[ation] more acceptable.

---

[122] Taxe sur la Valeur Ajoutée (TVA), the VAT-type tax in Belgium, France and Luxembourg.
[123] See Diary, 9 December 1964 for Clarke's sub-committee on the tax system.

DVA: Northern Regulator has full support of DEA.

Clarke Report (presumably later one)
Value of:

	Corp. Tax at 35%	At 40%	Pre-1965 syst[em]
20% Grant	15	14	
30% inv[estment] all[owances]	9½	14	15

Revenue effects would balance out in 1969–70. First two years loss of £200m–£250m. Plan E involves £350m. [Plan] D & F rejected Sunday before July, 22. Then came ill-fated Bagritry!

14 January Callaghan and Brown seem to have come to some (reluctant) agr[eemen]t on defl[ationary] package (JG). Approved of Tr[easury] article on economy (was it GB or ER?)

[Herbert] *Christie* on US

GDP to rise by 7½% in money terms and 5¼% in real terms.

Unemployment to fall to 3½ or 3¼%

Unemployment of 4% now = 3.7% thanks to Jobs Corps.

But greater pressure on wages and prices than in recent past.

BoP. Changes in liquid assets and liabilities all foreigners in 1965 was $1.3bn.

Target for 1966 is ±$0.25bn. *Likely* to be $1.25bn–$0.65bn.

17 January *Treasury WEP Paper on w[o]rld liquidity trends.*

	Scope for Reserve Gain $bn, annual averages				
	1960–4	1964	1965	1966	1967
US deficit	+2.0	+1.2	+0.9	+0.5	–0.5
UK deficit	+0.3	+1.9	+0.8	–0.1	–0.8
Monetary Gold	+0.6	+0.6	+0.5	+0.5	+0.5
Allow[ance] for statistical	(+0.1)				
exc. of surpluses		–0.3	+0.1	+0.1	+0.1
Total	+3.0	+3.5	+2.1	+1.0	–0.7

NB Deficit measured by official reserve positions.

Primary producers in surplus 1962–5 and 1966.

Prin[cipal] ind[ustrial] c[oun]tries other than UK or US heavy surpluses (varying from $1.5–$3.2, 1965 and 1964 [...?]).

But 1966 surplus will have to be only $0.8bn and 1967 –$0.3bn (And in 1967 primaries will have to be – $0.4bn).

Conclusions:

1. Effect of UK move to balance already mostly felt (through holding down imports — part of rest will be on cap[ital] acc[oun]t rather than trade presumably).

2. Reserve danger in 1967.
3. Something ab[ou]t slower growth of $ and £ assets (on financing of trade).

18 January *WEP Paper on World prod[uction] and trade*

	Movements through year % per annum		
	1965	1966	1967
World Ind[ustrial] Prod[ucers]	5½	6	5½
Exports of manufactures	11½	7½	7½
(to prim[ary] producers)	11	4	7½
(UK imports of m[anufactures]	+2		+7

Primary Producers Imports	Year to Yr %		
	1965	1966	1967
Total	8½	9½	5½
Non Sterling Area	7	7½	6½
Sterling Area	8½	4½	5½

Warning of 1967 slowdown through liq[uidity] factors.

Agonies over WPTIC

Draft Report complete victory for no-control approach. Adamantly rejected QRS. (DVA insisted that it should not consider wider q[uestio]ns involving internal defl[ation]. This had effect of making c[ommi]ttee solely concentrate on enumerating risks of restraints; no real attempt to compare differing degrees of risks of diff[eren]t sorts of restraint, which was only point of WPTIC. The real ec[onomic] study was being done by advisers. The latter […?] in turn was thought up by PM on earlier occasion. DVA welcomed it as way of getting advisers 'out of our hair'. Implied that if anything had to be done, might be the extension of the surcharge; but emphasised how risky and undesirable it was. Import deposits — transitional effect — way of reducing the £150m upsurge which would follow end of surcharge.

I drafted some amendments to suggest that there were circumstances in which risks of imposing restraint might have to be taken; and for longer haul QRS may be less damaging to sterling. (Incidentally a lot of vague unquantified talk about retaliation). All done on Thursday and Friday spanning my fantastic goodbye party. R. Opie (now on part-time) agr[ee]d amendments. Miss JM F[orsyth] put them up with covering note, agreeing to extent that QRS less explosive in EFTA than continued surcharge.

Gather that DVA said one could only put in amendments or minority report if wider support in DEA. [Keith] Stock* shrank back from anything so nasty to negotiate about! Nield asked 'to be excused' having to defend restraints internationally. Gather that at the following WPTIC meeting draft severely criticised, but on lines that it was not clear and forthright enough.

Whole thing was [...?] example of C[ivil] S[ervice] est[ablishment]. DVA prodded BoT when DEA seemed to be winning. Secretaries asked BoT for draft passages. (Their motivation 'good report').

[Henry] *Hardman* Affair*

Another perfect example of C[ivil] S[ervice] at worst.

After long interdepartmental neg[otiation]s draft note worked out for For[eign] Sec[retary] to send to PM suggesting not putting forward Brit[ish] cand[idate] for OECD Secretariat, while Wyndham-White* not available, because of Kennedy Round.

Then suddenly out of blue another letter was actually sent putting name of Hardman, who is retiring from MoD. Resulted from Helsby! talking to FO. Miss J. M. F[orsyth] scandalised at attempt to solve domestic Civil Service problem in this way. Wiggins advised me not to probe too closely into affair!

ER told Wiggins at my party that impropriety worth tolerating as part of really big changes in top personnel, as part of v[ery] important move (presumably going into Europe). J. Wiggins told me of corridor conversations about European move. PM said to be converted but afraid it would split Labour Party. Seems that some kind of exercise (à la Frank Lee)*[124] will be launched.

29 January *Reflection* Hull North:

    a. British elec. loves Cons. Gov[ernments]. Therefore voted Cons. for a long time and now votes for Cons. govt. under Mr Wilson.

    b. You can fool a lot of the people a lot of the time.

? January *Shepherd Revision of Godley article on l[ong] t[erm] growth.*[125]

Plan involves average increase of 65,000 in labour supply. But continuing falling trend in participation rate gives *fall* of 45,000 per annum (Godley-Shepherd eq[uatio]n gives even faster fall).

    1. 1% change in labour supply (compared with trend?) leads to ¾% change in prod[uctive] potential.

---

[124] Lee, who replaced the 'solidly Atlanticist and Eurosceptic Sir Roger Makins' as Treasury Permanent Secretary in 1960 has been credited with a key role in Britain's first application to join the EEC; for a balanced view, see N. P. Ludlow, 'A Waning Force: The Treasury and British European Policy, 1955–63', *Contemporary British History*, 17.4 (2003), pp. 94–5.

[125] This refers to W. A. H. Godley and J. R. Shepherd, 'Long-Term Growth and Short-Term Policy: The Productive Potential of the British Economy, and Fluctuations in the Pressure of Demand for Labour, 1951–1962', *National Institute Economic Review*, 29 (August 1964), pp. 26–38.

2. −1% change in nominal working week reduces prod[uctive] potential by 0.2%. With *continuous acceleration*, prod[uctive] pot[entail] increases over Plan period by:

    3.6% assuming original labour projections;

    3.0% with broken trend (two st[raight] line[s] equally justifiable);

    2.8%[with broken trend] plus continuation of reduced participation rate.

    Maybe ¼% too high because of assumption 1 above (because assumption too conservative?)

Postscript

But large increase in monthly employment figures since mid-1965 upsets some of above!

(And afterwards heard that MoL publishing mid-Feb revision of June employment figures with greater than average increase over earlier revision.)

Appendix I
Dramatis Personae

ABS, Dr Hermann Josef (1901–1994): banker; Chairman, Deutsche Bank, 1957–67; financial advisor to Konrad Adenauer; member, Bilderberg group.

AITKEN, Ian Levack (b. 1927): political staff, *Guardian*, 1964–92.

ALBU, Austen Harry (1903–94): engineer; MP (Labour) for Edmonton 1948–74; Minister of State, DEA, 1965–7.

ALLEN, Douglas A.V. (later Lord Croham) (b. 1917): Under Secretary, Treasury, 1960–2; Third Secretary, 1962–4; Deputy Under-Secretary, DEA, 1964–6; Second, then Permanent Under-Secretary, 1966–8; Permanent Secretary, Treasury, 1968–74.

ALLEN, George Cyril (1900–82): Professor of Political Economy, University College London, 1947–67.

ARMSTRONG, Sir William (later Lord Armstrong) (1915–80): Third Secretary, Treasury, 1958–62; Joint Permanent Secretary, 1962–8; Permanent Secretary, Civil Service Department, and Head of the Home Civil Service, 1968–74.

ATKINSON, Sir Fred (b. 1919): Economic Section, Treasury, 1949–69; Deputy Director, 1965–9; Chief Economic Adviser, Treasury, and Head, Government Economic Service, 1977–9.

BAGRIT, Sir Leon (1902–79): industrialist; member, Council for Scientific and Industrial Research, 1963–5; Advisory Council on Technology, 1964–9.

BALFOUR, Richard Creighton (1916–2009): Bank of England from 1935; Deputy Chief Cashier, 1965–70.

BALOGH, Dr Thomas (later Lord Balogh) (1905–85): Economic Adviser, Cabinet, 1964–7; Consultant to Prime Minister, 1968; Minister of State, Department of Energy, 1974–5.

BAREAU, Paul (1901–2000): financial journalist from 1926; in the 1960s a correspondent for the *Banker*, *Daily Mirror* and the *Economist*.

BARING, George (Lord Cromer) (1918–91): Barings, 1946–; Governor of the Bank of England, 1961–6, Ambassador to US, 1971–4.

BERKIN, John (1905–79): Managing Director, Royal Dutch Shell Group.

BERRILL, Kenneth (later Sir Kenneth) (1920–2009): economist; Fellow, St Catherine's College, 1949–62, King's College, Cambridge, 1962–9; special adviser, Treasury, 1967–9; Head, Government Economic Service and Chief Economic Adviser, Treasury, 1973–4; Head, Central Policy review Staff, 1974–80.

BLACKETT, Professor Patrick (Lord Blackett) (1897–1974): physics Nobel Laureate; Imperial College of Science and Technology, London, 1953–65; adviser, Department of Scientific and Industrial Research, 1956–60; National Research Development Corporation, 1949–64; President, Royal Society, 1965–70.

BOLTON, Sir George (1900–82): Bank of England, 1933–57; Executive Director, 1948–57; UK Director, IMF, 1946–52; Alternate UK Governor, IMF, 1952–7; Chairman, Bank of London and South America, 1957–70.

BOREHAM, (Arthur) John (later Sir John) (1925–94): CSO from 1958; Director, CSO and Head, Government Statistical Service, 1978–85.

BRAY, Dr Jeremy William (1930–2002): mathematician; ICI, MP (Labour) for Middlesbrough, 1962–70; Parliamentary Private Secretary to George Brown, 1965.

BRIDGES, Edward E. (Lord Bridges) (1892–1969): Treasury from 1917; Cabinet Secretary, 1938–45; Permanent Secretary, Treasury, and Head, Civil Service, 1945–56.

BROWN, George Alfred (later Lord George-Brown) (1914–85): MP (Labour) for Belper, 1945–70; Parliamentary Private Secretary to Minister of Labour and National Service, 1945–7 and to Chancellor of the Exchequer, 1947; Joint Parliamentary Secretary, Ministry of Agriculture and Fisheries, 1947–51; Minister of Works, 1951; Deputy Leader, Labour Party, 1960–70; First Secretary of State and Secretary of State for Economic Affairs, 1964–6; Foreign Secretary, 1966–8.

BROWN, (Marion) Patricia (b. 1927): Central Economic Planning Staff, 1947; Treasury, 1948–54; 1959–85; Economic Adviser, Economic Section, 1965; Senior Economic Adviser, Treasury, 1966; Under-Secretary, Treasury, 1972–85.

BROWN, Sophie (nee Levene) (1911–90): wife of George Brown (separated 1982).

BURGH, John Charles (later Sir John) (b. 1925): Private Secretary to Ministers of State, Board of Trade, 1954–7; Colonial Office, 1959–62; member, UK delegation to UNCTAD, 1964; Assistant Secretary, DEA, 1964; Principal Private Secretary to First Secretary of State and Secretary of State for Economic Affairs, 1965–8; Under-Secretary: Department of Employment, 1968–71; Deputy Secretary, Cabinet Office, 1972–4; Department of Prices and Consumer Protection, 1974–9; Department of Trade, 1979–80.

CAIRNCROSS, Dr Alexander Kirkland (later Sir Alec) (1911–98): economist; Economic Adviser, Board of Trade, 1946–50; Economic Adviser to HM Government, 1961–4; Head, Government Economic Service, 1964–9.

CALLAGHAN, (Leonard) James (later Lord Callaghan) (1912–2005): MP (Labour) for South Cardiff, 1945–50; for South East Cardiff, 1950–83; for South Cardiff and Penarth, 1983–7; Parliamentary Secretary, Ministry of Transport, 1947–50; Parliamentary Secretary and First Secretary, Admiralty, 1950–1; Chancellor of the Exchequer, 1964–7; Home Secretary, 1967–70; Foreign Secretary, 1974–6; Prime Minister, 1976–9.

CARNWATH, Sir Andrew Hunter (1909–95): Baring Brothers & Co. Ltd from 1928; Managing Director, 1955–74.

CASSELL, Frank (b. 1930): Assistant City Editor, *News Chronicle*, 1953–8; Deputy Editor, *Banker*, 1958–65; Treasury: Economic Adviser,

1965; Treasury, 1965–8; Senior Economic Adviser, 1968–9; Under-Secretary, 1974–83; Deputy Secretary, 1983–8.

CASTLE (née Betts), Barbara Anne (later Baroness Castle) (1910–2002): MP (Labour) for Blackburn, 1945–79; MEP, Greater Manchester, 1979–84; Greater Manchester West, 1984–9; Parliamentary Private Secretary, Sir Stafford Cripps, 1945–7; Harold Wilson, 1947–51; Minister for Overseas Development, 1964–5; Minister of Transport, 1965–8; Secretary of State for Employment, 1968–70; Secretary of State for Health and Social Services, 1974–6.

CATHERWOOD, (Henry) Frederick (Ross) (later Sir Frederick) (b. 1925): Managing Director, British Aluminium Co. Ltd, 1962–4; Chief Industrial Adviser, DEA, 1964–6; Director-General, NEDC, 1966–71.

CAULCOTT, Tom (b. 1927): Treasury, 1953–64; Private Secretary to Chancellors of the Exchequer, 1961–4; Principal Private Secretary to First Secretary of State, DEA, 1964–5; Assistant Secretary, Treasury, 1965–6; Assistant Secretary, Ministry of Housing and Local Government, 1967–9; Assistant Secretary, Civil Service Department, 1969–70; Under-Secretary, Machinery of Government Group, 1970–3; Principal Finance Officer, Local Government Finance Policy, Department of the Environment, 1973–6; Chief Executive, Association of Municipal Corporation, 1976–82.

CHAMBERS, Sir Paul (1904–81): Inland Revenue, 1927–47; ICI from 1947, Chairman, 1960–8; President, National Institute of Economic and Social Research, 1955–62.

CHARLES, S. T.: Assistant Secretary, External Relations, 1964–7, Industrial, Prices and Incomes, 1968, Regional Group, DEA, 1969.

CHRISTIE, Herbert (b. 1933): Economic Assistant, Treasury, 1960–3; First Secretary, Washington, 1963–6; Economic Adviser, NBPI, 1967–71 (seconded by J. Henry Schröder Wragg & Co Ltd); Senior Economic Adviser, Ministry of Posts and Telecommunications, 1971–4, Department of Prices and Consumer Protection, 1974–6; Economic Adviser, EEC Commission, 1976–8; Under-Secretary, Treasury, 1978–83.

CLARK, Percy (1917–85): Labour Party from 1947, Deputy Director of Information, 1960–4, Director of Information, 1964–70.

CLARKE, Sir Richard 'Otto' (1910–75): Second Permanent Secretary, Treasury, 1962–6; Permanent Secretary, Ministry of Aviation, 1966; Permanent Secretary, Ministry of Technology, 1966–70.

COCKFIELD, Arthur (later Lord Cockfield) (1916–2007): Director of Statistics and Intelligence to Board of Inland Revenue, 1945–52; Commissioner of Inland Revenue, 1951–2; Financial Director, Managing Director, Chairman, Boots Pure Drug Co. Ltd., 1953–67; member, NEDC, 1962–4, 1982–3; Chairman, Price Commission, 1973–7; Minister of State, Treasury, 1979–82; Secretary of State for Trade, 1982–3; Chancellor of the Duchy of Lancaster, 1983–4.

COLE, George James (later Lord Cole) (1906–79): Chairman, Unilever, 1961–70.

COOMBS, Dr H. C. 'Nugget' (1906–97): economist; Governor, Commonwealth Bank of Australia, 1949–60; Governor, Reserve Bank of Australia, 1960–8.

COPISAROW, Sir Alcon (b. 1920): Scientific Counsellor, British Embassy, Paris, 1954–60; Department of Scientific and Industrial Research, 1960–2; Chief Technical Officer, National Economic Development Council, 1962–4; Chief Scientific Officer, Ministry of Technology, 1964–6. Director, McKinsey & Co. Inc., 1966–76.

COUSINS, Frank (1904–86): General Secretary, Transport and General Workers Union, 1956–69; Minister of Technology, 1964–6.

CROSLAND (Charles) Anthony Raven (1918–77): MP (Labour) for South Gloucestershire, 1950–5; for Grimsby, 1955–77; Minister of State, Economic Affairs, 1964–5; Secretary of State for Education and Science, 1965–7; President of the Board of Trade, 1967–9; Secretary of State for Local Government and Regional Planning, 1969–70; Secretary of State for the Environment, 1974–6; Foreign Secretary, 1976–7.

CROSSMAN, Richard Howard Stafford 'Dick' (1907–74): Fellow and Tutor, New College, Oxford, 1930–7; MP (Labour) for Coventry East, 1945–74; Labour Party National Executive Committee, 1952–67; Party Chairman, 1960–1; Minister of Housing and Local Government, 1964–6; Lord President of the Council and Leader of the House of Commons,

1966–8; Secretary of State for Social Services, 1968–70; Editor, *New Statesman*, 1970–2.

CYRIAX, George (b. 1935): the *Economist*, 1957–60; *Financial Times*, 1960–6.

DEAN, Sir Maurice (1906–78): Permanent Secretary, Ministry of Technology, 1964–6.

DELL, Edmund Emanuel (1921–99): MP (Labour) for Birkenhead, 1964–79; Parliamentary Private Secretary to Chief Secretary to Treasury, 1964–5; Under Secretary of State for Economic Affairs, 1967–8.

DEMING, Fred (1912–2003): President, Federal Reserve Bank of Minnesota, 1957–65; Under-Secretary for Monetary Affairs, US Treasury and US representative, OECD Working Party 3, 1965–9.

DEVLIN, Patrick Arthur (later Lord Devlin) (1905–92): judge and legal philosopher; chairman, Committee of Inquiry into Certain Matters Concerning the Port Transport Industry, 1964–5.

DIAMOND, John [Jack] (later Lord Diamond) (1907–2004): MP (Labour) for Blackley Division Manchester, 1945–51; for Gloucester, 1957–70; Chief Secretary to the Treasury, 1964–70; Chairman, Royal Commission on the Distribution of Income and Wealth, 1974–9.

DIXON, Sir Pierson 'Bob' (1904–65): Foreign Office from 1929; Principal Private Secretary to Foreign Secretary, 1943–8; British Ambassador, Prague, 1948–50; Deputy Under–Secretary, 1950–4; UK Permanent Representative to UN, 1954–60; British Ambassador, Paris, 1960–5; leader, British delegation negotiating entry to EEC, 1961–3.

DUNNETT, Sir James (1914–97): Permanent Secretary, Ministry of Transport, 1959–62; Ministry of Labour, 1962–6.

ERHARD, Ludwig (1899–1977): Economics Minister, 1949–63; Chancellor, Federal Republic of Germany, 1963–6.

FFORDE, John Standish (1921–2000): Bank of England from 1957; Chief Cashier, 1966–70; Executive Director with responsibility for domestic monetary policy, 1970–82.

FOOT, Paul Mackintosh (1937–2004): journalist and writer; member, Socialist Workers' Party and antecedents; *Private Eye*; writer then editor, *Socialist Worker*, 1972–9; columnist, *Daily Mirror*, 1979–93.

FORSYTH, Jennifer Mary (1924–2005): Treasury from 1945; Assistant Secretary, External Relations, DEA, 1965–8; Economic Group, 1968–9.

FOWLER, Henry H. (1908–2000): Under-Secretary, US Treasury, 1961–4; Secretary of Treasury, 1965–8.

FRANCE, Sir Arnold (1911–98): Treasury from 1945, principally Overseas Finance; Third Secretary, 1960–3, assisting Edward Heath in application to join EEC; Deputy Secretary, 1963–4, Permanent Secretary, Ministry of Health, 1964–8; Chairman, Board of Inland Revenue, 1968–72.

FRANCK, M.: Economic Minister, French Embassy, London.

FRASER, Thomas (1911–88): MP (Labour) for Hamilton, 1943–67; Joint Parliamentary Under-Secretary of State, Scottish Office, 1945–51; Minister of Transport, 1964–5.

FRIEDMAN, Professor Milton (1912–2006): Nobel laureate, 1977; Professor of Economics, University of Chicago, 1948–82; economic columnist, *Newsweek*, 1966–84.

GAITSKELL, Hugh T. N. (1906–1963): academic economist; wartime civil servant; MP (Labour), Leeds South, 1945–63; Minister of Fuel and Power, 1947–50; Minister of Economic Affairs, 1950; Chancellor of the Exchequer, 1950–1; Leader, Labour Party, 1955–63.

GEDDES, Reay M. (later Sir Reay) (b. 1912): Director, Dunlop Rubber Company; member, NEDC, 1962–5.

GIBBS, R. M.: Economic Assistant, DEA, 1965.

GODLEY, Wynne A. H. (1926–2010): Economic Section, Treasury, 1956–70; Director, Department of Applied Economics, Cambridge, 1970–85; Professor of Applied Economics, Cambridge, 1980–93.

GORDON WALKER, Patrick Chrestien (later Lord Gordon-Walker) (1907–80): MP (Labour) for Smethick, 1945–64; for Leyton, 1966–74; Parliamentary Private Secretary to H. Morrison, 1946; Parliamentary Under-Secretary, Commonwealth Relations Office, 1947–50; Secretary of State for Commonwealth Relations, 1950–1; Foreign Secretary, 1964–5; Minister without Portfolio, 1967; Secretary of State for Education and Science, 1967–8.

GREIG, William 'Bill': political correspondent, *Daily Mirror*; Personal Press Adviser to George Brown, 1964–8.

GRIEVE SMITH, John (b 1927): Assistant Director, Economic Planning, DEA, 1964–7; Assistant Under-Secretary, General Planning Group, DEA, 1967–8.

GROVES, John Dudley (1922–2008): journalist, *The Times*, 1951–8; Head, Press Section, Treasury, 1958–62; Deputy Public Relations Adviser to Prime Minister, 1962–4; Chief Information Officer, DEA, 1964–8; Chief of Public Relations, Ministry of Defence, 1968–77; Director of Information, Department of Health and Social Security, 1977–8; Director-General, Central Office of Information, 1979–82.

GUNTER, Raymond Jones (1909–77): MP (Labour) for Essex South-East, 1945–50; for Doncaster, 1950–1; for Southwark, 1959–72; President, Transport Salaried Staffs' Association, 1956–64; National Executive, Labour Party, 1955–66; Minister of Labour, 1964–8; Minister of Power, 1968.

HALL, Robert Lowe (later Lord Roberthall) (1901–88): Lecturer in Economics, Trinity College, Oxford, 1926–47; Ministry of Supply, 1939–46; Adviser, Board of Trade, 1946–7; Director, Economic Section, Treasury, 1947–53; Economic Adviser to H.M. Government, 1953–61; Chairman, Executive Committee, National Institute of Economic and Social Research, 1962–70.

HANCOCK, David (later Sir David) (b. 1934): Treasury from 1959; Private Secretary to Chancellor of the Exchequer, 1968–70; Assistant Secretary, 1970; Financial and Economic Counsellor, Office of UK Permanent Representative to EC, 1972–4; Under Secretary, 1975–80; Deputy Secretary, 1980–2; Deputy Secretary, Cabinet Office, 1982–3; Permanent Secretary, Department of Education and Science, 1983–9.

HARDMAN, Sir Henry (b. 1905): economist; Permanent Under-Secretary, Ministry of Defence, 1964–6; member, Monopolies Commission, 1967–70.

HARROD, Roy (later Sir Roy) (1900–78): Student, Christ Church, Oxford, 1924–67; Joint Editor, *Economic Journal*, 1945–61; Reader in International Economics, Nuffield College, Oxford, 1952–67.

HEALEY, Denis (later Lord Healey) (b. 1917): MP (Labour) for Leeds South-East, 1952–92; Secretary of State for Defence, 1964–70; Chancellor of the Exchequer, 1974–9; Deputy Leader, Labour Party, 1980–3.

HEATH, Edward Richard George (later Sir Edward) (1916–2005): MP (Conservative) for Bexley, 1950–74; for Bexley Sidcup, 1974–83; for Old Bexley and Sidcup, 1983–2001; Chief Whip, 1955–9; Minister of Labour, 1959–60; Lord Privy Seal, 1960–3; Secretary of State for Industry, Trade, Regional Development and President Board of Trade, 1963–4; Leader of the Opposition, 1965–70, 1974–5; Prime Minister, 1970–4.

HELSBY, Sir Lawrence (later Lord Helsby) (1908–78): economist, 1930–45; Assistant Secretary, Treasury, 1944–7; Principal Private Secretary to Prime Minister, 1947–50; Deputy Secretary, Ministry of Food, 1950–4; First Civil Service Commission, 1954–9; Permanent Secretary, Ministry of Labour, 1959–63; Joint Permanent Secretary, Treasury and Head, Civil Service, 1963–8.

HENLEY, Sir Douglas (1919–2003): Treasury from 1949; Assistant Under-Secretary, DEA, 1964–9; Deputy Under-Secretary, 1969; Second Permanent Secretary, Treasury, 1972–6; Comptroller and Auditor General, 1976–81.

HESELTINE, Michael (later Lord Heseltine) (b. 1933): businessman; MP (Conservative) for Tavistock, 1966–74, Henley, 1974–2001; Secretary of State for the Environment, 1979–3, 1990–2, Defence, 1983–6, Trade and Industry, 1992–5; Deputy Prime Minister and First Secretary of State, 1995–7.

HOME, Sir Alec Douglas (previously Lord Home) (1903–95): Foreign Secretary, 1960–3, 1970–4; Prime Minister, 1963–4.

HOPKIN, W. A. B. (later Sir Bryan) (1914–2009): Deputy Director, Economic Section, Treasury, 1957–65; Director and Head, Government Economic Service, 1974–7; Professor of Economics, University of Cardiff, 1972–82.

HUDSON, Ian Francis (b. 1925): Customs and Excise, 1947–53; Ministry of Labour, 1953–6, 1959–61, 1963–4; Treasury, 1957–8; Establishments Officer, DEA, 1964–8; Department of Employment, 1968–73; Secretary, Pay Board, 1973–4; Secretary, Royal Commission (Diamond Commission) on Distribution of Income and Wealth, 1974–6.

HUGHES, Cledwyn (later Lord Cledwyn) (1916–2001): MP (Labour) for Anglesey, 1951–79; Minister of State for Commonwealth Relations, 1964–6; Secretary of State for Wales, 1966–8; Minister of Agriculture, Fisheries and Food, 1968–70.

HYMAN, Joe (1921–99): textile entrepreneur; Chairman and Chief Executive, Viyella International, 1961–9.

JACOBSSON, Per (1894–1963): Bank for International Settlements, 1931–56; Chairman of the Board and Managing Director, IMF, 1956–63.

JAMES, Mrs P. B. M.: Assistant Secretary, Regional Policy, DEA, 1964–8, Industrial Group, DEA, 1969.

JAY, Douglas Patrick Thomas (later Lord Jay) (1907–96): MP (Labour) for Battersea North, 1946–83; Economic Secretary, Treasury, 1947–50; Financial Secretary, Treasury, 1950–1; President Board of Trade, 1964–7.

JAY, Peter (b. 1937): Private Secretary to Joint Permanent Secretary, Treasury, 1964; Principal, 1964–7; Economics Editor, *The Times*, 1967–77.

JENKINS, Roy Harris (later Lord Jenkins) (1920–2003): MP (Labour) for Central Southwark, 1948–50; for Stechford, Birmingham, 1950–76; MP (SDP) Glasgow Hillhead, 1982–7; Parliamentary Private Secretary, Commonwealth Relations Office, 1949–50; Minister of Aviation, 1964–5; Home Secretary, 1965–7; Chancellor of the Exchequer, 1967–70; Home Secretary, 1974–6; President of European Economic Commission, 1977–81.

JOHNSON, Lyndon B. (1908–73): US President, 1963–9.

JONES, Aubrey (1911–2003): MP (Conservative) Birmingham Hall Green, 1950–65; Parliamentary Private Secretary to Minister of Economic Affairs, 1952–3; Minister of Fuel and Power, 1955–7; Minister of Supply, 1957–9; Chairman, National Board for Prices and Incomes, 1965–70.

JONES, Fred (b. 1920): Assistant to George Woodcock, TUC; Economist, NEDO, 1962–4; Senior Economic Adviser, DEA, 1964–6; Assistant Secretary, 1966–8; Assistant Under-Secretary, DEA, 1968–9; Assistant Under-Secretary, 1969–75, Deputy Secretary, 1975–80, Treasury.

JOSEPH, Sir Keith (later Lord Joseph) (1918–94): MP (Conservative) for Leeds North-East, 1956–87; Parliamentary Secretary, Ministry of Housing and Local Government, 1959–61; Minister of State, Board of Trade, 1961–2; Minister of Housing and Local Government and Minister for Welsh Affairs, 1962–4; Secretary of State for Social Services, 1970–4; Secretary of State for Industry, 1979–81; Secretary of State for Education and Science, 1981–6.

JUKES, John A. (b. 1917): Economic Adviser, Cabinet Office and Treasury, 1948–54; British Embassy, Washington, 1949–51; Economic Adviser to UKAEA, 1954–64 and Principal, Economics and Programming Office, UKAEA, 1957–64; Deputy Director-General, Economic Planning, DEA, 1964–7; Deputy Under-Secretary, DEA, 1967–9; Director-General, Research and Economic Planning, Ministry of Transport, 1969–70; Director-General, Economics and Resources, Department of the Environment, 1970–2; Deputy Secretary, Department of the Environment, 1972–4; Director-General, Highways, Department of the Environment, 1974–6, Department of Transport, 1976–7.

KAHN, Professor Richard F. (later Lord Kahn) (1905–89): Fellow, King's College Cambridge from 1930; Professor of Economics, Cambridge, 1951–72.

KALDOR, Nicholas (later Lord Kaldor) (1908–86): Reader in Economics, University of Cambridge, 1952–65; Professor, 1968–75; Special Adviser to Chancellor of the Exchequer, 1964–8, 1974–6.

KAUNDA, Dr Kenneth D. (b. 1924): President, Republic of Zambia, 1964–91.

KEARTON, (Christopher) Frank (later Lord Kearton) (1911–92): scientist and industrialist; ICI, 1933–46; Courtaulds, 1946–75, Chairman, 1962–75; member, NEDC, 1965–71; Chairman, Industrial Reconstruction Corporation, 1966–8.

KEITH, Kenneth A. (later Lord Keith) (1916–2004): merchant banker and industrialist; Managing Director, Phillip Hill, 1951–87; member, NEDC, 1964–71.

KEOGH, Jim: Deputy Chief Cashier, Bank of England, 1965–7; Principal, Discount Office, 1967–74.

KIPPING, Norman Victor (later Sir Norman) (1901–79): electrical engineer; Director-General, FBI, 1946–65.

KRISTENSEN, Professor Thorkil (1899–1989): Secretary-General, OECD, 1960–9.

LAING, (John) Maurice (later Sir Maurice) (1918–2008): Director, John Laing, 1939–88; NEDC, 1962–6; Director, Bank of England, 1963–80; President, CBI, 1965–6.

LANCASTER, Osbert (later Sir Osbert) (1908–86): cartoonist, *Daily Express*, 1938–81.

LAYTON, Christopher W. (b. 1929): Economist Intelligence Unit, 1953–4; the *Economist*, 1954–62; Economic Adviser to Liberal Party, 1962–9.

LEE, Sir Frank (1903–71): Treasury from 1940; Permanent Secretary, Ministry of Food, 1949–51, Board of Trade, 1951–60, Treasury, 1960–2.

LEE, M. I. 'Annabelle': Principal Information Officer, Information Division, Board of Trade, 1964–9.

LEVER, (Norman) Harold (later Lord Lever) (1914–95): MP (Labour) for Manchester Exchange, 1945–50; for Manchester Cheetham (later Manchester Central), 1950–79; Joint Parliamentary Under-Secretary of State, DEA, 1967; Financial Secretary to the Treasury, 1967–9; Paymaster-General, 1969–70; Chancellor of the Duchy of Lancaster, 1974–9.

LIESNER, Hans Hubertus (b. 1929): Economic Consultant, DEA, 1964–6; Under-Secretary, Treasury, 1970–6; Deputy Secretary and Chief Economic Adviser, Department of Trade and Industry, 1976–89.

LLOYD, (John) Selwyn Brook (1904–78): MP (Conservative) for Wirral, 1945–76; Minister of State, Foreign Office, 1951–4; Minister of Supply, 1954–5; Minister of Defence, 1955; Foreign Secretary, 1955–60; Chancellor of the Exchequer, 1960–2; Lord Privy Seal and Leader of the House of Commons, 1963–4; Speaker of the House of Commons, 1971–6.

LLOYD-HUGHES, Trevor Denby (later Sir Trevor) (1922–2010): Press Secretary to Prime Minister, 1964–9; Chief Information Adviser to Government, 1969–70.

MacDOUGALL, Sir Donald (1912–2004): economist; Prime Minister's Statistical Branch, 1940–5; Fellow, Wadham College, Oxford, 1945–50; Economic Director, OEEC, 1948–9; Fellow, Nuffield College, Oxford, 1947–64; Chief Advisor, Prime Minister's Statistical Section, 1951–3; Economic Director, NEDO, 1962–4; Director General, DEA, 1964–8; Head, Government Economic Service and Chief Economic Adviser to the Treasury, 1969–73; Chief Economic Adviser, CBI, 1973–84.

McINTOSH, Ronald (Robert Duncan) (later Sir Ronald) (b. 1919): Board of Trade from 1947; Assistant Under-Secretary, DEA, 1964–6; Deputy Under-Secretary, DEA, 1966–8; Deputy Secretary, Cabinet Office, 1968–70, Treasury, 1972–3; Director-General, NEDC, 1973–7.

MACLEOD, Iain Norman (1913–70): MP (Conservative) for Enfield West, 1950–70; Minister of Health, 1952–5; Minister of Labour, 1955–9; Secretary of State for Colonies, 1959–61; Chancellor of the Duchy of Lancaster and Leader, House of Commons, 1961–3; Chancellor of the Exchequer, 1970.

MACMILLAN, (Maurice) Harold (later Lord Macmillan) (1894–1986): MP (Conservative) for Stockton-on-Tees, 1924–9, 1931–45; and for Bromley, 1945–64; Minister of Housing and Local Government, 1951–4; Minister of Defence, 1954–5; Foreign Secretary, 1955; Chancellor of the Exchequer, 1955–7; Prime Minister, 1957–63.

McNAMARA, Robert S. (1916–2009): US Secretary of Defense, 1961–8; President, World Bank, 1969–81.

MACRAE, Norman (1923–2010): the *Economist*, 1949–88; retired as Deputy Chief Editor.

MARJORIBANKS, Sir James (1911–2003): Deputy Head of UK Delegation to High Authority of ECSC, 1952–5; Cabinet Office, 1955–7; HM Minister (Economic), Bonn, 1957–62; Assistant Under-Secretary, Foreign Office, 1962–5; Head, UK Delegation to EEC, European AEC and ECSC, 1965–71.

MAUDE, Evan Walter (1919–80): Treasury, 1946–64; Assistant Under-Secretary, DEA, 1964–6; Deputy Under-Secretary, 1966–7; Economic Minister, British Embassy, Washington, 1967–9; Third Secretary, Treasury, 1979–80.

MAUDLING, Reginald (1917–79): MP (Conservative) for Barnett, 1950–74; for Chipping Barnett, 1974–9; Parliamentary Secretary, Ministry of Civil Aviation, 1952; Economic Secretary to Treasury, 1952–5; Minister of Supply, 1955–7; Paymaster General, 1957–9; President of the Board of Trade, 1959–61; Secretary of State for the Colonies, 1961–2; Chancellor of the Exchequer, 1962–4; Home Secretary, 1970–2.

MAXWELL, (Ian) Robert (1923–91): 'publisher and swindler' (*Oxford DNB*); MP (Labour) for Buckingham, 1964–70.

MELVILLE, Eugene (1911–86): Economic Minister, Bonn, 1962–5; Permanent UK delegate to EFTA and GATT, 1965; Ambassador and Permanent UK representative to UN and other international organisations in Geneva, 1966–71.

MEYER, T. U.: Principal, Economic Co-ordination (Overseas), DEA, 1965–6.

MULLER, Anne (later Dame) (1930–2000): Private Secretary to Permanent Secretary, Ministry of Labour, 1959–63; Private Secretary to Permanent Secretary, Treasury, 1963–4; Principal, Growth, Incomes and Prices Policy Division, DEA, 1964–9; Principal, 1970–2, Under-Secretary, 1972–7, Deputy Secretary, 1977–84, Department of Trade and Industry (later Department of Industry); Second Permanent

Secretary, Cabinet Office, 1984–7; Second Permanent Secretary, Treasury, 1987–90.

MUNBY, Denys: economist, Oxford; Economic Planning Division, DEA; has article in *Oxford Economic Papers* (1959) on coal industry; point affiliated to Nuffield College.

MURRAY, Lionel (later Lord Murray) (1922–2004): Head, Economic Department, TUC, 1954–69; Assistant General Secretary, TUC, 1969–73; General Secretary, 1973–84.

NEILD, Robert Ralph (b. 1924): Economic Section, Treasury, 1951–6; Deputy Director, NIESR, 1958–64; Economic Adviser, Treasury, 1964–7; Director, Stockholm International Peace Research Institute, 1967–71; Professor of Applied Economics, Cambridge, 1971–84.

NEWTON, Gordon (later Sir Gordon) (1907–98): *Financial News*, 1935–9; war service; *Financial Times*, 1945–9; Editor, 1949–72.

NIELD, Sir William Alan (1913–94): Under-Secretary, Ministry of Agriculture, Fisheries and Food, 1959–64; Under-Secretary, 1964–5; Deputy Under-Secretary, 1965–6, DEA; Deputy Secretary, Cabinet Office, 1966–8; Permanent Secretary, 1969–72. He was a key official in the UK applications to join the EEC, 1963 and 1969–71.

O'BRIEN, Sir Leslie (later Lord O'Brien) (1908–95): Bank of England from 1927; Deputy Governor, 1964–6, Governor, 1966–73.

O'NEILL, Sir Con (1912–88): British Ambassador to the EEC, 1963–5; Under Secretary, Foreign Office, 1965–8; leader of delegation to negotiate British entry into EEC, 1969–72.

OPIE, Roger Gilbert (1927–98): Oxford economist; Economic Section, Treasury, 1958–60; Assistant Director, Economic Planning Division, DEA, 1964–6.

OWEN, John Glendwr (1914–77): Under Secretary, Overseas Finance, Treasury, 1959–73.

PADMORE, Sir Thomas (1909–96): Treasury from 1934; Second Secretary, Treasury, 1952–62; Permanent Secretary, Ministry of Transport, 1962–8.

PAISH, Frank Walter (1898–1988): Sir Ernest Cassel Professor of Economics, LSE, 1949–65.

PARSONS, Sir Maurice (1910–78): Bank of England from 1928; Private Secretary to Governor, 1939–43; Alternate Executive Director for UK on IMF, 1946–7; International Bank, 1947; Director of Operations, IMF, 1947–50; Deputy Chief Cashier, Bank of England, 1950; Assistant to Governors, 1955; Executive Director, 1957; Alternate Governor for UK of IMF, 1957–66; Deputy Governor, Bank of England, 1966–70.

PEART, Thomas Frederick 'Fred' (later Lord Peart) (1914–88): MP (Labour) for Workington, 1945–76; Parliamentary Private Secretary to Minister of Agriculture, 1945–51; Minister of Agriculture, 1964–8; Lord Privy Seal, 1968; Lord President of the Council, 1968–70; Minister of Agriculture, 1974–6; Lord Privy Seal, 1976–9.

PETERSON, Arthur (William) (later Sir Arthur) (1916–86): Home Office from 1938; Deputy Secretary, DEA, 1964–8; Permanent Under-Secretary, Home Office, 1972–7.

PITBLADO, David Bruce (later Sir David) (b. 1912): Treasury from 1942; Under-Secretary, Treasury, 1949; Principal Private Secretary to Prime Ministers, 1951–6; Vice Chairman, Managing Board, ECU, 1958–60; Third Secretary, Treasury, 1960–1; Economic Minister and Head, Treasury Delegation to Washington, 1961–3; Permanent Secretary, Ministry of Power, 1966–9; Ministry of Technology, 1969–70; and Civil Service Department, 1970–1; Comptroller and Auditor-General, 1971–6.

PLIATZKY, Sir Leo (1919–99): Treasury from 1950; Overseas Finance, 1953–66; Under-Secretary, 1967–71; Deputy Secretary, 1971–7; Joint Permanent Secretary, Department of Trade and Industry, 1977–9.

PLOWDEN, Edwin Noel Auguste (Lord Plowden) (1907–2001): industrialist and public servant; Chief Planning Officer, Central Economic Planning Staff, 1947–53; Chairman, Committee on Public Expenditure, 1959–61; on Aircraft Industry, 1964–5; Chairman, Tube Investments, 1963–76.

POWELL, Sir Richard (1909–2006): Under-Secretary, Ministry of Defence, 1946–8. Deputy Secretary, Admiralty, 1948–50; Deputy Secretary, Ministry of Defence, 1950–6; Permanent Secretary, Ministry of Defence, 1956–9; Permanent Secretary, Board of Trade, 1960–8.

PRYKE, Richard (b. 1923): economist, Fabian Society.

RAPHAEL, Chaim (1908–94): Deputy Head of Information Division, Treasury, 1957–9; Head, 1959–68; Civil Service Department, 1968–9.

READING, Brian: Bank of England; Economic Adviser, Economic Planning, DEA, 1964–6; economic adviser to Edward Heath, 1966–?; Economics Editor, the *Economist*, 1972.

REES-MOGG, William (later Lord Rees-Mogg) (b. 1928): *Financial Times*, 1952–60; *The Times*: Deputy Editor, 1960–7, Editor, 1967–81.

RICHARDSON, Gordon William Humphreys (later Lord Richardson) (1915–2010): Chairman, J. Henry Schroder Wagg & Co. Ltd, 1962–72; Schroders Ltd, 1966–73; Governor, Bank of England, 1973–83.

RICKETT, Sir Denis (1907–97): Treasury, 1947–68; Principal Private Secretary to the Prime Minister, 1950–1; Economic Minister in British Embassy, Washington, 1951–5; Third Secretary, Treasury, 1955–60; Second Secretary and Head of Overseas Finance Division, Treasury, 1960–8; Vice-President, IBRD, 1968–74.

ROBERTS, Professor Benjamin Charles (b. 1917): Professor of Industrial Relations, LSE, 1962–84.

RODGERS, William Thomas (later Lord Rodgers) (b. 1928): MP (Labour) for Stockton-on-Tees, 1962–74; for Teesside Stockton, 1974–83 (SDP/Alliance, 1981–3); Parliamentary Under-Secretary of State, DEA, 1964–7, Foreign Office, 1967–8; Minister of State, Board of Trade, 1968–9, Treasury, 1969–70, Ministry of Defence, 1974–6; Secretary of State for Transport, 1976–9.

ROLL, Sir Eric (later Lord Roll) (1907–2005): Deputy Secretary, Ministry of Agriculture, Fisheries and Food, 1959–61; Deputy Leader, UK Delegation for negotiations with the EEC, 1961–3; Economic Minister and Head of UK Treasury Delegation, Washington, 1963–4, also Executive Director for the UK, IMF and IBRD; Permanent Secretary, DEA, 1964–6.

RUNGE, Peter (1909–70): Vice-Chairman, Tate & Lyle Ltd; President, FBI, 1963–5; member, NEDC, 1964–6.

RUSK, (David) Dean (1909–94): US Secretary of State, 1961–9.

RUSSELL, A. C.: Private Secretary to Minister of State, DEA, 1964–6.

SCHWEITZER, Pierre-Paul (1913–94): Deputy Governor, Bank of France, 1960–3; Managing Director, IMF, 1963–73.

SHANKS, Michael James (1927–84): *Financial Times*, 1954–64; *Sunday Times*, 1964–5; Industrial Adviser, 1965–6, Industrial Policy Co-ordinator, 1966–7, DEA.

SHAWCROSS, Hartley (1902–2003): barrister, politician and businessman.

SHONE, Sir Robert Minshull (1906–92): Economic Director and Secretary, British Iron and Steel Federation, 1936–9, 1945–53; Executive Member, Iron and Steel Board, 1953–62; Director-General, NEDC, 1961–6.

SHORE, Peter D. (later Lord Shore) (1924–2001): Head, Labour Party Research Department, 1959–64; MP (Labour) Stepney, 1964–97; Parliamentary Secretary, Ministry of Technology, 1966; DEA, 1967; Secretary of State, DEA, 1967–9; Secretary of State for Trade, 1974–6; Secretary of State for Environment, 1976–9.

SHRIMSLEY, Anthony (1934–88): journalist; political correspondent, then political editor, *Sunday Mirror*, 1962–9; political editor, *Sun*, 1969–73, *Daily Mail*, 1973–83; Editor, *Now!*, 1979–81; Director, Press and Communications, Conservative Party, 1983–4.

SMITH, Ian Douglas (1919–2007): Prime Minister, Rhodesia, 1964–80.

SPAAK, Paul Henri (1899–1972): Secretary-General, NATO, 1957–61; Foreign Minister, Belgium, 1961–6.

STEVENS, Miss A. D.: Principal, Public Expenditure, 1965–7, General Planning Group, 1967–8, Economic Group, DEA, 1968–9.

STEVENS, John William (b. 1929): Executive Director, Bank of England, 1957–64; Economic Minister in Washington, 1965–7.

STEWART, Michael J. (b. 1933): Economic Assistant, Treasury, 1957–60; Secretary to Council on Prices, Productivity and Incomes, 1960–1;

Economic Adviser, Treasury, 1961–2; NIESR, 1962–4; Cabinet Office, 1964–7; Senior Economic Adviser, 1967; Reader in Political Economy, University College London, 1969–94.

STEWART, (Robert) Michael Maitland (later Lord Stewart) (1906–90): MP (Labour) for Fulham East, 1945–55; for Fulham, 1955–74; and for Hammersmith and Fulham, 1974–9; Secretary for Education and Science, 1964–5; Foreign Secretary, 1965–6; Secretary of State for Economic Affairs, 1966–7; First Secretary of State, 1966–8; Foreign and Commonwealth Secretary, 1966–8.

STOCK, Keith L. (1911–88): Under-Secretary, DEA, 1965–8.

THORNEYCROFT, (George Edward) Peter (later Lord Thorneycroft) (1909–94): MP (Conservative) for Stafford, 1938–45; for Monmouth, 1945–66; Parliamentary Secretary, Ministry of War Transport, 1945; President, Board of Trade, 1951–7; Chancellor of the Exchequer, 1957–8; Minister of Aviation, 1960–2; Minister of Defence, 1962–4; Secretary of State for Defence, 1964.

THORNTON, Peter Eustace (later Sir Peter) (b. 1917): Board of Trade from 1946; Assistant Under-Secretary, DEA, 1964–7; Under-Secretary, 1967–70, Deputy Secretary, 1970–2, Cabinet Office; Deputy Secretary, 1972–4, Second Permanent Secretary, Department of Trade and Industry, 1974.

VAN LENNEP, Emile (1915–96): Treasurer-General, Ministry of Finance, Netherlands, 1951–69; Chairman, OECD Working Party 3; Secretary-General, OECD, 1969–84.

VICE, Tony: *Sunday Times*.

WARBURG, Siegmund George (later Sir Siegmund) (1902–82): Director, S. G. Warburg & Co. Ltd, London, 1946–79; President, 1970–8.

WASS, Douglas (later Sir Douglas) (b. 1923): Treasury from 1946; Private Secretary to Chancellor of the Exchequer, 1959–61, to Chief Secretary to Treasury, 1961–2; Assistant Secretary, 1962–5; Alternate Executive Director, IMF, and Financial Counsellor, British Embassy, Washington, 1965–7; Under-Secretary, 1968–70, Deputy Secretary, 1970–3, Second Permanent Secretary, 1973–4, Permanent Secretary, Treasury, 1974–83; Joint Head, Home Civil Service, 1981–3.

WHITTOME, Leslie Alan (later Sir Alan) (1926–2001): Bank of England, 1951–64; Director, European Department, IMF, 1964–81.

WIGGINS, Anthony John (b. 1938): Treasury, 1961–4; Private Secretary to Permanent Secretary, 1964–6, Principal, 1966–7, DEA; Treasury, 1967–9; Assistant Secretary, Treasury, 1972–9; Principal Private Secretary to Chancellor of the Exchequer, 1980–1; Under Secretary, Department of Energy, 1981–4; Under Secretary, Cabinet Office, 1985–7; Under Secretary, 1987–8, Deputy Secretary, 1988–92, Department for Education and Science.

WILLIAMS, Marcia (later Lady Falkender) (b. 1932): Private Secretary to Harold Wilson, 1956–64; then Political Secretary and Head of Private Office to Harold Wilson, 1964–70, 1974–6.

WILLIAMS, Shirley (later Lady Williams) (b. 1930): General Secretary, Fabian Society, 1960–4; MP (Labour) for Hitchin, 1964–74; Hertford and Stevenage, 1974–9; Crosby (SDP), 1981–3.

WILLIAMS, Wynne: Press Officer, Bank of England.

WILSON, (James) Harold (later Lord Wilson) (1916–95): MP (Labour) for Ormskirk, 1945–50; for Huyton, 1950–83; Parliamentary Secretary, Ministry of Works, 1945–7; Secretary for Overseas Trade, 1947; President of the Board of Trade, 1947–51; Leader, Labour Party, 1963–76; Prime Minister, 1964–70, 1974–6.

WOODCOCK, George (1904–79): Assistant General Secretary, TUC, 1947–60; General Secretary, TUC, 1960–9; TUC member of NEDC, 1962–9.

WORKMAN, Robert Little (1914–94): Economist, Export Credit Guarantees Department, 1938–49; Principal, 1949–59; Assistant Secretary, 1959–66; Under-Secretary, Treasury, 1967–74.

WYNDHAM-WHITE, Eric (later Sir Eric) (1913–80): Executive Secretary, 1948–65, Director-General, GATT, 1965–8.

YOUNG, I. J.: Industrial Adviser, DEA, 1965–6.

Sources: personal information; *Oxford Dictionary of National Biography*; *The Times*, Digital Archive, 1785–1985; *Who Was Who*.

Appendix II

Department of Economic Affairs
Ministers and Senior Officials

The DEA lived long enough to have a fifth birthday party, but only just, being created on 16 October 1964 and disbanded on 16 October 1969.[1] In this Appendix we record as fully as is possible the ministerial (part A) and senior official (part B) appointments. Where exact dates are not known ? substitutes for the day and, if necessary, ? ? for day/month.

A1. Secretary of State:

16 October 1964	11 August 1966	George Brown
11 August 1966	29 August 1967	Michael Stewart
29 August 1967	6 October 1969	Peter Shore

A2. Minister of State:

20 October 1964	27 January 1965	Anthony Crosland [1]
27 January 1965	7 January 1967	Austen Albu
6 April 1968	6 October 1969	Thomas Urwin

A3. Parliamentary Under-Secretary of State

21 October 1964	6 April 1966	Maurice A. Foley
21 October 1964	7 January 1967	William T. Rodgers
7 January 1967	29 August 1967	Harold Lever
7 January 1967	29 August 1967	Peter Shore
29 August 1967	6 April 1968	Edmund Dell
29 August 1967	6 October 1969	Alan Williams

---

[1] 'DEA Throws a Birthday Party', *The Times*, 25 September 1969, p. 27; see also 'Sad Laughter as DEA Fades Out', *The Times*, 17 October 1969, p. 2 which recorded: 'A sardonic departmental circular was distributed [at the birthday party/wake], full of bitter jokes: "We announce with regret the death of the D.E.A. The body has been donated for further research. The heart is to go to the Treasury, the brains to the Ministry of Technology, the arms and legs to the Department of Local Government and Regional Planning. The soul will live on."'

A4. Parliamentary Private Secretary [2]:

Dr Jeremy W. Bray	(1964–5)
William Hannan	(1965–6)
Laurence Pavitt	(1966)
Jack Ashley	(1967–8)
Kevin McNamara	(1968)

B1. Permanent Under-Secretary of State:

18 October 1964	30 September 1966	Sir Eric Roll
1 October 1966	30 March 1968	Sir Douglas Allen
1 April 1968	16 October 1969	Sir William Nield

B2. Deputy Under-Secretary of State

19 October 1964	30 September 1966	Douglas Allen (Economic Co-ordination)
19 October 1964	? ? 1968	A.W. Peterson (Regional Planning)
? ? 1965	? ? 1966	William Nield
? ? 1966	? ? 1967	Evan Maude
? ? 1966	? ? 1967	Derek Mitchell
? ? 1967	30 August 1969	John Jukes
? ? 1969	6 October 1969	Douglas Henley

B.3 Under-Secretary of State

? ? 1964	? ? 1965	William Nield

B4. Assistant Under-Secretary of State

? ? 1964	? ? 1966	Evan Maude
? ? 1964	? ? 1969	Douglas Henley

B5. Director-General

18 October 1964	31 December 1968	Sir Donald MacDougall
1 January 1969	16 October 1969	W.A.B. 'Bryan' Hopkin

B6. Deputy Director General

19 November 1964	? ? 1967	John Jukes

B7. Chief Industrial Adviser

22 October 1964	30 April 1966	Sir Fred Catherwood

Notes:

[1]   Initially as Economic Secretary to the Treasury until 24 December 1964.

[2]   This is probably an incomplete list and no precise dates are possible; for example, 'Call for Planning Shake up', *The Times*, 5 July 1965, p. 6 records Dr Bray as formerly PPS to George Brown but provides no dates.

Sources: D.E. Butler and G. Butler, *Twentieth-Century British Political Facts, 1900–2000* (8th. edn, 2000), pp. 29–30, 302; *British Imperial Calendar and Civil Service List*, 1964–9; *The Times*, Digital Archive, 1785–1985; *Who's Who/Who Was Who*.

Appendix III
Calendar of Key Events

The following is taken from the 'Calendar of Economic Events', *National Institute Economic Review* (*NIER*) February issues for 1964–7, supplemented by S. Brittan, *Steering the Economy* (1969 edn), pp. 104–5 and 'Calendar of Main Economic Events' in A.K. Cairncross and F. Cairncross, eds, *The Legacy of the Golden Age: The 1960s and their Economic Consequences* (1992), pp. 186–8. The *NIER* in particular provides very much more detail than is recorded here and it is important to note that the quarterly *NIER* was (and remains today) a key resource for policy-makers and economists in the wider community.

1964 27 February	Bank Rate raised from 4 to 5%.
14 April	Budget; designed to reduce growth rate from current 5–6% to 4%.
4 May	GATT Kennedy Round begins.
16 July	Resale Price Maintenance Bill becomes law.
28 July	IMF renews for twelve months UK's $1bn stand-by credit.
11 September	Labour Party election manifesto published.
17 September	Conservative Party election manifesto published.
25 September	Dissolution of Parliament.
15 October	General election.
16 October	Harold Wilson forms government; main ministerial posts allocated and announced.
16 October	DEA established; George Brown as First Secretary of State and Secretary of State for Economic Affairs.
17 October	Decision made by new government not to devalue sterling.

18 October	DEA appointments: Donald MacDougall, Director-General, and Eric Roll, Permanent Secretary.
26 October	Government publishes White Paper (Prime Minister, *The Economic Situation*) announcing measures to reduce a balance of payments deficit estimated at £700m–£800m.
27 October	Government invokes article 12 of GATT after EFTA responds critically to the imports surcharge in 26 October measures.
30 October	GATT Council establishes committee comprising EEC and 11 other nations to investigate UK imports surcharge introduced in 26 October measures.
3 November	Lyndon B. Johnson elected US President.
6 November	S. Rhodesia votes for independence.
8 November	Paris Club provides $400m at the disposal of the IMF upon which Britain may draw.
11 November	Chancellor's first budget; tax increases and expenditure restraint in 1964/5; announcement of tax rises and tax reforms for 1965/6.
18 November	Government's draft 'statement of intention' on prices and incomes policy delivered to TUC and employers' associations.
19 November	EFTA Ministerial Council meets to consider UK imports surcharge.
23 November	Bank Rate raised from 5 to 7%, the highest since October 1961 and single largest increase since August 1939.
25 November	Bank of England announces $3bn credit line from 8 European central banks, Canada, US, Japan and BIS.
2 December	Government establishes Padmore Committee on the docks.
7 December	Prime Minister and US President meet, Washington.

7 December	Minister of Labour announces establishment of Royal Commission on trade unions and employers' associations (Donovan commission).
8 December	Bank of England announces credit restrictions.
9 December	TUC Economic Committee accepts final draft 'statement of intent' on incomes and prices policy.
16 December	Joint Statement of Intent on Productivity, Prices and Incomes' signed at Lancaster House by George Brown and representatives of the TUC, FBI, BEC and NABM and BCC.
18 December	GATT Council declares UK imports surcharge a violation of the Treaty.
1965 29 January	EFTA denounces UK export measures and demands immediate cut in the imports surcharge.
31 January	New export promotion measures.
10 February	Renewal of $3bn credit arrangement made in November 1964 for further 3 months.
11 February	White paper, *Machinery of Prices and Incomes* (Cmnd. 2577), published after discussions with trade unions and employers' associations.
16 February	Second Beeching report, *The Development of the Major Railway Trunk Routes*.
22 February	Announcement that imports surcharge will fall from 15 to 10% on 27 April.
22 February	Chancellor announces that real growth rate for public expenditure be limited to 4¼% between 1964–5 and 1969–70.
8 March	Bonn talks between Harold Wilson and Dr Erhard.
17 March	Aubrey Jones appointed first chairman, NBPI.
17 March	TUC Economic Committee agrees to 3–3½% pay norm proposed by NBPI.
6 April	MoD announces cancellation of TSR2 project.

6 April	Chancellor's second budget; deflating demand by £250m through additional taxation, both higher rates on existing taxes and prospective new taxes, including capital gains tax and corporation tax; also stricter controls over foreign investment and exchange.
8 April	White paper on criteria to be used by NBPI for referred cases and membership of Board.
27 April	Imports surcharge on most manufactured goods reduced from 15 to 10%.
29 April	Bank of England call for 1% special deposits.
30 April	TUC Conference votes to support government's policy on prices and incomes.
30 April	White paper on steel re-nationalisation published.
6 May	Opposition censure motion (steel re-nationalisation) defeated.
6 May	Bank of England instruction to London clearing banks on limiting credit expansion 1965–6.
12 May	IMF agrees to a further UK drawing of $1.4bn.
24 May	President of Board of Trade announces that government intends Britain to adopt metrification within 10 years.
3 June	Bank Rate reduced from 7% to 6%, but HP restrictions tightened.
27 July	Chancellor announces measures to strengthen balance of payments and to depress domestic demand, including public investment cuts, tighter exchange controls, further HP restrictions.
2 August	Iain Macleod appointed opposition spokesman on Treasury and economic affairs.
8 September	TUC Congress supports the voluntary 'early warning' system for wage claims and price increases.
10 September	Bank of England announces new support package for sterling by eight European countries, Canada and the US.

15 September	CBI accepts government proposals for strengthening prices and incomes policies.
16 September	National Plan published.
22 September	TUC sets up 'early warning' system for wage claims.
27 September	Washington meeting of G10.
30 September	Labour Party conference supports government's income and prices policy.
24 October	Bakers' union threatens strike action unless 40,000 members receive 30% pay rise.
4 November	Government advances financial assistance to Fairfield Shipbuilding & Engineering Co. to enable company to operate for further 4 months.
4 November	Paris meeting of G10.
9 November	Parliamentary session begins; steel re-nationalisation omitted from programme.
11 November	Southern Rhodesia IDI; immediate measures taken against illegal government.
11 November	White paper, *Prices and Incomes Policy: An 'Early Warning' system* (Cmnd. 2808).
18 November	NCB announces closure programme of 150 collieries and 120,000 miners redundant in 2–3 years.
18 November	Bakers' first strike.
25 November	Bakers' second strike.
28 November	Bakers' reject reference to NBPI.
1 December	Further sanctions against Southern Rhodesia.
2 December	Bakers' Union agrees to NBPI reference.
10 December	Fairfield workers agree to government-sponsored rescue programme.
14 December	FTA established between UK and Eire.
16 December	Report of Committee of Inquiry into the Aircraft Industry (Plowden Committee) (Cmnd. 2853).

	22 December	Minister for Economic Affairs announces plan for Fairfields comprising a government, trade union and industry partnership.
1966	1 January	As per schedule EEC cuts internal import duties by 10%.
	19 January	NBPI interim report on bakery pay (Cmnd. 2878).
	25 January	White paper on Industrial Reconstruction Corporation (Cmnd. 2889).
	1 February	Bank of England requests London clearing banks to freeze advances at 105% of March 1965 level.
	8 February	Tightening of HP restrictions.
	1 March	Chancellor announces intention to decimalise currency in February 1971.
	24 March	Geddes report (Cmnd. 2937) on reorganising shipbuilding published.
	31 March	General election: Labour increases majority from 5 to 97.
	14 April	National Union of Seamen reject employers' final wage offer.
	3 May	Callaghan third budget; deflationary measures; corporation tax fixed at 40%; introduction of SET; 10% imports surcharge to end 30 November.
	23 May	State of emergency declared to cover seamen's strike.
	9 June	TUC calls upon seamen to negotiate on basis of Pearson report.
	9 June	NBPI report on bakery pay published.
	13 June	Sterling rallies after annual BIS meeting announces $2bn credit arrangements.
	1 July	National Union of Seamen accepts Pearson report; strike ends after 46 days.
	13 July	Trade gap of £55m for June announced.
	14 July	Bank of England doubles special deposits and raises Bank Rate by 1 percentage point to 7%.

20 July   Prime Minister announces measures to meet
continuing pressure on sterling, including 'regulator' +10%, personal travel allowances outside
SA reduced to £50 per annum, tax changes and
expenditure restraint, voluntary price and wage
freeze.

30 July   White paper on prices and incomes; 6 month
standstill (Cmnd. 3073).

Appendix IV
Contemporary Economic Statistics
and Later Revisions

By the early 1960s, with the growth consciousness having taken root,[1] economic debate centred around a limited range of key statistics that tracked the four central macroeconomic policy objectives (full employment; price stability; 3–4 per cent economic growth; and a surplus on the current account balance of payments), these supplemented by a limited range of additional indicators, notably the industrial production index and certain components of the balance of payments, both current and capital account.

As Brittan reveals in the diary he was one of many, outside and inside of government, monitoring very closely indeed – if not obsessively – the daily flow of data. This was a basic input into the policy process, but more immediately, from the perspective of the DEA's Information Division, briefings were required constantly by senior civil servants and ministers needing at short notice either as a gloss for bad news or to maximise the potential benefits of good news, the latter seemingly always scarcer than the former. In this Appendix we reproduce the contemporary estimates and (where appropriate) later revisions (both 1967 and current ONS) of the main series that Brittan and his contemporaries monitored and used for policy; those that were reproduced in Figure 4 (panels A–D) of the Introduction. Additionally, we supplement these data with daily estimates for the foreign exchange reserves, a key anxiety for policy-makers and one upon which Brittan reflected much in the diary.[2]

---

[1] R. Middleton, 'Economists and Economic Growth in Britain, c.1955–65', in L. A. Black and H. Pemberton, eds, *Affluent Britain: Britain's Postwar 'Golden Age' Revisited* (Aldershot, 2004), pp. 129–47. This Appendix builds upon work started in my *Charlatans or Saviours? Economists and the British Economy from Marshall to Meade* (Cheltenham, 1998), pp. 257–61.

[2] Diary, 24 November, 9 and 17 December 1964; 11 May, 2 July, 4 August and 30 December 1965.

Our starting point is the observation made in 1991 by Douglas Allen, by now Lord Croham, who had been Deputy Under-Secretary at the DEA during Brittan's term as an irregular, that:[3]

> Anyone trying to recount the history of a period in which he was active, relying on memory and the material available at the time, would be totally astonished to find that most of the figures for the same period produced by other people twenty or thirty years later were quite unrecognizable. The most important instrument lacking was a position-finder to tell us exactly where we were at any given moment. Nearly all statistics, and especially those made on the basis of trends, are subsequently changed and yield quite a different picture with the passage of time. It might well be, therefore, that many of the things that happened in the 1960s took place because of inadequate guidance and information.

It has been estimated that during the 1960s and 1970s the average range of revisions to the GDP and current account balance of payments series were 1.2 per cent for the former and £268 million for the latter, with the revisions upwards for the former in seventeen out of the twenty years enumerated and improvements in the latter in eighteen years. Thus, there was 'a tendency for revisions in the statistics to make our review of the economy look rosier with hindsight than it looked at the time', and so much so that 'these statistical revisions could have considerable importance for the interpretation of policy actions since they may make policy interventions which appeared quite rational at the time look misconceived in the light of the data now at our disposal.'[4] A classic, much cited case in point was the July 1966 deflationary measures, the final nail in the coffin of the National Plan, which were precipitated by forecasts[5] that there would be a substantial current account deficit by the end of the year whereas by 1969 revisions were showing a surplus and the latest ONS estimate is for a surplus approaching £150 million.[6]

In considering the main categories of data used by Brittan and his contemporaries we are severely handicapped by the absence of systematic

---

[3] Lord Croham, 'Were the Instruments of Control for Domestic Economic Policy Adequate?', in F. Cairncross and A. K. Cairncross, eds., *The Legacy of the Golden Age: the 1960s and Their Economic Consequences* (1992), p. 92.

[4] P. Mosley, *The Making of Economic Policy: Theory and Evidence from Britain and the United States since 1945* (Brighton, 1984), p. 243.

[5] In sequence, between February and November 1966, the NIESR forecasts for the current balance for calendar 1966 were deficits of £80 million, £55 million, £40 million and £173 million, with the last two incorporating the effects of the July measures; see Middleton, *Charlatans or Saviours?*, p. 260 n. 69.

[6] Office for National Statistics, *Economic Trends, Annual Supplement*, 32 (2006), table 2.13A.

research on the supply-side of statistics,[7] for we lack a proper history of the CSO[8] and have only partial accounts of Treasury economic forecasting for this period.[9] The demand side is naturally more developed, although an obvious research topic remains how economic and financial journalists used official and other statistics to construct the economic discourse.

(i) Balance of payments

Table 2 panel A reproduces a matrix of the current account balance (NSA) on a quarterly basis for the period 1964.I–1966.IV. The first estimate for 1964.I was published in the CSO's June 1964 *Monthly Digest of Statistics* (*MDS*).[10] This estimated a deficit for the quarter of £67 million (£62 million on a SA basis), but this was then revised every quarter through to the September 1966 *MDS*, at which point the NSA deficit had been reduced to £52 million. The current ONS estimate for this quarter is a deficit of £34 million, only half that of the original estimate. The 1967 revisions in Figure 4 panel A1 are those published between September 1966, when the 1964 estimates stabilised, and March 1968, when the 1966 estimates stabilised. For each quarter the range of estimates between the first published and the 1967 estimates is considerable.

---

[7] The 1950s saw the publication of three key studies: M. G. Kendall, *The Sources and Nature of the Statistics of the United Kingdom*, 2 vols (1952; 1957); C. F. Carter and A. D. Roy, *British Economic Statistics: A Report* (Cambridge, 1954); and E. Devons, *An Introduction to British Economic Statistics* (Cambridge, 1956). These remain relevant to the 1960s but in important respects were severely outdated, and particularly with respect to national accounts (including the balance of payments) and financial statistics; see also Government Statistical Service, 'Developments in Official Economic Statistics, 1957–1963', *Economic Trends*, 124 (February 1964), pp. xxii–xxxii; and F. M. M. Lewes, *Statistics of the British Economy* (1967).

[8] R. Ward and T. Doggett, *Keeping Score: The First Fifty Years of the Central Statistical Office* (1991) is highly abbreviated.

[9] 'Short-Term Economic Forecasting in the United Kingdom', *Economic Trends*, 130 (August 1964), pp. ii–xi and 'Government Economic Research', *Economic Trends*, 142 (August 1965), pp. ii–xii. R. F. Bretherton, *Demand Management, 1958–64* (1999), pp. 61–75 provides a useful review of the forecasts for 1958–64, while there are occasional references in A. K. Cairncross, *The Wilson Years: A Treasury Diary, 1964–1969* (1997).

[10] In practice, this was published with, or very slightly later than, the monthly *Economic Trends* (*ET*); see 'United Kingdom Balance of Payments in the First Quarter of 1964', *Economic Trends*, 128 (June 1964), pp. ii–xiii which first discusses the seasonally adjusted current account. It was *ET* that was monitored more by journalists (it had charts as well as tables!), so that for example the 1964.I first GDP estimate was first picked up by *The Times* ('Expansion Slackening but Incomes still Rising', 31 July 1964, p. 15) from that source ('National Income and Expenditure in the First Quarter of 1964', *Economic Trends*, 129 (July 1964), pp. ii–xi). Additionally, there were daily press notices publicising the major series.

Table 2. Balance of payments (NSA): current account balance; balance of long-term capital, balance of capital and long-term capital transactions and balancing item, 1964.I-1966.IV.

MDS/Month	Jun-64	Sep-64	Dec-64	Mar-65	Jun-65	Sep-65	Dec-65	Mar-66	Jun-66	Sep-66	Dec-66	Mar-67	Jun-67	Sep-67	Dec-67	Mar-68	Jun-68	Estimates: First	Min	Max	Final	range	as % of 1st est
A. Current account balance																							
1964.I	-67	-52	-49	-54	-54	-56	-56	-56	-56	-52	-52	-52						-67	-49	-67	-52	-18	26.9
1964.II		-73	-67	-60	-60	-63	-63	-63	-59	-57	-57	-57						-73	-57	-73	-57	-16	21.9
1964.III			-183	-182	-182	-192	-192	-192	-192	-191	-191	-191						-183	-182	-192	-191	-10	5.5
1964.IV				-78	-78	-101	-101	-99	-99	-93	-93	-93						-78	-78	-101	-93	-23	29.5
1965.I					-7	-41	-35	-38	-38	-26	-26	-35	-34	-35	-35	-35		-7	-7	-41	-35	-34	485.7
1965.II						25	-8	-5	-5	-11	-11	-10	-11	-12	-12	-12		25	25	-12	-12	-37	-148.0
1965.III							-128	-118	-118	-110	-110	-107	-107	-103	-103	-103	-103	-128	-103	-128	-103	-25	19.5
1965.IV								25	25	43	43	43	34	40	40	40		25	43	25	40	-18	-72.0
1966.I									-26	-24	-21	-33	-35	-31	-31	-27	-27	-26	-21	-35	-27	-14	53.8
1966.II										-74	-82	-74	-76	-76	-76	-66	-66	-74	-66	-82	-66	-16	21.6
1966.III											-131	-111	-112	-121	-121	-119	-119	-131	-111	-131	-119	-20	15.3
1966.IV												157	164	169	169	181	181	157	181	157	181	-24	-15.3
B. Balance of long-term capital																							
1964.I	-91	-95	-93	-86	-86	-86	-86	-93	-93	-96	-96	-96						-91	-86	-96	-96	-10	11.0
1964.II		-121	-120	-114	-114	-107	-107	-112	-112	-109	-109	-109						-121	-107	-121	-109	-14	11.6
1964.III			-100	-69	-69	-57	-57	-61	-61	-59	-59	-59						-100	-57	-100	-59	-43	43.0
1964.IV				-102	-102	-94	-94	-97	-97	-104	-104	-104						-102	-94	-104	-104	-10	9.8
1965.I					-90	-89	-63	-66	-66	-77	-77	-88	-88	-85	-85	-85		-90	-63	-90	-85	-27	30.0
1965.II						3	-11	-33	-33	-16	-16	-25	-25	-24	-24	-24		3	3	-33	-24	-36	-1200.0
1965.III							-108	-92	-92	-94	-94	-96	-96	-96	-96	-96		-108	-92	-108	-96	-16	14.8
1965.IV								-27	-27	-28	-28	-30	-30	-27	-27	-27		-27	-27	-30	-27	-3	11.1
1966.I									-73	-60	-54	-73	-73	-65	-65	-52	-52	-73	-52	-73	-52	-21	28.8
1966.II										21	28	9	9	9	9	10	10	21	28	9	10	-19	-90.5
1966.III											-22	-28	-28	-27	-27	-25	-25	-22	-22	-28	-25	-6	27.3
1966.IV												-36	-36	-33	-33	-35	-35	-36	-33	-36	-35	-3	8.3

C. Current account balance and balance of long-term capital

Quarter	Successive estimates				
1964.I	-158 -147 -142 -140 -142 -142 -149 -149 -148 -148 -148 -148	-140	-158	-148	-18	11.4
1964.II	-194 -187 -174 -170 -170 -175 -171 -166 -166 -166 -166	-166	-194	-166	-28	14.4
1964.III	-283 -251 -249 -249 -253 -250 -250 -250 -250 -250	-249	-283	-250	-34	12.0
1964.IV	-180 -195 -196 -197 -197 -197 -197 -197 -197	-180	-197	-197	-17	9.4
1965.I	-97 -130 -104 -98 -103 -103 -122 -120 -120 -120	-97	-130	-120	-33	34.0
1965.II	28 -19 -38 -27 -35 -36 -36 -36 -36	28	-38	-36	-66	-235.7
1965.III	-236 -210 -204 -203 -203 -199 -199 -199 -199	-199	-236	-199	-37	15.7
1965.IV	-2 15 15 13 4 13 13 13	15	-2	13	-17	850.0
1966.I	-99 -84 -75 -106 -108 -96 -96 -79 -79	-75	-108	-79	-33	33.3
1966.II	-53 -54 -65 -67 -67 -56 -56	-53	-67	-56	-14	26.4
1966.III	-153 -139 -140 -148 -148 -144 -144	-139	-153	-144	-14	9.2
1966.IV	121 128 136 136 146 146	146	121	146	-25	-20.7

D. Balancing item

Quarter	Successive estimates				
1964.I	89 56 47 45 45 58 58 45 46 49 49 49	89	45	49	-44	-49.4
1964.II	29 27 17 17 7 7 3 3 2 2 2	29	2	2	-27	-93.1
1964.III	35 11 11 2 2 6 6 17 17 17	35	2	17	-33	-94.3
1964.IV	-72 -72 -32 -32 -33 -33 -41 -41 -41	-32	-72	-41	-40	55.6
1965.I	-31 0 -1 -1 -1 15 17 18 18 18	18	-31	18	-49	158.1
1965.II	-19 33 48 48 49 56 55 58 58 58	58	-19	58	-77	405.3
1965.III	19 19 4 4 1 1 -1 -1 -1	19	-4	-1	-23	-121.1
1965.IV	54 54 38 38 33 37 29 29 29	54	29	29	-25	-46.3
1966.I	77 77 58 32 64 68 57 57 49 49	77	32	49	-45	-58.4
1966.II	42 -38 -26 -26 -27 -33 -33	-26	-42	-33	-16	38.1
1966.III	44 35 34 38 38 37 37	44	34	37	-10	-22.7
1966.IV	-62 -61 -69 -69 -66 -66	-61	-69	-66	-8	12.9

Source: MDS, July 1966–June 1968.

The problem of the accuracy and timeliness of balance of payments statistics had featured in Macmillan's 1956 budget speech discussed earlier (p. 32). Later that year Macmillan announced a programme for the improvement of official statistics,[11] and O'Hara has detailed how the Treasury and the Bank responded to the challenge, by 1959 establishing a Standing Committee for Statistics on Economic Policy under the head of the CSO.[12] The case for further improvements was made by the Radcliffe committee's report as part of its modernisation agenda,[13] and in the following year the CSO began publication of what became known as the 'pink book'.[14] Notwithstanding these improvements, considerable difficulties remained in estimating the components of the current account, being evident most in terms of the invisible account though the visible account was not without its own problems. Cumulatively, these were such that the NIESR at this time operated a rule of thumb that the first estimate undervalued credit items by £100 million.[15]

Systematic under-recording was one problem, but it was compounded by a press which did not routinely flag the fragility of the first estimates and the importance of the balancing item, with *The Times* and the *Economist* as notable exceptions.[16] As is clear from Table 2 panel D (and as was shown in Figure 4 panel A2) the balancing item (a measure of our statistical ignorance, being the difference between the balance of monetary movements, category E8 in Table 3, and the balance of current and long-term capital transactions, category C in Table 3) was anything but trivial. For example, in 1964.I, at which point the first current account balance estimate was

[11] 'Economic Statistics', *Parliamentary Debates* (House of Commons), 5th ser. 557 (1 August 1956), cols 1400–4.

[12] G. O'Hara, 'Towards a New Bradshaw?: Economic Statistics and the British State in the 1950s and 1960s', *Economic History Review*, 60.1 (2007), p. 14.

[13] Committee on the Workings of the Monetary System (Radcliffe Committee), *Report*, BPP 1958–9 (827), esp. ch. x.

[14] Before 1960 responsibility for the balance of payments statistics lay with the Bank of England which compiled them on the basis of data supplied by the Board of Trade and as a result of its own exchange control operations: Ward and Doggett, *Keeping Score*, p. 62. The first annual CSO publication of *United Kingdom Balance of Payments* began in 1960, but the *Bank of England Quarterly Bulletin* remains an equally important source, and especially for capital account transactions.

[15] Middleton, *Charlatans or Saviours?*, p. 258.

[16] For example, for *The Times*, 'UK Balance of Payments in Deficit', 30 June 1964, p. 10 and 'More Cheerful View of the Deficit', 26 January 1965, p. 16 are exemplars of good economic journalism, reporting the first estimates (which showed a deteriorating current account due to import growth, itself a function of a rapidly expanding economy) with the caveats about first estimates and then a technical discussion of the importance of the balancing item and of how capital account transactions might be interpreted.

–£67 million, the balancing item was +£89 million. Indeed, in five of the twelve quarters here surveyed, the balancing item exceeded the current account balance.

Current scholarship, which builds upon the scepticism of a few contemporary writers,[17] has it that much of the balance of payments problem of the 1960s was constructed in an unnecessarily febrile mood of crisis (see pp. 17, 22, 28, 32–3, 39, 42). Certainly, contemporary debate too often conflated developments in the current account, itself not a homogenous accounting category, with the capital account (Table 2 panel B) and the combined current account and balance of long-term capital transactions (Table 2 panel C). We reproduce in Table 3 the complete balance of payments accounts for 1963 using the then new standard presentation with two differences: first, that we have augmented the invisible account with its component accounts (government and private); and, secondly, to assist the analysis category letters and item numbers have been added.

Taking each in turn, the visible account (A1) presents the least conceptual and measurement difficulties. It is also very straightforward: Britain has run a visible trade deficit (A4) since early in the nineteenth century and no negative significance should thereby be applied. All that varied was the size of the deficit which was positively related to the pressure of demand and thus part of the Stop-Go discourse. The invisible account (A5), however, reflects both economic and political forces, comprising a government account (A6, the summation of A6.7, A6.12 and A6.13–6.15) which was very strongly in deficit due to Britain's geo-political posture (upon which Brittan had very strong views),[18] and a private account (A7, the summation of A7.1–7.2) which principally but not exclusively measured trade in services. As can be seen from the example for 1963, the overall invisible balance was a surplus of £162 million (A8), but this would have been much larger had government net transactions (A6) not been so strongly negative, for example through reduced military payments abroad (A6.1) which was of course one of the issues that the Wilson government had to confront, resulting eventually in the 1967 decision to

---

[17] Notably, A. R. Conan, *The Problem of Sterling* (1966), F. Hirsch, *The Pound Sterling: A Polemic* (1965) and W. A. P. Manser, *Britain in the Balance: The Myth of Failure* (1971).

[18] S. Brittan, *The Treasury under the Tories* (1964) contained an assessment of defence expenditure, including in relation to GDP relative to other countries, and much incidental discussion of the balance of payments and balance of payments statistics (pp. 88, 138–9), but it was not until *Steering the Economy* (1969 edn) that these topics received detailed treatment, including the burden of overseas expenditure (pp. 251–5) and developing scepticism about sterling's international role (pp.260–2).

Table 3. UK balance of payments (£m), standard presentation, 1963 [1]

A. Current Account

A1	*Visible account:*				
A2	Imports (fob)	4,335			
A3	Exports and re-exports (fob)	4,286			
A4	Visible trade balance [A2-A3]	-49			
A5	*Invisible account:*				
A6	Government (net)	-509		Payments:	
			A6.1	Military	-251
			A6.2	Economic grants	-69
			A6.3	Other grants	-26
			A6.4	Subscriptions & contributions to international organisations	-29
			A6.5	Administration, diplomatic, etc.	-35
			A6.6	Pensions	-19
			A6.7	Total	-429
				Receipts:	
			A6.8	US & Canadian forces expenditure	+12
			A6.9	Other military receipts	+25
			A6.10	Defence aid	
			A6.11	Other	+5
			A6.12	Total	+42
				Interest and dividends (net):	
			A6.13	Interest on North American loans	-38
			A6.14	Interest on aid loans	+16
			A6.15	Other	-100
			A6	Total current invisible expenditure:	-509
A7	Private (net)	671	A7.1	Interest, profits and dividends (net)	+499
A8	Invisibles balance [A6+A7]	+162	A7.2	Other invisibles (net)	+172
			A7	Invisible balance	+671
A9	*Current balance [A4+A8]*	+113			

B. Long-term capital account

B1	Inter-govnmental loans (net)	-97
B2	Other UK official long-term capital (net)	-8
B3	*Private investment:*	
B4	Abroad	-309
B5	In the UK	+259
B6	*Balance of long-term capital [B1+B2+B3+B4+B5]*	-155

C. Balance of Current and long-term capital transactions [A9+B6] -42

D. Balancing item [E8-C] -111

E. Monetary movements

E1	Miscellaneous capital (net)	-49
E2	*Changes in:*	
E3	External liabilities; SA and OSA currencies (net)	144
E4	Offical holdings of non-convertible currencies	

E5	UK balance in EPU	
E6	Account with IMF	5
E7	Gold and convertible currency reserve	53
E8	*Balance of monetary movements* [E1+E3+E4+E5+E6+E7]	153

Note: [1] A decrease in liabilities or an increase in assets is shown -; an increase in liabilities or a decrease in assets shown +.

Source: The Balance of Payments: Methods of Presentation', *Bank of England Quarterly Bulletin*, 4.4 (December 1964), tables I, III.

withdraw east of Suez.[19] From the perspective of the current account as a whole and over a longer period, the private sector balance of payments was always in surplus in the 1950s and 1960s; it was the deficit on the government account which pushed the current account into deficit during boom years.[20]

The long-term capital account has also a government and private dimension. The former (B1, B2) comprised liabilities on the balance of payments amounting to £105 million, these relating to the legacy of past events as well as newer obligations such as foreign assistance for LDCs. The private account (B3), which in 1963 was in deficit to the tune of £50 million (B4+B5), reflected the balance of direct and portfolio investment by British companies abroad and foreign companies in Britain. It was official policy that the current account balance of payments surplus be sufficiently large to accommodate the higher propensity of British companies to invest overseas than for foreigners to reciprocate with the British economy.[21] Britain had traditionally been a substantial net exporter of capital, and the balance of payments implications of these capital flows and the issue of whether British firms' investment overseas was at the expense of domestic investment and employment were current topics of debate, and especially for a Labour government.[22]

Finally, we chart in Figure 8 daily changes in the total reserves for the period from just before Labour's election to the day of devaluation in November 1967, annotating the chart with the major event history. Brittan would very much like to have had access to this series which has been compiled retrospectively from Bank of England records,[23] not least that one can marry his entries in the Diary with the exact position. We have

[19] S. Dockrill, *Britain's Retreat from East of Suez: The Choice between Europe and the World?* (2002).

[20] R. Middleton, *Government versus the Market: The Growth of the Public Sector, Economic Management and British Economic Performance, 1890–c.1979* (Cheltenham, 1996), pp. 534–5.

[21] According to Bretherton, *Demand Management,* p. 3 it was Treasury doctrine by the late 1950s that there should be a surplus of c£350 million to cover net investment overseas and to build up the reserves.

[22] J. D. Tomlinson, 'The Labour Party and the Capitalist Firm, c.1950–1970', *Historical Journal,* 47.3 (2004), pp. 685–708.

[23] The Bank published end month data on gold and convertible currency reserves in the Exchange Equalisation Account in the statistical annex to each of its *Quarterly Reviews* during this period. There was no published daily data, though this did not stop press speculation about reserve movements. My thanks to Michael Oliver for allowing me to use these data which formed the basis for figure 3 of M. D. Bordo, R. MacDonald and M. Oliver, 'Sterling in Crisis, 1964–1967', *European Review of Economic History,* 13.3 (2009), pp. 437–59.

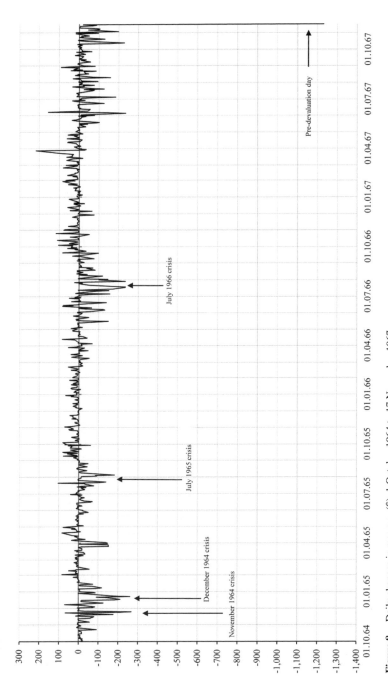

Figure 8. Daily changes in reserves ($), 1 October 1964 to 17 November 1967.

Source: M. D. Bordo, R. MacDonald and M. J. Oliver, 'Sterling in crisis, 1964-1967', *European Review of Economic History*, 13.3 (2009), pp. 437-59, figure 3.

not calculated his 'strike rate' but clearly his information sources could be very well informed.[24]

(ii) GDP

The quarterly GDP series, both at current and constant (1958) prices, was published by the CSO four months in arrears, i.e. the 1964.I first estimate was published in *MDS*, July 1964. Table 4 reproduces these first estimates, the 1967 revisions and current ONS estimates in a fashion which aids direct comparison (the current ONS estimate obviously does not use 1958 prices and thus resort has been made to index numbers).

As was revealed in Figure 4 panel B1, the 1964 first estimates were subject to unusually large revisions by 1967, this part of a larger problem (centred on the industrial production index) that policy-makers and commentators were perplexed by what was happening to the economy for the greater part of 1964.[25] We reproduce in Table 5 an 'at the time' and 'hindsight' assessment of October 1964 made as part of a bigger exercise by John Boreham*, a professional statistician and long-time member of the CSO. This was the first month of the new government; retrospectively this is how Boreham characterised their understanding of the economy on the basis of the position-finders then available:[26]

> At the time GDP looked as though it had stopped growing at about the turn of the year. From 1963 III to 1964 I there was a sharp 'up and down' owing a great deal to the figures for stockbuilding and exports of goods and services. Even if the up and down is discounted because of the perennial timing problems with figures of stockbuilding, the flatness of the GDP figures for 1964 I and II seemed at the time to confirm the end of growth. However, the up and down has vanished with hindsight because stockbuilding and exports of goods and services have been smoothed out to some extent and a small, offsetting, 'down and up' (in relation to trend) has been inserted into consumers' expenditure. As a result there seems to be a fairly steady growth of some 9 per cent between 1962 IV and 1964 II (that is based on the average estimate for GDP, which is available with hindsight). There was a kink (down-up-down in relation to trend) from 1962 IV to 1963 III in the GDP (Expenditure) series, but that is not of significance except for the way it could have misled in 1963.
>
> The rate of growth of about 1¼ per cent a quarter from 1962 IV to 1964 IV, together with a much less marked deterioration in real resources for the balance

---

[24] Comparisons can also be made with Cairncross, *The Wilson Years*, e.g. diary entry for 25 November 1964 'We lost over £90m. today more even than yesterday' (p. 17). According to Oliver's data, the loss was £267 million.

[25] For early in the new government, see for example in *The Times*, 'Industrial Output held on Plateau', 22 October, 1964, p. 19 which reported on the August 1965 industrial production index and 'National Output Stagnating', 3 November 1964, p. 15 on the 1964.II first GDP estimate.

[26] A. J. Boreham, 'A Statistician's View', in M. V. Posner, ed., *Demand management* (1978), p. 144.

Table 4. GDP at constant factor cost (SA), £ millions and index numbers, first estimate, 1967 revisions and current ONS estimates, 1963-6

	Constant 1958 prices					Current estimate [1]	
	First estimate £m	Index First estimate 1964.I=100	1967 estimate £m	Index 1967 estimate 1964.I (first estimate)=100	Difference between first and 1967 estimate (%)	2003 prices, £m (YBHH)	Index 1963=100
1963	23,205		23,744		2.32	377,107	100.0
1964	24,798		25,137		1.37	398,271	105.6
1965	25,621		25,774		0.60	409,167	108.5
1966	26,175		26,175		0.00	416,658	110.5
% change 1963-6	12.8		10.2			10.5	10.5
1964.I	6,007	100.0	6,205	103.3	3.30	98,400	100.0
1964.II	6,070	101.0	6,249	104.0	2.95	99,384	101.0
1964.III	6,160	102.5	6,282	104.6	1.98	99,574	101.2
1964.IV	6,329	105.4	6,401	106.6	1.14	100,913	102.6
1965.I	6,372	106.1	6,440	107.2	1.07	101,233	102.9
1965.II	6,315	105.1	6,388	106.3	1.16	101,950	103.6
1965.III	6,390	106.4	6,440	107.2	0.78	102,647	104.3
1965.IV	6,458	107.5	6,506	108.3	0.74	103,337	105.0
1966.I	6,538	108.8	6,570	109.4	0.49	103,523	105.2
1966.II	6,485	108.0	6,501	108.2	0.25	104,020	105.7
1966.III	6,500	108.2	6,523	108.6	0.35	104,743	106.4
1966.IV	6,556	109.1	6,556	109.1	0.00	104,372	106.1
% change 1964.I-1966.IV	9.1	9.1	5.7	5.7		6.1	6.1

Note: [1] GDP at factor cost no longer provided by ONS; GVA at factor cost (series YBHH) substituted.

Sources: MDS, March 1964-April 1967; ONS, *Economic Trends Annual Supplement*, 32 (2006).

Table 5. October 1964: 'at the time' and 'hindsight' data and assessment.

	At the time	Hindsight
A. Activity and unemployment	The pace of economic expansion appears to have been slow since the beginning of 1964, in contrast with the rapid expansion in 1963; indeed industrial production has been flat all year. The underlying trend of the volume of exports is now flat after the rapid rise in 1963, but the volume of imports is still rising, though less rapidly than at the turn of the year.	GDP, which grew by over 5 per cent during 1963, has progressively slowed down this year and, if as we believe, stockbuilding has passed its peak, it is now increasing at an annual average rate of no more than 2 per cent. Domestic consumption, private and public, as well as fixed investment are rising moderately. The volume of exports is not changing but the volume of imports is still growing moderately.
	Some of the rise in unemployment in July and August may have owed something to the influx of school-leavers and the renewed fall in September tends to confirm that judgement. Nevertheless it is now likely that the sharp drop in unemployment since early 1963 is over and that the underlying trend is at best flat and may be rising a little.	It is now likely that most of the sharp drop in unemployment since early 1963 is now over and that the underlying trend is a very slow fall or even flat.
B. Inflation and costs	Wages seem to be rising at about 0.5 per cent per month. Although seasonal food prices are now moving favourably and the sharp rise in the index of retail prices that took place in the Spring (0.5 per cent a month, on average, between January–February and June–July) It is unlikely to reappear, increases of 0.2 or 0.3 per cent a month are still possible.	Average earnings are rising at a little over 1 per cent a quarter which is not out of line with the settlement at something under 5 per cent which is taking place. Wholesale prices of materials and fuel bought by manufacturing industry, after the rather sharp rise at the end of 1963, seem to have stabilised for the time being. Although seasonal food prices are now moving favourably and the sharp rise in the index of retail prices that took place in the Spring (0.5 per cent a month, on average, between January–September and June–July) is unlikely to reappear, increases of 0.2 or 0.3 per cent a month are still possible.
C. Balance of Payments	The trends in export and import volumes have produced a sharp deterioration in the current balance.	The trends in export and import volumes have produced a sharp deterioration in the current balance from a small surplus at the end of 1963 to a deficit now of about £40 million a month..

Source: A.J. Boreham, 'A Statistician's View', in M.V. Posner, ed., *Demand Management* (1978), 99. 141-2.

of payments, bring about the changed assessment of activity. Indeed, if the assessment had not been that stockbuilding had reached a peak about mid-1964, it would have been reasonable to assess that GDP was still growing briskly in 1964 III. In the event, as we all know, GDP went on growing into 1965, though not so fast as in 1963. (The fourth quarter to fourth quarter rates were 6 per cent from 1962 to 1963, 4 per cent from 1963 to 1964, 2½ per cent from 1964 to 1965, all based on the average estimate of GDP.)

Such were the problems in 1963–4 that the NIESR proposed that a new compromise estimate for GDP be derived,[27] and in 1964–5 CSO staff refined the quarterly series,[28] but in addition there was a major difficulty with another statistical series which was both an important input into the GDP series (output estimate in particular) and a position-finder in its own right, that of the index of industrial production.

(iii) Industrial production

In 1964 the principal monthly aggregate activity indicator was the seasonally adjusted all industries index of industrial production which was published two months in arrears in *ET* and *MDS*. (Importantly, it was published as an integer.) This series encompassed manufacturing, construction, and the gas, electricity and water sectors. This covered some 11 million workers out of a total employed (Great Britain) labour force of 24.8 million, some 44 per cent. Whilst manufacturing, by far the largest element (8.8 million), had not quite attained its peak in the labour force, either absolutely or relatively, it is very much the case that with no service sector activity index available the policy community was dependent upon a very partial measure of aggregate economic activity.

Here we highlight that the index of industrial production on an SA basis remained flat for at least the first two quarters of 1964 (the precise time period is a function of whether we take the first estimates for the first five months or the slightly revised series being published in *MDS* from September 1964 onwards). Whichever is the case, the essential point is that after what appeared to be strong growth in 1963.IV growth appeared to have stalled, with this a cause of increasing concern within the Treasury

---

[27] W. A. H. Godley and C. Gillion, 'Measuring National Product', *National Institute Economic Review*, 27 (February 1964), pp. 61–7 and idem. 'What has Really Happened to Output?: A Comment', *Bulletin of the Oxford University Institute of Economics and Statistics*, 26.3 (1964), pp. 271–3.
[28] 'Quarterly Estimates of the Gross Domestic Product based on Output Data', *Economic Trends*, 148 (February 1966), pp. ii–xi.

and press speculation.[29] For Bretherton, 'In retrospect it is clear that the index ... was indeed very misleading over this period' and successive revisions have produced a very different picture which we show in Table 6, different both with respect to the growth rate between 1963.IV and 1964. IV and the timing of change once 1963 weights were substituted for those of 1958. Bretherton further notes:[30]

> If the later revisions are more to be trusted than the original figures, it seems that total industrial production was in fact rising during the first nine months of 1964 at an annual rate of 5 to 6 per cent, instead of remaining almost stationery. Had this been known at the time, the Budget Committee's recommendations for restraining action in July might well have prevailed.

Table 6.   Index (all industries) of industrial production (SA), 1963.IV–1964.IV.

	1963–5 First Estimate (1958 base) [A]	1968 Revisions (1958 base) [B]	1969 Revision (1963 weights) (1963 base) [C]
1963.IV	124	124.0	104.1
1964.I	127	126.2	106.1
1964.II	127	127.9	108.0
1964.III	127	128.6	108.6
1964.IV	130	130.2	110.7
% rise	4.8	5.0	6.3

Sources: A: *MDS*, June 1964–March 1965; B: Bretherton, *Demand Management*, p. 49.

(iv) Unemployment and Retail Price Index

Neither of these series were subject to significant changes after the first estimate which was published one month in arrears.

The unemployment series is for Great Britain,[31] NSA and is a measure of registered unemployed, both wholly unemployed and temporarily stopped;

---

[29] For example, A. K. Cairncross, *Diaries: The Radcliffe Committee and the Treasury, 1961–64* (1999), p. 93, diary entry for 3 July 1964; 'It was not easy to convince the Chancellor that he should take further action to check demand when he believed, on the strength of the index, that the economy was stuck.' See also the observation 'the British economy is not apparently keeping to the rules' in 'What is Happening to Industrial Output', *The Times*, 26 November 1964, p. 18.

[30] Bretherton, *Demand Management*, p. 48. Cairncross, *Diaries* reflects in subsequent entries on the developing economic situation in the three months preceding the election; see also idem, *Managing the British Economy in the 1960s: A Treasury Perspective* (1996), pp. 83–7.

[31] Northern Ireland had very much higher unemployment, at roughly four times the average for Great Britain.

it is thus a by-product of an administrative system and not designed as such to measure the pressure of demand in the labour market. There was also data available on vacancies to aid analysis of activity levels.

The RPI series (base 16 January 1962 = 100) was slightly reweighted each year for ascertained changes in consumption as between 10 major categories (including housing).

(v) Conclusions

That the economic house was built on friable statistical sands was an axiom that Brittan knew full well before he joined the DEA, but in his fourteen months he experienced it even more directly. We have in this Appendix made a modest start in staring down the microscope on to the detail, including the publishing life cycle, of 1960s economic data. To understand more fully policy disappointments of this period much further work in this area is necessary. Meanwhile, it is not difficult to see why in the diary, and especially towards the end, Brittan spent so much time trying to get a feel for the economy through devouring the statistics and forecasts that came his way.

Select Bibliography

All places of publication London, unless otherwise stated.

Archival sources
(with abbreviations)

Brittan, Samuel, papers: London School of Economics and Political Science (BLPES) Coll. Misc. 745/1–5 Diary

The National Archives of the United Kingdom: Public Record Office, London
TNA volumes from the CAB, EW and PREM classes followed by series and volume/piece numbers.

Cabinet Office records (CAB):
CAB 124/1433 Central Economic Planning, 1961–3.
CAB 124/1440 National Productivity Year, 1962–3.
CAB 129/111 C (62) 201, Prime Minister, Modernisation of Britain, 30 November 1962.
CAB 129/121 C (65) 53, 'The Outline Plan', 30 March 1965.
CAB 147/9 Organisation for evolving and implementing political decisions in economic field: usefulness of HM Treasury in economic field.

Department of Economic Affairs records (EW):
EW 1/26 Functions of DEA: draft article.
EW 1/72 Review of the work of DEA and possible changes in its role, 1966.
EW 4/50 Cooperation with the Treasury, 1964–6.
EW 8/1 Papers leading up to Joint Statement of Intent on Productivity, Prices and Incomes: papers 3 November 1964 to 27 January 1965.
EW 24/93 The Future of Planning, 1965–6.
EW 24/96 National Plan: 1966 review.
EW 25/100 The National Plan: draft.

Dominion Office papers (DO):
DO 121/273 Visit reports by Cledwyn Hughes, Minister of State for Commonwealth Relations: visits to Malta, October 1965, the Caribbean, April 1965, Washington, Rhodesia, July 1965 and Zambia, December 1965.
DO 183/778 Constitution Council of Southern Rhodesia,1965.

Prime Minister's records (PREM):
PREM 13/275 Relations between HM Treasury and Department of Economic Affairs: speech by Governor, Bank of England, 15 February 1965; ministerial comment.
PREM 13/2126 Division of functions between HM Treasury and Department of Economic Affairs: future of DEA.

PREM 13/3151 UK Drawing from the International Monetary Fund, 1965.

Treasury records (T):
T 171/755 Economic and Financial Situation in Summer and Autumn of 1964.

Other Archives

Lord George-Brown papers (LGBP): Bodleian Library, University of Oxford:
MS Eng c4867 Desk Diary, 1964
MS Eng c4986 General Political Correspondence
MS Eng c4998 Political Correspondence, 1964
MS Eng c5000 Machinery of Economic Policy, 1964

MacDougall, Sir Donald, papers (MACD): Churchill College, Cambridge:
MACD 32 iii NEDC
MACD 40 ix Autobiography 'Don and Mandarin', reviews

Penguin Archive (PA): University of Bristol:
DM1107/A722 Editorial file, The Treasury under the Tories, 1962–7.
DM1107/A1252 Editorial file, Steering the economy, 2nd edn, 1969–73.

Published diaries and papers

Cairncross, A. K., *The Robert Hall Diaries*, I: *1947–53* (1989).
—— *The Robert Hall Diaries*, II: *1954–61* (1991).
—— *The Wilson Years: A Treasury Diary, 1964–1969* (1997).
—— *Diaries: the Radcliffe Committee and the Treasury, 1961–64* (1999).
Castle, B., *The Castle Diaries, 1964–1970* (1986).
Crossman, R. H. S., *The Diaries of a Cabinet Minister*, I: *Minister of Housing, 1964–66* (1975).
—— *The Diaries of a Cabinet Minister*, II: *Lord President of the Council and Leader of the House of Commons, 1966–68* (1976).
—— *The Diaries of a Cabinet Minister*, III: *Secretary of State for Social Services, 1968–70* (1977).
Howson, S. K. and Moggridge, D. E., eds, *The Wartime Diaries of Lionel Robbins and James Meade, 1943–45* (1990).
—— and —— eds, *The Collected Papers of James Meade*, IV: *The Cabinet Office Diary, 1944–46* (1990).
Morgan, J., eds, *The Backbench Diaries of Richard Crossman* (1981).

Newspapers, journals etc

Bank of England, *Quarterly Bulletin*, 4.1–6.4, March 1964–December 1966.
Economist, Historical Archive, <http://www.tlemea.com/economist/home.asp>.
National Institute Economic Review, quarterly, 27–39, February 1964–February 1967.
The Times, Digital Archive, 1785–1985.

Parliamentary debates

'Budget Proposals', *Parliamentary* Debates (House of Commons), 5th ser. 551 (17 April 1956), cols 852–89.

'Economic Statistics', *Parliamentary Debates* (House of Commons), 5th ser. 557 (1 August 1956), cols 1400–4.

'Budget Statement', *Parliamentary Debates* (House of Commons), 5th ser. 701 (11 November 1964), cols. 1023–45.

'Budget Statement', *Parliamentary Debates* (House of Commons), 5th ser. 710 (6 April 1965), cols. 243–391.

'Budget Resolution and Economic Situation', *Parliamentary Debates* (House of Commons), 5th ser. 710 (7 April 1965), cols. 490–625.

'Steel Nationalisation', *Parliamentary Debates* (House of Commons), 5th ser. 711 (6 May 1965), cols. 1571–1694.

'Labour Party (Election Pledges)', *Parliamentary Debates* (House of Commons), 5th ser. 717 (29 July 1965), cols. 713–832.

'Censure Motion', *Parliamentary Debates* (House of Commons), 5th ser. 717 (2 August 1965), cols 1070–1198.

'Civil Service (Pay)', *Parliamentary Debates* (House of Commons), 5th ser. 721 (25 November 1965), cols 774–8.

Official publications

British Imperial Calendar and Civil Service List, annual, 1964–9.

Central Statistical Office, *Monthly Digest of Statistics*, January 1964–June 1967.

Committee of Inquiry into the Aircraft Industry (Plowden Committee), *Report*, BPP 1965–6 (2853), iv, 189.

Committee of Inquiry into Certain Matters Concerning the Port Transport Industry (Devlin Committee), *First Report*, BPP 1964–5 (2523), xxi, 811; *Final Report*, BPP 1964–5 (2734), xxi, 827.

Committee on the Civil Service (Fulton Committee), I: *Report of the Committee, 1966–68*, BPP 1967–8 (3638), xviii, 129.

Committee on Higher Education (Robbins Committee), *Report*, BPP 1962–3 (2154), xi, 639.

Committee on Turnover Taxation (Richardson Committee), *Report*, BPP 1963–4 (2300), xix, 299.

Committee on the Workings of the Monetary System (Radcliffe Committee),
Report, BPP 1958–9 (827), xvii, 389;
Principal Memoranda of Evidence Submitted to the Committee on the Working of the Monetary System, 3 vols (1960).

'Government Economic Research', *Economic Trends*, 142 (August 1965), pp. ii–xii.

Government Statistical Service, 'Developments in Official Economic Statistics, 1957–1963', *Economic Trends*, 124 (February 1964), pp. xxii–xxxii.

Machinery of Prices and Incomes Policy, BPP 1964–5 (2577), xxx, 615.

'Memorandum Submitted on Behalf of the Secretary of State for Economic Affairs' for the Estimates Committee Sub-Committee on Economic Affairs 1964–5, *Fourth Report from the Estimates Committee, Government Statistical Services*, HC 246 (1966–7), pp. 283–316.

'National Income and Expenditure in the First Quarter of 1964', *Economic Trends*, 129 (July 1964), pp. ii–xi.

National Ports Council, *Annual Report and Statement of Accounts, 1964*, HC 241 (1964–5).

The National Plan, BPP 1964–5 (2764), xxx, 1.

NEDC, *Growth of the United Kingdom Economy to 1966* (1963).

NEDC, *Conditions Favourable to Faster Growth* (1963).

NEDC, *The Growth of the Economy* (1964).

Office for National Statistics, *Economic Trends, Annual Supplement 2006*, 32 (2006).

Prime Minister's Office, *The Economic Situation* (1964).

'Quarterly Estimates of the Gross Domestic Product based on Output Data', *Economic Trends*, 148 (February 1966), pp. ii–xi.

Royal Commission on the Civil Service (Priestley Commission), *Report*, BPP 1955–6 (9613), xi, 925.

Shipbuilding Inquiry Committee, 1965–1966 (Geddes Committee), *Report*, BPP 1965–6 (2937), vii, 45.

'Short-Term Economic Forecasting in the United Kingdom', *Economic Trends*, 130 (August 1964), pp. ii–xi.

Sixth Report from the Estimates Committee together with the Minutes of Evidence taken before Sub-Committee E and Appendices, HC 308 (1964–5).

'United Kingdom Balance of Payments in the First Quarter of 1964', *Economic Trends*, 128 (June 1964), pp. ii–xiii.

Unpublished sources

Allan, L. M., 'Thatcher's Economists: Ideas and Opposition in 1980s Britain', University of Oxford DPhil thesis (2008).

Articles and Books

Albu, A., 'Lessons of the Labour Government: I, Economic Policies and Methods', *Political Quarterly*, 41.2 (1970), pp. 141–6.

Bagrit, L., *The Age of Automation* (1965).

Bale, T., 'Harold Wilson, 1963–76', in K. Jefferys, ed., *Leading Labour: From Keir Hardie to Tony Blair* (1999), pp. 116–32.

Balogh, T., 'The Apotheosis of the Dilettante: The Establishment of Mandarins', in H. Thomas, ed., *The Establishment* (1959), pp. 83–126.

—— *Planning for Progress: A Strategy for Labour* (1963).

—— *Unequal Partners*, 2 vols (Oxford, 1963).

Beckerman, W., ed., *The Labour Government's Economic Record, 1964–1970* (1972).

Beckerman, W., 'Wilfred Beckerman (b. 1925)', in R. E. Backhouse and R. Middleton, eds, *Exemplary Economists* (Cheltenham, 2000), II, pp. 146–97.

Blackaby, F. T., 'Narrative, 1960–74', in F. T. Blackaby, ed., *British Economic Policy, 1960–74* (Cambridge, 1978), pp. 11–76.

Blank, S., *Industry and Government in Britain: The Federation of British Industries, 1945–65* (1973).

Bordo, M. D., MacDonald, R. and Oliver, M., 'Sterling in Crisis, 1964–1967', *European Review of Economic History*, 13.3 (2009), pp. 437–59.

Boreham, A. J., 'A Statistician's View', in M. V. Posner, ed., *Demand Management* (1978), pp. 139–50.

Bretherton, R. F., *Demand Management, 1958–64*(1999).

Bridges, E. E., *Portrait of a Profession: The Civil Service Tradition* (1950).

—— *The Treasury* (2nd edn, 1966).

Brittan, S., *The Treasury under the Tories, 1951–1964* (Harmondsworth, 1964).

—— 'The Irregulars', *Crossbow*, 10 (1966), pp. 30–3.

—— 'Inquest on Planning', *Broadsheet*, 33.499 (January 1967), pp. 1–60.

—— *Left or Right?: The Bogus Dilemma* (1968).

—— 'The Irregulars', in R. Rose, ed., *Policy-Making in Britain: A Reader in Government* (1969), pp. 329–39.

—— *Steering the Economy: The Role of the Treasury*, (rev edn, 1969).

—— *Steering the Economy: The Role of the Treasury*, (rev edn, Harmondsworth, 1971).

—— *Second Thoughts on Full Employment* (1975).

—— 'Samuel Brittan (b. 1933), in R. E. Backhouse and R. Middleton, eds, *Exemplary Economists* (Cheltenham, 2000), II, pp. 270–95.

—— 'A Backwards Glance: The Reappraisal of the 1960s', <www.samuelbrittan.co.uk/spee4_p. html>, 14.03.03.

—— *Against the Flow: Reflections of an Individualist* (2005).

—— 'The Moral of the Department of Economic Affairs', 22 October 2007 <http://www.samuelbrittan.co.uk/spee52_p.html>, 22.07.10.

Brown, C., 'Heseltine Becomes a Lion to Roar in Whitehall's Jungle, *Independent*, 10 July 1995 <http://www.independent.co.uk/news/heseltine-becomes-a-lion-to-roar-in-whitehalls-jungle-1590707. html>, 23.07.10.

Brown, G., *In my Way* (1971).

Burnham, P., *Remaking the Postwar World Economy: ROBOT and British Policy in the 1950s* (2003).

Butler, D. E. and Butler, G., *Twentieth-Century British Political Facts, 1900–2000* (8th. edn, 2000).

—— and Rose, R., *The British General Election of 1959* (1960).

—— and King, A., *The British General Election of 1964* (1965).

—— and —— *The British General Election of 1966* (1966).

Cairncross, A. K., *Economic Ideas and Government Policy: Contributions to Contemporary Economic History* (1995).

—— *Managing the British Economy in the 1960s: A Treasury Perspective* (1996).

—— and Cairncross, F., eds, *The Legacy of the Golden Age: The 1960s and their Economic Consequences* (1992).

Cairncross, F., 'Roll, Eric, Baron Roll of Ipsden (1907–2005)', *Oxford Dictionary of National Biography*, <www.oxforddnb.com/view/article/96608>, 29.06.10.

Callaghan, J., *Time and Chance* (1987).

Capie, F. H., *The Bank of England, 1950s to 1979* (Cambridge, 2010).

Carter, C. F. and Roy, A. D., *British Economic Statistics: A Report* (Cambridge, 1954).

Catherwood, H. F. R., *Britain with the Brakes Off* (1966).

—— *At the Cutting Edge* (1995).

—— 'The National Economic Development Council: A View from Industry', *Contemporary British History*, 12.1 (1998), pp. 77–81.

Catterall, P., 'Handling the Transfer of Power: A Note on the 1964 Origins of the Douglas-Home Rules', *Contemporary British History*, 11.1 (1997), pp. 76–82.

—— *et al.*, 'Editing Political Diaries', *Contemporary Record*, 7.1 (1993), pp. 103–31.

Clarke, P., *A Question of Leadership: Gladstone to Blair* (rev. edn. 1999).

Clarke, R. W. B., 'The Plowden Report, I: The Formulation of Economic Policy', *Public Administration*, 41.1 (1963), pp. 17–24.

—— 'The Machinery of Government', in W. Thornhill, ed., *The Modernization of British Government* (1975), pp. 63–95.

—— *Public Expenditure Management and Control: The Development of the Public Expenditure Survey Committee (PESC)*, ed. A. K. Cairncross (1978).

Clifford, C., 'The Rise and Fall of the Department of Economic Affairs, 1964–69: British Government and Indicative Planning', *Contemporary British History*, 11.2 (1997), pp. 94–116.

—— and McMillan, A., eds, 'Witness Seminar: The Department of Economic Affairs', *Contemporary British History*, 11.2 (1997), pp. 117–42.

Clift, B. and Tomlinson, J. D., 'Whatever Happened to the Balance of Payments "Problem"?': The Contingent (Re)construction of British Economic Performance Assessment', *British Journal of Politics and International Relations*, 10.4 (2008), pp. 607–29.

Conan, A. R., *The Problem of Sterling* (1966),

Coopey, R. 'Industrial Policy in the White Heat of the Scientific Revolution', in R. Coopey, S. Fielding and N. Tiratsoo, eds., *The Wilson Governments, 1964–1970* (1993), pp. 102–22.

Croham, Lord, 'Were the Instruments of Control for Domestic Economic Policy Adequate?', in F. Cairncross and A. K. Cairncross, eds., *The Legacy of the Golden Age: The 1960s and Their Economic Consequences* (1992), pp. 81–93.

Cronin, J., 'Labour's "National Plan": Inheritances, Practice, Legacies', *The European Legacy*, 6.2 (2001), pp. 215–32.

—— *New Labour's Pasts: The Labour Party and its Discontents* (2004).

Crosland, S., *Tony Crosland* (1982).

Crouch, C., 'The Place of Public Expenditure in Socialist Thought', in D. Lipsey and D. Leonard, eds, *The Socialist Agenda: Crosland's Legacy* (1981), pp. 156–85.

Denton, G., Forsyth, M. and MacLellan, M., *Economic Planning and Policies in Britain, France and Germany* (1968).

Devons, E., *An Introduction to British Economic Statistics* (Cambridge, 1956).

Dockrill, S., *Britain's Retreat from East of Suez: The Choice between Europe and the World?* (2002).

Dow, J. C. R., *The Management of the British Economy, 1945–60* (Cambridge, 1964).

Elliott, L. and Treanor, J., 'Cable and Osborne are the odd couple who could make or break the coalition', *Guardian*, 13 May 2010 <http://www.guardian.co.uk/politics/2010/may/13/cameron-cable-osborne-visit-banks/print>, 22.07.10.

English, R. and Kenny, M., eds, *Rethinking British Decline* (2000).

Fabian Society, *The Administrators: The Reform of the Civil Service* (1964).

Favretto, I., '"Wilsonism" Reconsidered: Labour Party Revisionism, 1952–64', *Contemporary British History*, 14.4 (2000), pp. 54–80

Fellner, W., Gilbert, M., Hansen, B., Kahn, R. F., Lutz, F. A. and de Wolf, P., *The Problem of Rising Prices* (Paris, 1961).

Fforde, J. S., *The Bank of England and Public Policy, 1941–1958* (Cambridge, 1992).

Fielding, S., '"White Heat" and White Collars: The Evolution of "Wilsonism"', in R. Coopey, S. Fielding and N. Tiratsoo, eds, *The Wilson Governments, 1964–1970* (1993), pp. 29–47.

Findley, R., 'The Conservative Party and Defeat: The Significance of Resale Price Maintenance for the General Election of 1964', *Twentieth Century British History*, 12.3 (2001), pp. 327–53.

Foley, M., *The Rise of the British Presidency* (Manchester, 1993).

Foot, P., *The Politics of Harold Wilson* (Harmondsworth, 1968).

—— 'Obituary: Pipe Dreams', *Socialist Review*, June 1995 <http://pubs.socialistreviewindex.org.uk/sr187/foot.htm> 07.06.10.

Fry, G. K., *Reforming the Civil Service: The Fulton Committee on the British Home Civil Service of 1966–1968* (1993).

—— 'Whitehall in the 1950s and 1960s', *Public Policy and Administration*, 13.1 (1998), pp. 2–25.

Fry, R., ed., *A Banker's World: The Revival of the City, 1957–70; Speeches and Writings of Sir George Bolton* (1970).

Gamble, A. M. and Walkland, S. A., *The British Party System and Economic Policy, 1945–1983: Studies in Adversary Politics* (Oxford, 1984).

George, V. and Wilding, P., *Ideology and Social Welfare* (1985).

Godley, W. A. H. and Gillion, C., 'Measuring National Product', *National Institute Economic Review*, 27 (February 1964), pp. 61–7.

—— and —— 'What has Really Happened to Output?: A Comment', *Bulletin of the Oxford University Institute of Economics and Statistics*, 26.3 (1964), pp. 271–3.

—— and Shepherd, J. R., 'Long-Term Growth and Short-Term Policy: The Productive Potential of the British Economy, and Fluctuations in the Pressure of Demand for Labour, 1951–1962', *National Institute Economic Review*, 29 (August 1964), pp. 26–38.

Goldsworthy, D., 'Macleod, Iain Norman (1913–1970)', *Oxford Dictionary of National Biography*, <www.oxforddnb.com/view/article/34788>, 18.11.04.

Goodhart, C. A. E. and Bhansali, R. J., 'Political Economy', *Political Studies*, 18.1 (1970), pp. 43–106.

—— 'A Central Bank Economist', in P. Mizen, ed., *Central Banking, Monetary Theory and Practice: Essays in Honour of Charles Goodhart* (Cheltenham, 2003), pp. 13–61.

Graham, A. W. M., 'Thomas Balogh (1905–1985)', *Contemporary Record*, 6.1 (1992), pp. 194–207.

Green, E. H. H., *Ideologies of Conservatism: Conservative Political Ideas in the Twentieth Century* (Oxford, 2002).

Hackett, J. W., 'Britain and France: Two Experiments in Planning', *Political Quarterly*, 37.4 (1966), pp. 429–40.

Hague, D. C. and Wilkinson, G. C. G., *The IRC: An Experiment in Industrial Intervention. A History of the Industrial Reorganisation Corporation* (1983).

Harrod, R., *Towards a New Economic Policy* (1967).

Healey, D., *The Time of My Life* (1989).

Heclo, H. and Wildavsky, A., *The Private Government of Public Money: Community and Policy inside British Politics* (1974).

Hennessy, P, *Cabinet* (1986).
—— *Whitehall* (rev. edn, 1990).
Heppell, T., 'The Labour Party Leadership Election of 1963: Explaining the Unexpected Election of Harold Wilson', *Contemporary British History*, 24.2 (2010), pp. 151–71.
Hirsch, F., *The Pound Sterling: A Polemic* (1965).
Hoekman, B. and Kostecki, M., *The Political Economy of the World Trading System: From GATT to WTO* (Oxford, 1995).
Honeyman, V., 'The Leadership of Harold Wilson Assessed Using the Greenstein Model', POLIS Working Paper no. 25, University of Leeds (2007).
Howard, A., 'Fallen on Stony Ground', *Times Literary Supplement*, 23 May 1997, p. 27.
—— and West, R., *The Making of the Prime Minister* (1965).
Hutchison, T. W., *Economics and Economic Policy in Britain, 1946–1966: Some Aspects of their Interrelations* (1968).
Hutton, W., *The State We're In* (1995).
James, H., *International Monetary Cooperation since Bretton Woods* (1996).
Jay, D. P. T., 'Government Control of the Economy: Defects in the Machinery', *Political Quarterly*, 39.2 (1968), pp. 134–44.
—— *Change and Fortune: A Political Record* (1980).
Jay, P., 'Left, Right, Left', *Financial Times Magazine*, 92 (12 February 2005), pp. 25–7.
Johnman, L. and Murphy, H., *British Shipbuilding and the State since 1918: A Political Economy of Decline* (Exeter, 2002).
Jones, A., *The New Inflation: The Politics of Prices and Incomes* (Harmondsworth, 1973).
Jones, R., *Wages and Employment Policy, 1936–1985* (1987).
Jones, T., *Remaking the Labour Party: From Gaitskell to Blair* (1996).
Kaplan, J. J. and Schleiminger, G., *The European Payments Union: Financial Diplomacy in the 1950s* (1959).
Kaufman, G., *How to be a Minister* (rev. edn, 1997).
Kavanagh, D., *Political Science and Political Behaviour* (1983).
Keegan, W., *The Prudence of Mr Gordon Brown* (2003).
Kendall, M. G., *The Sources and Nature of the Statistics of the United Kingdom*, 2 vols (1952; 1957).
King, A., 'Do Leader's Personalities Really Matter?', in A. King, ed, *Leader's Personalities and the Outcomes of Democratic Elections* (Cambridge, 2002), pp. 1–43.
Kipping, N., *Summing Up* (1972).
Kirby, M. W., 'Blackett in the "White Heat" of the Scientific Revolution: Industrial Mobilisation under the Labour Governments, 1964–1970', *Journal of the Operational Research Society*, 50.10 (1999), pp. 985–93.
Knight, A., *Private Enterprise and Public Intervention: The Courtaulds Experience* (1974).
Kynaston, D., *The Financial Times: A Centenary History* (1988).
Labour Party, *Labour in the Sixties* (1960).
—— *Signposts for the Sixties* (1961).
—— *The New Britain* (1964).
Leruez, J., *Economic Planning & Politics in Britain* (Oxford, 1975).
Lewes, F. M. M., *Statistics of the British Economy* (1967).
Lowe, R., 'The Core Executive, Modernization and the Creation of PESC, 1960–64', *Public Administration*, 75.4 (1997), pp. 601–15.

—— *The Official History of the British Civil Service*, I: *Reforming the Civil Service, the Fulton years, 1966–81* (2010).

—— and Rollings, N., 'Modernising Britain, 1957–64: A Classic Case of Centralisation and Fragmentation?' in R. A. W. Rhodes, ed., *Transforming British Government* (2000), I, pp. 99–118.

Ludlow, N. P., 'A Waning Force: The Treasury and British European Policy, 1955–63', *Contemporary British History*, 17.4 (2003), pp. 87–104.

MacDougall, G. D. A., 'The Machinery of Economic Government: Some Personal Reflections', in D. Butler and A. H. Halsey, eds, *Policy and Politics: Essays in Honour of Norman Chester* (1978), pp. 169–81.

—— *Don and Mandarin: Memoirs of an Economist* (1987).

Mackintosh, J. P., *The British Cabinet* (1962).

Macrae, N., *Sunshades in October: An Analysis of the Main Mistakes in British Economic Policy since the Mid Nineteen-Fifties* (1963).

Manser, W. A. P., *Britain in the Balance: The Myth of Failure* (1971).

Marr, A., *A History of Modern Britain* (2007).

McAllister, I., 'The Personalization of Politics', in R. J. Dalton and H.-D. Klingemann, eds, *The Oxford Handbook of Political Behavior* (Oxford, 2007), pp. 571–88.

Mercer, H., *Constructing a Competitive Order: The Hidden History of British Antitrust Policies* (Cambridge, 1995).

—— 'The Abolition of Resale Price Maintenance in Britain in 1964: A Turning Point for British Manufacturers?', *LSE Working Paper in Economic History* no. 39/98 (1998).

Middlemas, K., *Industry, Unions and Government: Twenty-One years of NEDC* (1983).

Middleton, R., *Government versus the Market: The Growth of the Public Sector, Economic Management and British Economic Performance, 1890–c.1979* (Cheltenham, 1996).

—— *Charlatans or Saviours?: Economists and the British Economy from Marshall to Meade* (Cheltenham, 1998).

—— 'Struggling with the Impossible: Sterling, the Balance of Payments and British Economic Policy, 1949–72', in A. Arnon and W. L. Young, eds, *The Open Economy Macromodel: Past, Present and Future* (Boston, MA, 2002), pp. 103–54.

—— 'Economists and Economic Growth in Britain, c.1955–65', in L. A. Black and H. Pemberton, eds, *Affluent Britain: Britain's Postwar 'Golden Age' Revisited* (Aldershot, 2004), pp. 129–47.

—— 'Brittan on Britain "The economic contradictions of democracy" redux', *Historical Journal*, 54.4 (2011), pp. 1141–68.

—— 'Brittan on Britain: decline, declinism and the "traumas of the 1970s"', in L. A. Black, H. Pemberton and P. M. Thane, eds, *Reassessing 1970s Britain: a benighted decade* (Manchester, 2012), in press.

Morgan, A., *Harold Wilson* (1992).

Mosley, P., *The Making of Economic Policy: Theory and Evidence from Britain and the United States since 1945* (Brighton, 1984).

Newton, C. C. S. 'The Two Sterling Crises of 1964 and the Decision not to Devalue', *Economic History Review*, 62.1 (2009), pp. 73–98.

—— 'The Sterling Devaluation of 1967, the international economy and post-war social democracy', *English Historical Review*, 125.3 (2010), pp. 912–45.

—— 'The Defence of Sterling, 1964–67', unpublished paper (2010).

O'Hara, G., '"Planned Growth of Incomes": or "Emergency Gimmick": The Labour Party, the Social Partners and Incomes Policy, 1964–70', *Labour History Review*, 69.1 (2004), pp. 59–81.

—— 'Towards a New Bradshaw?: Economic Statistics and the British State in the 1950s and 1960s', *Economic History Review*, 60.1 (2007), pp. 1–34.

—— *From Dreams to Disillusionment: Economic and Social Planning in 1960s Britain* (2007).

Opie, R. G., 'The Making of Economic Policy', in H. Thomas, ed., *Crisis in the Civil Service* (1968), pp. 53–82.

—— 'Economic Planning and Growth', in W. Beckerman, ed., *The Labour Government's Economic Record, 1964–1970* (1972), pp. 157–77.

Paish, F. W., *Studies in an Inflationary Economy: The United Kingdom, 1948–1961* (1962).

—— *How the Economy Works and Other Essays* (1970).

Panitch, L., *Social Democracy and Industrial Militancy: The Labour Party, the Trade Unions and Incomes Policy, 1945 to 1974* (Cambridge, 1976).

Parkinson, J. R., 'The Financial Prospects of Shipbuilding after Geddes', *Journal of Industrial Economics*, 17.1 (1968), pp. 1–17.

Paterson, P., *Tired and Emotional: The Life of Lord George-Brown* (1993).

Pemberton, H., *Policy Learning and British Governance in the 1960s* (2004).

Pimlott, B., *Harold Wilson* (1992).

Pliatzky, L., *Getting and Spending: Public Expenditure, Employment and Inflation* (2nd edn., Oxford, 1984).

—— 'The Treasury's Mission under Gordon Brown', *Political Quarterly*, 68.1 (1997), pp. 91–4.

Political and Economic Planning, *Growth in the British Economy: A Study of Economic Problems and Policies in Contemporary Britain* (1960).

Pollitt, C. *Manipulating the Machine: Changing the Pattern of Ministerial Departments, 1960–83* (1984).

Ponting, C., *Breach of Promise: Labour in Power, 1964–1970* (1989).

Postan, M., 'A Plague of Economists?: On Some Current Myths, Errors and Fallacies', *Encounter*, 30.1 (January 1968), pp. 42–7.

Pressnell, L. S., *External Economic Policy since the War*, I: *The Post-War Financial Settlement* (1987).

Preston, R., *Brown's Britain* (2005).

Price, R. W. R., 'Budgetary Policy', in F. T. Blackaby, ed., *British Economic Policy, 1960–74* (Cambridge, 1978), pp. 77–134.

Rhodes, R. A. W., 'The Changing Nature of Central Government in Britain: The ESRC's Whitehall programme', *Public Policy and Administration*, 13.4 (1998), pp. 1–11

—— 'A Guide to the ESRC's Whitehall Programme, 1994–1999', *Public Administration*, 78.2 (2000), pp. 251–82.

Ringe, A., 'Background to Neddy: Economic Planning in the 1960s', *Contemporary British History*, 12.1 (1998), pp. 82–98.

—— and Rollings, N., 'Responding to Relative Decline: The Creation of the National Economic Development Council', *Economic History Review*, 53.2 (2004), pp. 3 31–53.

——, —— and Middleton, R., *Economic Policy under the Conservatives, 1951–64: A Guide to Documents in the National Archives of the UK* (2004).

—— *et al.*, 'The National Economic Development Council, 1962–67', *Contemporary British History*, 12.1 (1998), pp. 99–130.

Roll, E. 'The Machinery for Economic Planning: I. The Department of Economic Affairs', *Public Administration*, 44.1 (1966), pp. 1–11.

—— *Crowded Hours: An Autobiography* (1985).

Rooth, G., *Occupation and Pay in Great Britain, 1906–60* (Cambridge, 1965).

Roy, R., 'No Secrets between "Special Friends": America's Involvement in British Economic Policy, October 1964-April 1965', *History*, 89.3 (2004), pp. 399–423.

Sampson, A., *Anatomy of Britain*. (1962).

Schenk, C. R., 'The Empire Strikes Back: Hong Kong and the Decline of Sterling in the 1960s', *Economic History Review*, 57.3 (2004), pp. 551–80.

—— *The Decline of Sterling: Managing the Retreat of an International Currency, 1945–1992* (Cambridge, 2010).

Shanks, M., *The Stagnant Society: A Warning* (1961).

—— 'The "Irregular" in Whitehall', in P. Streeten, ed., *Unfashionable Economics: Essays in Honour of Lord Balogh* (1970), pp. 244–62.

—— *Planning and Politics: The British Experience, 1960–76* (1977).

Sherman, A. J., 'Warburg, Sir Siegmund George (1902–82)', *Oxford Dictionary of National Biography*, <www.oxforddnb.com/view/article/31800>, 27.07.10.

Shone, R., 'The Machinery for Economic Planning: II, The National Economic Development Council', *Public Administration*, 44.1 (1966), pp. 13–27.

Shonfield, A., *British Economic Policy since the War* (1958).

Shrimsley, A., *The First Hundred Days of Harold Wilson* (1965).

Smith, D. C., 'Incomes Policy', in R. E. Caves and Associates, eds, *Britain's Economic Prospects* (1968), pp. 104–44.

Stewart, M., *Life and Labour: An Autobiography* (1980).

Stewart, M. J., 'A Plague of Politicians?' *Encounter*, 30.5 (May 1968), pp. 54–6.

—— 'A Plague of Economists?' *Encounter*, 31.5 (November 1968), pp. 94–5.

—— *The Jekyll and Hyde Years: Politics and Economic Policy since 1964* (1977).

Tew, J. H. B. 'Policies Aimed at Improving the Balance of Payments', in F. T. Blackaby, ed., *British Economic Policy, 1960–74* (Cambridge, 1978), pp. 304–59.

Theakston, K., *The Labour Party and Whitehall* (1992).

—— *The Civil Service since 1945* (Oxford, 1995).

—— 'Comparative Biography and Leadership in Whitehall', *Public Administration*, 75.4 (1997), pp. 651–67.

—— *Leadership in Whitehall* (1999).

—— 'Richard Crossman: The Diaries of a Cabinet Minister', *Public Policy and Administration*, 18.4 (2003), pp. 20–40.

—— 'Whitehall Reform', in P. Dorey, ed., *The Labour Governments, 1964–1970* (2006), pp. 147–67.

Thompson, N., 'The Fabian Political Economy of Harold Wilson', in P. Dorey, ed., *The Labour Governments, 1964–1970* (2006), pp. 53–72.

Tolstóy, L., *War and Peace: A Novel*, trans. L. and A. Maude. (Oxford, 1932).

Tomlinson, J. D., *The Politics of Decline: Understanding Post-War Britain* (2000).

—— *The Labour Governments, 1964–70*, III: *Economic Policy* (Manchester, 2004).

—— 'The Labour Party and the Capitalist Firm, c.1950–1970', *Historical Journal*, 47.3 (2004), pp. 685–708.

—— 'Balanced Accounts? Constructing the Balance of Payments Problem in Post-War Britain', *English Historical Review*, 124.4 (2009), pp. 863–84.

de Vries, M. G., *The International Monetary Fund, 1966–1971: The System under Stress*, 3 vols (Washington, DC, 1976).

Walker, D., 'The First Wilson Governments, 1964–1970', in P. Hennessy and A. Seldon, eds, *Ruling Performance: British Governments from Attlee to Thatcher* (Oxford, 1987), pp. 186–215.

Walters, A. A., 'The Radcliffe Report – Ten Years After: A Review of the Empirical Evidence', in D. R. Croome and H. G. Johnson, eds, *Money in Britain, 1959–1969* (Oxford, 1970), pp. 39–68.

Ward, R. and Doggett, T., *Keeping Score: The First Fifty Years of the Central Statistical Office* (1991).

Warner, G., 'Why the General said No', *International Affairs*, 78.4 (2002), pp. 869–82.

Wilson, H., 'A Four-Year Plan for Britain', *New Statesman*, 24 March 1961, pp. 462–8.

—— *The New Britain: Labour's Plan* (Harmondsworth, 1964).

—— *Purpose in Politics: Selected Speeches* (1964).

—— *The Labour Government, 1964–1970: A Personal Record* (1971).

Index

Page numbers in bold refer to biographical details in Appendix I.